PENGUIN  CLASSICS

LYSISTRATA AND OTHER PLAYS

ARISTOPHANES was born, probably in Athens, *c.* 449 BC and died between 386 and 380 BC. Little is known about his life, but there is a portrait of him in Plato's *Symposium*. He was twice threatened with prosecution in the 420s for his outspoken attacks on the prominent politician Cleon, but in 405 he was publicly honoured and crowned for promoting Athenian civic unity in *The Frogs*. Aristophanes had his first comedy produced when he was about twenty-one, and wrote forty plays in all. The eleven surviving plays of Aristophanes are published in the Penguin Classics series as *The Birds and Other Plays*, *Lysistrata and Other Plays* and *The Wasps/ The Poet and the Women/The Frogs*.

ALAN H. SOMMERSTEIN has been Professor of Greek at the University of Nottingham since 1988, and is Director of Its Centre for Ancient Drama and its Reception. He has written or edited over twenty books on Ancient Greek language and literature, especially tragic and comic drama, including *Aeschylean Tragedy* (1996), *Greek Drama and Dramatists* (2002), and a complete edition of the comedies of Aristophanes with translation and commentary. For the Penguin Classics he has also translated Aristophanes' *The Knights*, *Peace*, and *Wealth* in the volume *The Birds and Other Plays*.

ARISTOPHANES

Lysistrata and Other Plays

THE ACHARNIANS,
THE CLOUDS, LYSISTRATA

Translated with an Introduction and Notes by
ALAN H. SOMMERSTEIN

REVISED EDITION

PENGUIN BOOKS

PENGUIN BOOKS

Published by the Penguin Group
Penguin Books Ltd, 80 Strand, London WC2R 0RL, England
Penguin Putnam Inc., 375 Hudson Street, New York, New York 10014, USA
Penguin Books Australia Ltd, 250 Camberwell Road, Camberwell, Victoria 3124, Australia
Penguin Books Canada Ltd, 10 Alcorn Avenue, Toronto, Ontario, Canada M4V 3B2
Penguin Books India (P) Ltd, 11, Community Centre, Panchsheel Park, New Delhi – 110 017, India
Penguin Books (NZ) Ltd, Cnr Rosedale and Airborne Roads, Albany, Auckland, New Zealand
Penguin Books (South Africa) (Pty) Ltd, 24 Sturdee Avenue, Rosebank 2196, South Africa

Penguin Books Ltd, Registered Offices: 80 Strand, London WC2R 0RL, England

www.penguin.com

Original translation first published 1973
This revised edition first published 2002
033

Copyright © Alan H. Sommerstein, 2002
All rights reserved

The moral right of the translator has been asserted

Set in 10.25/12.25 pt PostScript Adobe Sabon
Typeset by Rowland Phototypesetting Ltd, Bury St Edmunds, Suffolk
Printed in England by Clays Ltd, St Ives plc

ISBN-13: 978-0-14-044814-6

www.greenpenguin.co.uk

MIX
Paper from
responsible sources
FSC™ C018179

Penguin Books is committed to a sustainable
future for our business, our readers and our planet.
This book is made from Forest Stewardship
Council™ certified paper.

Contents

Chronology   vii
Introduction   xi
Further Reading   xlix
Translator's Note   li
Note on the Text   liv

Preface to *The Acharnians*   3
THE ACHARNIANS   13

Preface to *The Clouds*   65
THE CLOUDS   75

Preface to *Lysistrata*   133
LYSISTRATA   141

Notes   195

Chronology

449/8 BC? Aristophanes born.

441 Euripides' first victory at the City Dionysia.

438 Production of Euripides' *Telephus* and *Alcestis*.

431 Outbreak of Peloponnesian War.

430–426 The Great Plague of Athens.

430–428 Aristophanes trains to be a dramatist, collaborating anonymously with other authors.

429 Death of Pericles.

428 Aristophanes submits *The Banqueters* to Archon for production, in the name of Callistratus.

427 *The Banqueters* (D): second prize.

426 *The Babylonians* (D): first prize.
Cleon attempts to prosecute Aristophanes for 'slandering the City'.

425 *The Acharnians* (L): first prize.
Pylos–Sphacteria campaign; Spartan invasions of Attica cease.

424 *The Knights* (L), the first play Aristophanes produced himself: first prize.
Cleon indicts Aristophanes for falsely pretending to be a citizen, but the prosecution is withdrawn.

423 *The Clouds* (D) proves a failure.
Truce of one year (begins day after City Dionysia).

422 *The Preview* and *The Wasps* (L): first and second prizes.
Truce expires; fighting resumed (in Thracian region only).

Cleon killed at Amphipolis (summer); peace negotiations follow.

421 *Peace* (D): second prize.

Peace of Nicias (takes effect twelve days after City Dionysia).

419/18 Aristophanes revises *The Clouds*, but the new version is not produced.

415 Sicilian expedition sets out.

414 *The Birds* (D): second prize.

413 Total destruction of Sicilian expedition.

411 *Lysistrata* (L?).

The Poet and the Women (*Thesmophoriazusae*) (D).

Oligarchic coup of Four Hundred, who rule for four months (summer).

410 Restoration of full democracy.

406 Death of Euripides.

Athenian victory at Arginusae; successful commanders tried and executed for failing to pick up shipwrecked men.

Death of Sophocles.

405 *The Frogs* (L): first prize.

Athenian fleet annihilated at Aegospotami (summer); Athens besieged.

405/4 Public honours awarded to Aristophanes, and *The Frogs* restaged (404, L).

Surrender of Athens. Installation of junta of Thirty.

403 Expulsion of Thirty. Restoration of democracy.

399 Trial and execution of Socrates.

395 Outbreak of Corinthian War (Athens/Thebes/Corinth/Argos vs. Sparta).

391 *The Assemblywomen* (*Ecclesiazusae*).

c. **390** Aristophanes chosen by lot to serve on the Council of Five Hundred.

388 *Wealth* (*Plutus*).

387 *Cocalus* (D), produced by Aristophanes' son Araros: first prize.

386? *Aeolosicon*, produced by Araros: Aristophanes' last play.

386 End of Corinthian War; Sparta retains her hegemonic position.

c. 385 Death of Aristophanes, leaving two sons, Araros and Philippus, who later become comic dramatists themselves.

384–379 Plato makes Aristophanes a character in the *Symposium*.

Introduction

The eleven surviving plays of Aristophanes are all that we have, apart from fragments preserved on papyri or quoted by other ancient writers, of one of the most remarkable branches of the literature of antiquity, the Old Comedy of Athens. Of Old Comedy I will say more presently: first something on Aristophanes himself, his life, times, work and ideas.

ARISTOPHANES' LIFE AND WORK

Aristophanes, son of Philippus, of the 'deme' or district of Cydathenaeum within the urban area of Athens,[1] was born close to the mid-point of the fifth century BC. He may have served an apprenticeship in the early 420s helping other dramatists with their scripts and production;[2] his own first comedy, The Banqueters, was written presumably in 428 and produced (by a collaborator, Callistratus) at the showpiece festival of the City Dionysia in the spring of 427, where it was placed second in the comic competition. The following year Aristophanes won first prize with The Babylonians (again produced by Callistratus), and afterwards either he or his producer was threatened with prosecution by Cleon, the most powerful politician of the day, for allegedly slandering the Athenian people and state, though the case apparently never came to court. In 425 the team of Aristophanes and Callistratus won another first prize with The Acharnians, the earliest of his plays to survive,[3] and in 424 Aristophanes for the first time produced a play in his own name when he made his most ferocious attack yet on Cleon in The

Knights. This apparently resulted in another threat of prosecution by Cleon; Aristophanes' (anonymous) ancient biographer says it was on the serious charge of falsely pretending to be an Athenian citizen, for which the penalty on conviction was sale into slavery. A rather obscure passage in *The Wasps* (lines 1284–91) suggests that Aristophanes saved himself (probably, once again, before the matter got as far as the courts) by promising to treat Cleon more mildly in future; if so, the promise was not kept.

Altogether in a career of some forty years Aristophanes wrote at least forty plays.[4] Only eleven of these were still being read to any significant extent in late antiquity,[5] but these eleven all survived through the Middle Ages[6] to reach the security of printed editions between 1498 and 1525 and to be read and performed today: *The Acharnians*, *The Knights*, *The Clouds* (423, but revised later), *The Wasps* (422), *Peace* (421), *The Birds* (414), *Lysistrata* and *The Poet and the Women*[7] (both 411), *The Frogs* (405), *The Assemblywomen*[8] (probably 391), and *Wealth*[9] (388). Of these, *The Acharnians*, *The Knights* and *The Frogs* are known to have won first prize, and *The Wasps* was only defeated because Aristophanes had entered another play for the same competition; *Peace* and *The Birds* came second, *The Clouds* failed badly, and in the other four cases the competition result is not known. Some months after the production of *The Frogs*, when the Assembly decided to implement a proposal, advocated in the play (lines 686–705), to restore citizen rights to many who had lost them on political and other grounds, they also passed a decree commending Aristophanes, conferring upon him a crown of sacred olive,[10] and ordering the play to be restaged; in one sense this was the climax of Aristophanes' career, but he may have recalled it afterwards with somewhat mixed feelings, since many of those to whom rights were restored proceeded to use them to overthrow the democratic regime and install the rule of a narrow and bloody junta (the Thirty). Aristophanes himself, however, does not seem to have been regarded as one of the Thirty's supporters, since around 390 his name appears on an inscribed list of members of the Council of Five Hundred, who had to undergo, before entering office, a scrutiny at which any dubious aspect of their past life might be brought up against them.

Wealth was the last play that Aristophanes produced in his own name. He wrote two more comedies subsequently; these were produced by his son Araros,[11] and one of them won first prize. Aristophanes probably died between 386 and 380.

ARISTOPHANES PORTRAYED BY
A CONTEMPORARY

It was most likely not long after Aristophanes' death that Plato wrote his *Symposium*,[12] which purports to be an account of a dinner party given by the tragic poet Agathon in 416 at which both Socrates and Aristophanes were present. This work, fictional though it no doubt is, is nevertheless the only source we have that might give us a glimpse of Aristophanes independently of his plays; and it is a source with some authority, since Aristophanes was only recently dead at the time of writing, had been a prominent figure in Athenian life for four decades, and will have been well known both to Plato and to many of his readers.

The first we hear of Aristophanes in the *Symposium* is that like all the other guests (except Socrates), he has a hangover from the previous night's party, or, as he puts it, 'I had a bit of a dip yesterday too' (176b). When his neighbour Eryximachus, a medical man, proposes that all the guests should make speeches in praise of Love (Eros), Socrates comments that Aristophanes can hardly refuse, 'seeing that he devotes his whole life to Dionysus and Aphrodite'[13] (177e). Aristophanes' turn to speak eventually comes, but he is in the middle of an attack of hiccups (185c), and Eryximachus has to speak before him, as well as prescribing treatment for his complaint (185d–e). By the end of the doctor's speech Aristophanes has recovered, and is ready to begin (188e–189a); but he is almost immediately accused of trying to be funny at Eryximachus' expense (189a–b). He apologizes, but says (189b) that he *is* afraid his speech may seem – not funny (*geloia*), since 'that would be a plus point, and just right coming from me, artistically speaking' – but contemptible (*katagelasta*). He then makes his speech (189c–193e). Originally, he says, human beings were spherical in shape, with four legs and double the present number of all the other organs, and there were three sexes, male, female and hermaphrodite; but when they tried to fight against the gods Zeus punished them. Rather than destroy them (which would have deprived him and the other gods of their sacrificial offerings), he sliced them all in half, thus simultaneously increasing their numbers (and hence the number of sacrifices they offered) and reducing their strength; and subsequently, finding that the separated halves of each former individual passionately sought each other out and were ready to stay locked in permanent embrace until they died of starvation, he made such anatomical adjustments as were necessary to enable them to give each other sexual satisfaction as we know it today. And that is why even now there are three kinds of persons – straights, gays and lesbians as we would call them[14] – because 'each of us is always looking for his other half' (191d); and it is this desire and pursuit that we call love, and in its fulfilment that the hope of happiness lies.

There is a good deal that is ludicrous here, some of it repeating themes frequent in Aristophanes' comedies (such as that gods would starve if mortals did not sacrifice to them, or that all politicians had been homosexually promiscuous in adolescence); nobody, to be sure, derides Aristophanes, but this may well be because it would not be appropriate to do so in this convivial atmosphere. What is perhaps more significant is Aristophanes' own anxiety to be taken seriously: at the end of Socrates' speech, the climax of the whole dialogue, everybody congratulates him except Aristophanes, who 'tried to raise a point about the reference that Socrates had made to his speech' (212c) – for Socrates, or rather the wise woman Diotima whom he professed to be quoting, had criticized Aristophanes, without naming him, on the ground that 'neither a half nor a whole can be the object of love unless it is something good' (205d–e). Socrates never has to answer him, because the proceedings are immediately interrupted by the arrival of the drunken Alcibiades; but whether we are to see Aristophanes as hoping to rebut Diotima's criticism or just as wanting to draw the company's attention to the fact that she had taken notice of his thesis, the effect is still to portray him as someone who wanted to be thought of as something more than a laughter-maker.

It is striking that Socrates is not made to show any resentment, nor Aristophanes any embarrassment, on the subject of *The Clouds* – even though Plato believed, as we know from his *Apology*, that *The Clouds* was a significant factor in creating the prejudice against Socrates that contributed to his condemnation and execution in 399, and even though there is significant further evidence that contemporary Athenians took it for granted that comic satire, at least if large-scale or persistent, was likely to be believed and to injure the reputation of the person satirized.[15] We should remember that Socrates is elsewhere represented by Plato as caring very little for his reputation (unlike most ancient Greeks) and as believing it wrong to retaliate for an injury received; the Socrates that Plato portrays simply would not have regarded Aristophanes as an enemy, and those who knew him well would have been aware of this. Neither he nor Aristophanes could be supposed to have had any idea in 416 of what was to happen in 399, a lost war and five revolutions later.

THE POLITICAL BACKGROUND

Aristophanes' lifetime was a time of extreme political turbulence. When he was in his teens, Athens was at the height of her power and fame. For a generation the city had been governed by a radical form of democracy, under which all adult male citizens had an equal share in policy decisions (which were taken by an Assembly of the whole citizen body, voting by show of hands), while those over thirty had also an equal opportunity to take an active part in the administration of justice (most trials being held before popular juries numbering several hundred, who judged both factual and legal issues and from whom there was no appeal) and an equal chance of appointment (by lot) to executive office[16] or to the Council of Five Hundred which dealt with routine public business and prepared the agenda for the Assembly. During most of this time Athenian politics had in practice been dominated by a single man, Pericles ('Zeus' as he was dubbed by Cratinus and other comic dramatists), through his personality, his oratory, his popular policies and the power that comes from success. Under his leadership Athens survived a war[17] in which at one time she was fighting half Greece and Persia too, on three continents at once; she converted what had been a military alliance directed against the Persian empire into a league of subject states paying tribute to herself; and while using a large part of this revenue to build and maintain an unchallengeable navy, she spent much of the rest on a programme of public building then unparalleled anywhere in Greece. The peace of the Greek world depended, however, on the balance of strength between Athens as the greatest sea-power and Sparta as the greatest land-power, and in the 430s it increasingly seemed to Spartans (and even more to their allies, the Corinthians) that this balance was tipping too much Athens' way; at any rate, when a series of disputes arose between Athens and various members of the Spartan alliance, the outcome, in the spring of 431, was war.[18]

Despite occasional sanguinary or spectacular episodes, despite regular invasions and devastations of Athenian territory, despite the great plague of 430–426 which probably killed more Athenians than all the campaigns of the war combined, and despite a heavy run-down of Athenian financial resources, the conflict was indecisive, since Sparta could not defeat Athens at sea and Athens could not defeat Sparta on land. It was ended in 421 by a compromise peace – psychologically a heavy defeat for Sparta, whom at the outset most neutrals had expected to be victorious within three years – and before long a supremely confident Athens was forming alliances, and deploying her troops, in the heart of the Peloponnese. In 415 the Athenians invaded Sicily, some of them at least aiming at the conquest of the whole island, and the next year, by an attack on Spartan home territory in conjunction with their Argive allies, they casually provoked the Spartans into a new war. Then, in 413, everything went wrong. The Sicilians defeated and destroyed the Athenian expedition; Sparta, on the advice of the brilliant former Athenian general Alcibiades (in exile for alleged offences against religion), seized and fortified a permanent base a few miles from Athens; and the crisis resulted which forms the background to *Lysistrata*. A few months later, in the early summer of 411, a strictly constitutional *coup d'état* overthrew the Athenian democracy; the new regime of the 'Four Hundred', however, failed to make peace as its leaders had hoped to do, and was soon itself deposed, in favour first of a broader oligarchy (the 'Five Thousand') and then, early in 410, of an even more radical version of the old democracy. By now many of Athens' subject states were in revolt, but she more than held her own at sea until, in 407, the Persian king, Darius II, decided to back Sparta. From then on the Athenians could survive only by winning every naval battle until such time as Darius died; in summer 405 they suffered a catastrophic defeat at the Hellespont, were soon subjected to a land and sea blockade, and in spring 404 surrendered unconditionally. Darius II died a few weeks later.

Athens was not destroyed, as many Athenians feared it would be, but she was deprived of all her overseas possessions and of all but an insignificant remnant of her navy, and subjected, with Spartan approval, to the rule of a junta of thirty.[19] Other neighbouring states, however, seem to have feared that Athens would become an instrument of Spartan policy to control and coerce them, and supported the initially small band of rebels who, within eighteen months, had overthrown the Thirty, restored democracy, and enacted a wide-ranging amnesty for past offences. The political settlement of 403 ushered in eighty-one years of unbroken internal peace and unchallenged democracy which ended only when Athens fell under Macedonian domination. Externally Athens spent most of this period in a series of attempts, always with inadequate resources, to regain something like her old position of power; the first of these, known as the Corinthian War, began in 395 with an alliance of all the leading Greek states (Athens, Argos, Corinth, Thebes), with Persian backing, against Sparta – but the Persians changed sides, and the war ended in 387/6 with a peace dictated by them which gave Sparta everything she wanted, Athens a little, and the other allies nothing. At just about the same time, Plato was founding the first permanent school of philosophy near the park and gymnasium called the Academy. Athenians did not yet recognize the fact, but the transformation of their city from the political to the intellectual centre of Greece was under way.

Aristophanes' later work reflects the early stages of this transformation. His last two surviving plays, as much as their predecessors, are concerned with real, identifiable evils afflicting society; but the comic remedy for these evils is not (as in *The Acharnians*, *The Knights*, *Peace* or *Lysistrata*) a single political act ('make peace', 'get rid of Cleon'), nor (as in *The Clouds* or *The Frogs*) the rejection of contemporary trends in thought and literature in favour of an idealized past, but the construction of a new society on the basis of a theoretical principle (in one case communism, in the other universal and equal wealth), much as was done by Plato in his *Republic* a decade or two later.[20] The audience of these plays, while recognizing the evils (and recognizing that they *need* to be remedied), is certainly not expected to endorse the actual remedies applied. It is otherwise in Aristophanes' earlier works, where, for the most part, we find not only real evils but practicable prescriptions for them.

ARISTOPHANES' IDEAS

The statement made in the last sentence of the preceding section is a controversial one. Probably the dominant trend in present-day Aristophanic criticism[21] is one that stresses (with every justification) Aristophanes' immense, kaleidoscopic artistry and inventiveness in word and image, theme and structure, sound and sight, but denies to him any serious aims in the political and social fields.[22] The evidence clearly shows, however, that fifth- and fourth-century Athenians themselves thought that comedy could exert an influence on public opinion and even sometimes on public policy, and it must be presumed that comic dramatists were aware of this. The comic dramatists, too, were themselves Athenian citizens, to whom, as to most of their audiences, it was of literally vital importance that the Athenian citizen body should take the right decisions on key political issues – for a wrong decision, especially in wartime, could only too easily lead to Athens suffering the same fate that she inflicted on Scione in 421 and on Melos in 415, the destruction of the city, the extermination of its adult male inhabitants, and the enslavement of the rest. And the dramatic festivals gave them perhaps the biggest citizen audience that any kind of public discourse could ever hope to have in Athens.[23] If, then, a comic dramatist seems on the face of it to be giving his plays a consistent slant in a particular direction on one or several political issues, it is not unreasonable to suppose that this slant represents his own opinion and that he is hoping that after the performance, this opinion will be shared more widely and more strongly among his audience than it had previously been. Such hopes were doubtless not always fulfilled, and even if they were, this certainly did not always, or even usually, result in policy changes even when the play was well enough received to win first prize: peace was not made after *The Acharnians*, Cleon was not discarded after *The Knights* (indeed, he was soon elected to a generalship), and the proposal in *The Frogs* to restore rights to the disfranchised was adopted only several months later when the war situation had become desperate. This, however, may well be due to differences in social composition between the Assembly and the theatre audience: one had to pay to attend the theatre, and the poorer and less educated sections of the citizen body are likely to have been under-represented. It is no coincidence that Old Comedy typically has a right-wing political agenda.[24]

Aristophanes takes care never to express open opposition to the democratic system itself; that is only to be expected, since, so far as we can tell, no one addressing the Athenian public ever did express such opposition except at times (such as in 411 and 404) when there seemed a real prospect that the system might be overthrown.[25] Repeatedly, however, above all in *The Wasps* but also elsewhere, he ridicules a crucial feature of the system, the use of mass juries dominated (according to the stereotype

he presents) by the elderly poor, and treats the daily pay-
ments made for jury service (but for which juries would have
consisted mainly of the well-to-do and leisured) as a waste of
public money. And though individual politicians may seem to
be satirized indiscriminately, those who are singled out most
persistently and extensively for hostile treatment, both in Aristophanes' plays and in our fragmentary evidence for those of his
rivals – notably Cleon (till his death in 422), Hyperbolus (till
his exile in 417 or 416) and Cleophon (in the last years of the
war) – are regularly described as relying mainly on the support
of the poor,[26] gained through financial and other favours, while
the rare cases in which politicians receive *favourable* mention
in comedy invariably relate to persons described, in comedy or
elsewhere, as opponents of these figures or of their brand of
politics.[27] The intended beneficiaries of the restoration of political rights advocated in *The Frogs* are explicitly (though euphemistically) identified with those who had taken part in the
oligarchic regime of 411, and the chorus go on to recommend
that the direction of affairs should be entrusted to 'men of good
birth and breeding' – and these two categories would certainly
overlap at a number of points. Aristophanes – and his rivals too
– may well, most of the time, have accepted democracy as the
only political system on offer or likely to be; but the evidence
suggests that they had no great love for it.

The attitude of Aristophanes to peace and war is coloured by
the same political tendencies. It is an egregious mistake to portray him as a pacifist.[28] He fully shares, or at least regularly
voices, the pride felt by all Athenians in their victories over the
Persians at Marathon in 490 and Salamis in 480; he believes
Athens may soon have to fight them again (*Peace* 108, 406–13;
Lysistrata 1133); and even when it comes to relations with other
Greek states, we find that in *The Birds*, whenever current or
recent campaigns are mentioned or alluded to, the tone is a
hawkish one – the only thing wrong with the Sicilian expedition,
apparently, is that victory is not coming quickly enough (line
639). But when *The Birds* was produced, Athens was not, and
did not expect to be, at war with Sparta; and whenever Athens
is at war with Sparta, it is taken for granted that what is needed

is to make peace as quickly as possible – although in *Lysistrata*, given the current situation, it is recognized that it will take a miracle to achieve this on acceptable terms. This is not an anti-war but a pro-Spartan orientation – and it is significant that in the early part of *The Acharnians* the hero, Dikaiopolis, is spoken of half a dozen times, by himself and others, as speaking 'in defence of Sparta'. Sparta was an oligarchic state; she had attempted to strangle Athenian democracy at birth in 508/7, Athenian anti-democrats had intrigued treasonably with Sparta during the war of the 450s, the Four Hundred hoped (in vain) that Sparta would be readier to make peace with them than with the democrats, and in 404 Spartan generals were intimidatingly present at the Assembly which voted the Thirty into power.[29] Aristophanes' ideal vision of Greek politics, briefly mentioned in *Peace* (line 1082) and given concrete form in dance and song at the end of *Lysistrata*, is of Athens and Sparta 'ruling Greece together' in friendly collaboration. It never happened, and never could have happened – and Aristophanes knows very well how deeply many of his fellow-citizens hate and distrust Sparta;[30] but at least until 404 and the experience of the Thirty, he never gives up the ideal.

In the literary and intellectual sphere, as we see from *The Clouds* and *The Frogs*, Aristophanes saw a marked contrast between old and new, Aeschylus and Euripides, traditional and sophistic education. His own position is ambivalent. He was, after all, one of the new generation himself – Euripides was old enough to be his father, and had been writing tragedies before he was born – and his characters are quite willing to use sophistic methods of argument when it suits them; his older rival Cratinus thought that it would make an effective thumbnail characterization of an imaginary intellectual spectator to call him 'a bit of a quibbler, a hunter of clever ideas, a Euripid-aristophanist'.[31] At the same time, he was very conscious that the intellectual had a social responsibility. He felt that responsibility strongly himself: he was, so far as we know, the only Old Comic dramatist who openly prided himself on being, through his plays, a benefactor of the Athenian people,[32] and in *The Frogs* he makes Aeschylus and Euripides agree that it is every poet's duty to 'make people into better citizens' (*The Frogs* 1008–9) – after which Aeschylus argues that Euripides, who has previously made a proud boast of having encouraged his public to question and test received wisdom, accept nothing on authority, and see two sides to every issue, has singularly failed to fulfil this duty. The same criticism would apply to the sophistic thinkers and educators, various (and sometimes conflicting) aspects of whose ideas and interests were embodied in the Socrates of *The Clouds*: it is all very well to deconstruct traditional certainties, but if one deconstructs an edifice without constructing a viable new one, one is left with a useless heap of rubble. And however unfair *The Clouds* may be to the real Socrates, Socrates' own disciple Plato makes him insist that he teaches no positive doctrine, asserts no propositions, does nothing but ask questions – or, as a hostile interpreter might well put it, that he is a negative critic without a constructive idea in his head.

Euripides and Socrates are also both accused of atheism – or rather of not believing in the gods of the community. This may seem surprising, coming from a dramatist who regularly himself portrays the gods in a manner which to modern religious sensibilities seems exceedingly irreverent, and who in three of his eleven surviving plays (*Peace*, *The Birds* and *Wealth*) makes his heroes defeat the designs of Zeus and the Olympians and, in the latter two plays, depose them from power. In none of this, however, was there anything impious. Undignified, even mocking, portrayals of the gods are to be found in Greek poetry all the way back to Homer. The possibility of Zeus falling from power, as his predecessors Uranus and Cronus had done, was a crucial element in such well-established myths as those of the birth of Athena and the wedding of Peleus and Thetis;[33] there was no reason why it should not be played with as a comic fantasy, an amusing impossibility like the building of a city of birds in mid air or the transfer of political power in Athens from men to women – particularly since (as Hesiod had long ago emphasized, and as most Athenians would say they knew from bitter experience) Zeus seemed so persistently and unreasonably hostile to mortals' natural aspirations for security and prosperity.[34] What was dangerous, and forbidden, was to do any-

thing calculated to deprive the established gods of the worship
to which they were traditionally entitled; for this would be likely
to anger the gods, and they might well take revenge not only on
the offender but on his entire community, all the more so if it
had failed to punish him. And nothing could be more certainly
calculated to deprive the gods of worship than an assertion that
they did not exist or (as Strepsiades in *The Clouds* is sometimes
made to understand, or misunderstand, Socrates as believing)
that they had already been expelled from power. To *imagine* a
scenario in which such an expulsion takes place is harmless,
precisely because we know it is only imaginary: we would love
not to be ruled by a capricious and spiteful Zeus (just as we
would love it today if there were no Inland Revenue), we enjoy
taking a dream-trip to a world in which he can no longer trouble
us, but when we wake up, as it were, at the end of the play,
we know Zeus is still going to be there. Accordingly, while
Aristophanes often makes fun of the gods in large and small
ways, he never lets any sympathetic character mock at religious
observances. After all, the very performance of an Aristophanic
comedy was itself part of a religious observance.

THE DRAMATIC FESTIVALS

Comedy at Athens, like tragedy, was always performed in connection with one of the festivals of the god Dionysus – the
Lenaea in the lunar month of Gamelion (corresponding roughly
to January) and the City Dionysia in Elaphebolion (corresponding roughly to March). The Lenaea, at which *The Acharnians*
and probably *Lysistrata* were produced, was essentially a local
Athenian affair, since visitors from abroad were unable to attend
in any numbers owing to the extreme difficulty of sea travel in
winter;[35] the City Dionysia was the occasion when the wealth
of Athens, political, literary and musical, was displayed to the
world. Comedy, to be sure, had relatively greater prominence
at the Lenaea, since the tragic contest there was a much slighter
affair (probably only four plays were presented, as against
twelve at the City Dionysia); nevertheless, for comic as well as

tragic poets, a victory at the City Dionysia, or even permission
to compete, carried significantly greater prestige than it did at
the Lenaea.[36]

The City Dionysia lasted four or five days.[37] Before the festival
began, the statue of its patron god, Dionysus Eleuthereus, was
brought in procession from a temple lying just outside the city,
near the Academy, to the Theatre of Dionysus, close under the
south face of the Acropolis, where the competitions were held;
here the god remained throughout the festival, watching the
performances and sometimes (as in *The Frogs*) seeing himself
take part in them. On the day after this procession there was
another, when numerous sacrifices were offered; the sponsors
(*choregoi*: see below) of the various performances took a leading
part in the procession and dressed themselves magnificently.
The rest of this day appears to have been devoted to contests of
boys' and men's choruses (representing the ten tribes into which
the citizen body was divided) singing and dancing the lyric
performances in honour of Dionysus and known as dithyrambs.

Possibly on this day, possibly at the start of the next day when
the dramatic performances began, an important civic ceremony
was performed: a parade was held of those young men, just
reaching their majority, whose fathers had been killed in battle,
and they were presented with a set of armour at the public
expense; increasingly too, the opportunity of so vast a gathering
was exploited to stage other public ceremonials for which the
widest publicity was desired.[38] Thus the audience which, on
the second day of the festival proper, settled down to watch
(probably) three tragedies and a satyr-play by one poet, and two
comedies by two other poets, could not help being well aware
that it (or rather the most important part of it) was also the
People of Athens, that courage and public spirit had made their
city great, and that it was up to them to keep it so.

This audience was enormous by most modern theatrical
standards (though not by those of, say, the amphitheatre of
Verona). The capacity of the Theatre of Dionysus was about
14,000, and there can be little doubt that it was always full
during the Dionysia. There seem to have been no restrictions of
age, gender or citizen status governing attendance: Plato in his

Gorgias (502d) makes Socrates say that 'poets in the theatres' direct their eloquence at a public 'consisting of children, women and men, slave and free, all at once', and one passage in *Lysistrata* (line 1051) – though only one – makes explicit reference to the presence of women. The audience, to be sure, can sometimes be addressed as if it consisted only of men; but then it can also be addressed as if it were identical with the Athenian citizen body, which it certainly was not, since it always contained many resident foreigners (metics)[39] and, at the City Dionysia, many visiting foreigners too. Both foreigners and women, in classical Athens, will have been familiar with the experience of being treated, especially on public occasions, as though they did not exist; and the women, in particular, may well have been largely of low status[40] – both in *The Birds* (793–6) and in *The Poet and the Women* (395–7) it is taken for granted that when a citizen goes to the theatre his wife normally stays at home, and when the women in the latter play are discussing the alleged iniquities of Euripides, none of them ever claims to have actually seen any of his tragedies. Women may have been segregated in the back rows;[41] many seats near the front[42] were reserved for Athenian priests and officials, the most privileged seat of all, the centre place in the front row, being that of the priest of Dionysus.

Preparations for the festival had begun several months before. Soon after taking office in the summer, the Archon[43] took in hand the arrangements for the City Dionysia, and his colleague the Basileus[44] those for the Lenaea. In connection with tragedy and comedy these magistrates had two main duties. On the one hand, they had to select the poets who were to be allowed to compete (to be 'given a chorus', as the expression was). It is not known how they did this or what advice, if any, they took; being chosen by lot, they would not normally have any special qualifications for the task themselves, and they may well have chosen expert assessors to assist them, though the final responsibility was their own. There are hints that poets, at least sometimes, would recite samples of their work to the magistrate. The task, at any rate, was a very delicate one, and a magistrate who made an unpopular choice (such as one we hear of who refused a tragic chorus to Sophocles) might never be allowed to forget it. The presiding magistrate also had to nominate sponsors (*choregoi*) to equip the choruses, bear the expenses of their training, and organize the performances generally. He chose men of considerable means, who were then required to undertake the task as a compulsory civic duty. Sometimes he received applications from men volunteering to be *choregoi*, for despite the expense involved, a *choregia* was widely regarded as an honour, and defendants in lawsuits often pointed to the number and magnificence of their *choregiai* as proof of their public spirit.[45]

Each comic *choregos* was responsible for one play. Acting on the advice of the poet (and/or the producer, if the two roles were not combined – see below), he had to organize and finance the training of the chorus, supply costumes and properties, hire the piper who accompanied them and any non-speaking performers who might be required – and, if he valued his reputation (unlike Antimachus, cursed by the chorus of *The Acharnians* for his stinginess), provide a dinner afterwards for all concerned in the production. In the formal competition records, the name of the winning *choregos* regularly appears before that of the producer.

It is not altogether clear how and by whom the actors who played individual parts were selected. It is known that in early times poets had acted in their own plays, and that towards the middle of the fifth century BC they began instead to employ professional actors of their own choice. It is also known that by the early fourth century five principal actors ('protagonists') were being chosen by the state and allocated by lot, one to each poet; but it is not known when this system was introduced. At the Lenaea a prize was awarded to the best comic protagonist (not necessarily the one who had acted in the winning play); surprisingly, it was not till a century after Aristophanes' time that a similar prize was introduced at the City Dionysia.

Traditionally poets had produced their own plays, and it was as producers (*didaskaloi*, literally 'trainers' of the chorus) that their names appeared in the official records of the festivals. By Aristophanes' time, however, it had become common for poets,

especially comic poets,[46] to collaborate with a specialist producer (and often also with an assistant producer in charge of
the chorus), and many of his plays were produced for him either
by Callistratus (who was responsible for *The Acharnians* and
Lysistrata among others), by Philonides (who was also a comic
poet himself), or (at the end of his career) by his own son Araros.
There can be little doubt that audiences were well aware of the
real identity of the author; indeed in *The Knights*, the first play
he produced himself, Aristophanes, through the mouth of the
chorus-leader, says that many members of the public have been
asking him 'why he had not long ago asked for a chorus in his
own name',[47] and the poet Plato[48] may have presented himself
openly, in his comedy *Peisander*, as the author-but-not-
producer of the play.[49]

When *choregos*, poet and producer (if any) had completed
their preparations, two days before the festival, a preview (*pro-
agon*) was held in the Odeon, not far from the theatre. The poet
(or the producer, or both?) presented the actors and chorus,
without their masks and costumes, and announced the title of
the play. In some cases this will have given the public a fairly
good idea of what the play was about: after the hints given in
The Acharnians (7–8, 299–302), they will not have been very
surprised when a play announced as *The Knights* turned out to
be an attack on Cleon. In other cases the audience would have
been put in a mood of mystified expectation (a play called *The
Clouds* might have been about anything) or even positively
misled (in view of the strong tradition of animal choruses in
comedy, no one would have expected the chorus of *The Wasps*
to consist, as it did, of elderly jurymen).

Productions at the dramatic festivals were normally always
competitive; the only exception that we know of, in Aristophanes' time, was the restaging of *The Frogs*, which was ordered
by a special Assembly decree. The prizes were allotted by a panel
of judges selected by a complicated procedure designed to ensure
that the judging should be both competent and fair: a large pool
of candidates was selected by the Council (some of them on
the nomination of the competing *choregoi*) and the ten actual
judges, one from each tribe, were chosen by lot from this pool

just before the contest. It appears, furthermore, that normally only five of the ten votes (again chosen by lot) were read and counted; this may have been done partly as a further precaution against corruption (doubling the odds against a bribe doing any good to its giver) and partly in order to give the god a share in deciding the destination of the prize (for the decision of the lot was not due to human choice and therefore logically had to be due to divine choice).[50] Many remarks in comedy, in Aristophanes' time and long after, indicate that the judges were thought likely to be strongly influenced by the perceived preferences of the audience as a whole, though dramatists also often made their choruses address the judges directly to appeal for a favourable verdict.[51]

PERFORMERS AND PRODUCTION

Technically the competition at the City Dionysia or Lenaea was not between plays or between poets but between choruses; thus when all was ready for a play to begin, the crier proclaimed *Eisage ton choron* ('Bring on your chorus') – even though it had long been the regular practice for a play to begin with dialogue and for the chorus to come on only later. The comic chorus consisted of twenty-four members. Normally each chorus is given a distinctive identity, but it need not retain this identity consistently throughout the play. In *The Acharnians*, for example, the chorus at its first entry is very plainly identified as consisting of elderly, bellicose charcoal-burners from Acharnae, and it speaks and sings in that capacity for most of the first half of the play; in the second half, however, there is nothing in the script to distinguish it from any other comic chorus (indeed in one song it seems to identify itself with a comic chorus that had performed at the Lenaea in a previous year)[52] and even before this it speaks at one moment (as other Aristophanic choruses sometimes also do) in the name of the author in the first person.[53] Even in *The Clouds*, where the plot requires that the chorus should retain to the end their character as cloud-goddesses, they can speak (lines 1115–30) as a group of performers taking part in a competition, and demand, with menaces, to be given the first prize.[54]

Lysistrata is exceptional among surviving plays[55] in having two choruses, presumably of twelve each (though they eventually unite into one). The motive for this is dramatic, not musical, since all female parts whatever were played by men.[56]

The normal expectation was that once the chorus had appeared on the scene it would remain until the end of the play – indeed that its departure *was* the end of the play.[57] This imposed some restrictions on the plot: in particular, after the first entry of the chorus, nothing could be done of which they disapproved and which they were willing and able to stop. In tragedy this could be a nuisance, and choruses were sometimes made to take oaths whose implications they did not fully realize, so that when they understood the situation and wished to intervene they could not do so without perjuring themselves. In Old Comedy the chorus very frequently does strongly disapprove of what one or another character is doing, and does try to stop them, often by force, as in *The Acharnians*. Only in *The Clouds*, of the three plays in this volume, does the chorus not intervene in the action; and there it turns out that its non-intervention was deliberate, and has far graver consequences than any intervention could have had.

The chorus normally danced as it sang, and the dance-movements were regarded as an important part of the total effect of a choral ode, but unfortunately we know very little about them.[58]

There appears to have been a competition rule limiting the number of actors who could have speaking parts. For tragedy, in Aristophanes' time, the limit was three, but for comedy it was four.[59] This restriction meant that the author could not, like a modern dramatist, carry a large number of characters through the play, unless he was prepared to have the same part played by different actors in different scenes; some Athenian dramatists did split parts in this way,[60] but Aristophanes' scripts strongly suggest that he never did. He regularly has only one character, or at most two, who appear in all or most scenes of a play; and characters whom one might have expected to be of some importance, such as Lampito in *Lysistrata*, can simply vanish. *The Clouds*, with three characters carried through the play, is exceptional in this respect, and presented Aristophanes with a problem for which he found no satisfactory solution – though perhaps he would have found one, had he not abandoned his revision of the play before it was completed. With only four actors at his disposal, he could not have a debate between Right and Wrong with Strepsiades, Pheidippides and Socrates all present; so before the debate begins, Socrates, without giving a reason, has to excuse himself.[61]

Another scene in which Aristophanes stretches the four-actor limit as far as it will go is the opening Assembly scene in *The Acharnians*. Here one actor (doubtless the protagonist) takes the part of Dikaiopolis, another that of the Crier (who has relatively little to say, but, given his official role in the proceedings, must be present throughout the Assembly meeting); the other two actors must therefore share the scene's four other roles. This can only be worked if one plays Amphitheus and the Ambassador, the other Pseudartabas and Theorus; and it will be observed that the Ambassador is got off stage fifteen lines before Pseudartabas, to give his actor a chance to change mask and costume.[62] Even so, two quite rapid changes are required: one actor must exit as Amphitheus at line 55 and return as the Ambassador at line 64, the other must exit as Pseudartabas at line 125 and return as Theorus at line 134.[63]

The rule about number of actors was rigid, the rule about the continuous presence of the chorus nearly so. More elastic were certain conventions about the structure of the play. The basic form was something like this:

(1) An initial scene or series of scenes (called by modern scholars the *prologue*), in which the opening situation was made clear and the movement of the plot begun.

(2) The *parodos* or entry of the chorus, often marked by a long and varied song-and-dance movement.

(3) A series of scenes interspersed with songs by the chorus; the central scene was usually a formal debate (*agon*) on the crucial issue of the play, containing two opposing speeches each introduced by a choral song.

(4) The *parabasis*, in which the chorus partially or completely abandoned its dramatic role and addressed the audience directly, usually in the absence of the actors. It normally consists of three songs (*S*) and three speeches (*s*), in the order *S1-s1*, *S2-s2*, *S3-s3*; *S2* corresponds metrically to *S3* and *s2* to *s3*, and the first speech (*s1*) usually ends with a passage to be rattled off very rapidly (theoretically in one breath), called a *pnigos*.

(5) Another series of scenes interspersed with choral songs. The songs in this section generally contained satirical jibes at prominent individuals (the chorus of *Lysistrata* [lines 1042–8] draws attention to the fact that it is departing from this custom); one of them was normally, in Aristophanes' earlier plays, expanded into a brief second *parabasis*.[64]

(6) A concluding scene of general rejoicing, often associated with a banquet or a wedding.

None of the plays in this volume corresponds exactly to this pattern, and it is evident that poets regarded it only as a basic framework on which variations could be played. The *parados* of *The Clouds*, for example, consists of only a single song (and the chorus are probably not even on stage to sing it; they make their entry a little later [lines 323–8], in silence). *The Acharnians* has no *agon*; this is certainly because, had there been one, somebody would have had to argue in favour of war, and Aristophanes is careful, in all his plays on the theme of peace, not to allow the case for war to be presented.[65] For the same reason, although *Lysistrata* contains a scene in the form of an *agon*, it is completely one-sided: the Magistrate is hardly allowed to get a word in edgeways.[66] Again, *Lysistrata*, with its divided chorus, can have no *parabasis*; in place of this we find a scene between the two choruses, with alternating song, dance, speeches and violence – though the speeches are still directed mainly at the audience. Even the final scene of rejoicing is dispensable. The audience of *The Clouds* may well have assumed that when the triumphant Strepsiades took his son home and put his creditors to flight, an ending of that kind was coming, and they have already been told (line 1213) that there is going to be a feast; but the chorus have already (lines 1113–14) given a hint that things are going to develop differently, and instead

of rejoicing the play ends in destruction – after which the leader
of the chorus says that it is time to go, and the chorus simply
walk off.

More consistent, though less formalized, than the 'technical'
structure described above is a 'functional' structure which
appears with little variation in every surviving Aristophanic
play.[67] Each play begins with a person, a situation and an idea.
The person is the comic hero or heroine – in our three plays,
Dikaiopolis, Strepsiades and Lysistrata, respectively. The situation is one which from this person's point of view (and often
from that of many others as well) is profoundly unsatisfactory.
And the idea is the hero(ine)'s plan for putting things right, for
restoring happiness to himself,[68] or his family, or his city, or (as
in *Lysistrata*) the whole Greek world, or even the whole of
humanity. In relation to this idea, each play can be analysed
into four phases:

(1) *Conception*: we learn about the initial situation, and discover what the idea is. Sometimes, as in *The Acharnians*, the idea
strikes the hero, like an inspiration, as we watch; sometimes, as
in *Lysistrata*, it is evidently already well formed, and in course
of being put into practice, before the play begins – but we are
always kept mystified for a considerable time as to its exact
nature.

(2) *Struggle*: the hero(ine) meets with, and overcomes, diffi-
culties or dangers standing in the way of implementing the idea,
often taking the form of the opposition of some person or group.
Lysistrata has to face not only male opposition (from the men's
chorus and the Magistrate) but also, more than once, that of
her own followers.

(3) *Realization*: the idea is put into effect.

(4) *Consequences*: a series of scenes illustrating the effects
that follow from the implementation of the idea, effects that are
usually highly beneficial, at least in terms of the comic concept
of happiness;[69] occasionally, as in *The Clouds*, the idea proves
a failure or worse – but this only (and always) happens when it
was purely selfish in aim and could never have brought any
benefit to the community generally.[70]

At both the City Dionysia and the Lenaea, comedy and

tragedy were performed in the Theatre of Dionysus south of the Acropolis. The present layout of the theatre dates from long after Aristophanes' time, and the detailed reconstruction of the fifth-century BC theatre remains a matter of great dispute, but certain points are clear, not least from the evidence of the tragic and (especially) comic texts themselves. Centrally placed, with the spectators' seating encompassing it on three sides, was the *orchestra* ('dance-floor') where the chorus usually performed; in the centre of this there was probably an altar, round which the 'circular choruses' of dithyramb danced, and which often served in tragedy, and sometimes in comedy, as a place of sanctuary for the persecuted. Behind (i.e., south of) the *orchestra* stood a building called the *skene* ('booth'), originally perhaps no more than a dressing-room, but in Aristophanes' time regularly representing, both in tragedy and in comedy, a house, temple, cave, thicket or other 'interior' space – or more accurately, perhaps (since only its façade could normally be seen), the boundary between that interior and the exterior space represented by the performing area itself. The *skene* probably had three doors; part of it was on two floors, with a window on the upper storey (used in several comedies), and the remaining, single-storeyed section had a flat roof (on which Dikaiopolis' wife stands in *The Acharnians* to watch the Dionysiac procession, and which in *Lysistrata* represents the battlements of the Acropolis). Painted panels hung on the front walls could be used to indicate unusual scene settings, such as the Hoopoe's thicket in *The Birds*; it is possible that the west front of the Acropolis was thus visually represented in *Lysistrata*, and that when the *skene* had to represent two or more houses at once (e.g. the houses of Dikaiopolis and Lamachus towards the end of *The Acharnians*) an appropriately placed panel gave a *trompe l'oeil* effect of a passageway between buildings.

It was long a matter of controversy whether there was a raised platform in front of the *skene*, but the evidence of vase-paintings, both from Athens and (a little later) from southern Italy, makes it fairly certain that in Aristophanes' time there was an oblong wooden platform, about three feet above *orchestra* level and approached by sets of steps[71] at the corners and possibly also in the centre. Before the central door stood a small altar (dedicated, it seems, like the altars in front of many real Athenian houses, to Apollo Agyieus), much used in tragedy for prayer and the burning of incense.

The platform was at times a convenient device for marking off the actors visually from the chorus, but the actors were certainly not at this time confined to it, and movement between platform and *orchestra* was easy. On one south Italian vase a character, apparently the centaur Cheiron, is being helped or forced up the corner steps, a slave pushing from behind and another man pulling him from above by the back of the head.[72]

Between the ends of the platform and the spectators' seating there were broad side passages (*eisodoi*[73]) for the entrance and exit of the chorus and of actors coming from, or going to, places other than the 'house' or 'houses' in the *skene*. In later comedy the two *eisodoi* were treated as leading to different parts of the offstage world (one to the city centre, the other to the countryside or the harbour), but there is no clear evidence that any such convention existed in Aristophanes' time. It seems likely, however, that the chorus normally entered along the western *eisodos* (on the spectators' right side), so that when they marched in in three files and then turned to face the audience, the left file became the front row.[74]

Two major special-effects devices were available for use in tragedy and comedy. One, known to modern scholars as the *ekkyklema*,[75] served primarily to bring tableaux and immobile characters (such as dead bodies in tragedy) out of the *skene* into view; it is appropriately employed in *The Acharnians* to bring an immobile tragic poet into view, but Aristophanes seems also to have put it to a wide variety of other uses. It was probably nothing more complex than a wheeled platform or trolley which could be rolled out of the central door of the *skene*. The other device, probably known already in Aristophanes' time simply as 'the machine' (*mechane*), was a crane which was used to stage flying entries by gods and heroes in tragedy[76] – and by Socrates in *The Clouds*.

The comic actor's costume was traditionally characterized by grotesque padding, and it seems that this was still normal for

most characters in Aristophanes' time; right through the fourth
century, vase-paintings and terracotta figurines continue to
endow most comic characters with ludicrous paunches. Over
this actors wore close-fitting bodysuits, and those playing male
parts generally wore a very short tunic which left uncovered a
large leather phallus. Sometimes this was made unobtrusive by
being curled into a loop and tied up to itself; sometimes it was
left to hang loose;[77] sometimes, notably in the second half of
Lysistrata and for Dikaiopolis in the final scene of *The Acharnians*, it was shown erect. Certain male characters who were
presented, or who presented themselves, as persons of superior
dignity, wore full-length garments (as did almost all females[78]);
the Magistrate in *Lysistrata* will have been one of these, so that
he can be made to appear like a woman without changing his
clothes, merely by kitting him out with some suitable accessories.

Certain characters would wear special costumes, or carry
marks of their identity or profession. Lamachus in *The Acharnians* probably wore a red military cloak (*phoinikis*). In
Lysistrata, Lampito and her Peloponnesian companions will
have worn 'Doric' garments which were considerably more
revealing than those worn by Athenian women (hence the comments on their physical endowments in lines 78–92); the Scythian policemen would be recognized by their distinctive costume
(known from art) and their bows and quivers, the Spartan herald
by his wand of office.

The costumes of the chorus, if they represented human beings,
were similar to those of the actors, with phalli if appropriate.
Choruses of animals or birds,[79] on the other hand, gave the
costume designer plenty of opportunity to exercise his imagination – though he did not, it seems, make as much use of it as he
might have done in the case of *The Clouds*, where, on the
contrary, Strepsiades is made to say a great deal about the fact
that the chorus do *not* look like clouds (lines 340–55).

Actors and chorus all wore masks, which were typically made
with grotesque exaggeration of features. This custom was
almost certainly inherited from a long tradition associating
masked impersonation with the worship of Dionysus (on
vase-paintings a mask, standing by itself, sometimes actually

represents the god), but it also had distinct practical advantages: it made face visibility and recognition easy in a very large theatre where the spectator had no artificial optical aids, and it also facilitated the playing of many different roles, sometimes in quick succession, by the same actor. The masks, though they were called 'faces' (*prosopa* or *prosopeia*), are better described as headpieces, since they also included hair (or a bald crown, as the case might be) and, for most adult males, a beard.[80] By the late fourth century there was a repertoire of stock masks available for any play, but this may well have been a development associated with the tendency of comic characters themselves, by that time, to be classifiable into a rather limited number of well-recognized types. Certainly in Aristophanes' time some masks must have been unique or nearly so (that of Pseudartabas in *The Acharnians*, with its single gigantic eye, is an obvious example[81]). When a living individual was caricatured on stage, it was normal to commission a mask recognizably like him: in *The Knights* Aristophanes goes out of his way to make one of the characters explain why this has not been done in the case of Cleon.[82] One reason for the choice of Socrates to represent the whole class of contemporary intellectuals in *The Clouds* may well have been that, as we know from other sources, Socrates had an unusually ugly face which lent itself easily to caricature.

The masks and the unchanging back-scene are not the only features of Athenian theatre production that would have been offensive to an audience brought up on early-twentieth-century naturalism. Since the performances took place in the daytime and in the open air, it was not possible to indicate visually whether the action was supposed to be taking place in daylight or darkness. *The Clouds* begins at night; but the Athenian audience will only have known this because the characters are asleep and one of them, on waking, complains how long the nights are, and presently asks for a lamp. Again, it was impossible, except by the use of the *ekkyklema*, to show action taking place indoors. In general this would not be too disturbing, because much more of the business of ancient Greek than of modern western life was in any case done in the open air; and audiences seem to have readily accepted some stretching of plausibility to enable scenes to be performed in front of them which in 'reality' would more likely have taken place out of their sight – scenes like the debate between Right and Wrong in *The Clouds*[83] or the unconsummated love-scene between Cinesias and Myrrhine in *Lysistrata*.[84]

In any case, the imaginary location of the action is often left vague, and its imaginary time is often gappy. *The Acharnians* begins on the Pnyx, where the Assembly was held, but when Dikaiopolis walks 'home' (i.e., probably, up the steps towards the *skene*) we find we are in front of his house – and he says, moreover, that he has returned to his country village; he proceeds to celebrate the Country Dionysia, yet at the end of the play we find we are in the middle of the Anthesteria – which was held two months later. In *Lysistrata*, the action is continuous up to the ignominious retreat of the Magistrate; when the younger women next appear, we find that five days have elapsed (line 881). So long as the audience knows those facts about the imaginary situation which matter for the understanding of the current scene, they are evidently not expected to bother their heads with those which do not.

COMEDY IN LANGUAGE

Aristophanes' merits as a comedian can for the most part be left to speak for themselves; but one matter which has to be mentioned here, because in a translation it cannot be reproduced but only imitated, is his dexterity at all forms of juggling with words. I shall give some examples of this from the beginning of *The Acharnians* – a passage that provides a favourable opportunity for word-play, because nothing whatever is happening: Dikaiopolis is merely whiling his time away, waiting to see if the Assembly will begin less than five hours late. While he is waiting, he fires off a few (as we can call them) warm-up jokes. One of the first of these occurs almost at once. 'The number of things that have pained me', says Dikaiopolis, 'is *psammakosio-gargara*', literally 'sand-hundred-heaps'. The Greek language provided excellent facilities for the invention of novel compound words, and Aristophanes exploits them with gusto; in *Lysistrata* (lines 457–8) 'lettuce-seed-pancake-vendors of the Market Square' and 'innkeepers, bakers and garlic-makers' are just one word each (each word filling eleven-twelfths of a verse line). The idea is carried to its extreme of extremes at the end of *The Assemblywomen*, where the main item on the menu for the concluding feast is described in one word of seventy-nine syllables.[85]

Another and very common trick is the so-called *para prosdokian*, 'contrary-to-expectation': the speaker makes us quite sure what we are going to hear next – and then says something quite different. Dikaiopolis recalls a long list of theatrical joys and sorrows, and then says that never in all the years he's . . . – and we expect to hear that in all the years he's lived – never has he been so distressed as now; in fact we hear that in all the years he's washed, he's never been so stung by soap in the eyes as now – that is, as he is 'stung' (wounded, enraged) by the emptiness of the Pnyx on the day of so important a meeting.

The simple (and not so simple) pun is also frequent – and particularly challenging for the translator. A little later in Dikaiopolis' speech (lines 32–6) he is reflecting on the difference between life in the city, where everything one needs must be purchased for cash, and peasant self-sufficiency; I here translate his words literally:

yearning for my village, where no one said 'buy [*priō*] charcoal', nor vinegar or oil; it knew not 'buy' [*priō*], but provided everything for itself, and The Sawyer [*ho Priōn*] was not there.

Probably 'The Sawyer' (or 'The Saw') was the nickname of a politician who either had a rasping voice, or had allegedly once had to make a living as a woodcutter:[86] politicians, like market traders, were creatures of the city, who were not to be found in Dikaiopolis' village.

On another pun, of rather a different kind, the whole plot of *The Acharnians* depends. Two lines early in the play – one spoken by the demigod Amphitheus to the Assembly (line 52), the other later on by Dikaiopolis to Amphitheus (line 131) – are identical: *spondas poiēsai pros Lakedaimonious monōi*, 'to make peace with the Spartans, only'. But from the one passage to the other the construction of *monōi*, 'only', has changed. In the earlier passage Amphitheus is saying 'The gods have commissioned me *to make peace with the Spartans, only* me', i.e., I am the only person authorized to do so; in the later one, Dikaiopolis is saying 'I want you *to make peace with the Spartans, only* for me and my wife and children', i.e., I and my family are to be its only beneficiaries. It need only be added that when the peace-treaty (*spondai*) is finally brought by Amphitheus, it takes the very agreeable form of three wine-skins suitable for pouring libations (also *spondai*).[87]

Michael Silk has recently written that the central features of 'the comic vision of Aristophanes' are unlimited *possibility*, unlimited *inclusivity*, 'the necessity of *connection*' with cultural tradition, and 'a deep instinct for the *particular*, the concrete, the immediate'.[88] Or to paraphrase: nothing is beyond imagination; no one is contemptible (except those who choose to make themselves so); everything that can be seen and felt and experienced is of interest, and capable of generating happiness through laughter; and we are what our past has made us, though our nature also impels us to reach out for an ideal future. It is not a bad vision for the twenty-first century, or for any other.

AHS

NOTES

1. This does not necessarily imply that Aristophanes was born or lived in the district of Cydathenaeum, since deme affiliation was hereditary from father to son.
2. If this apprenticeship is what he means by a reference in *The Wasps* (lines 1018–20) to his 'unseen . . . ventriloquial' contributions to other poets' work at the beginning of his career.
3. For further information about *The Acharnians*, and likewise on *The Clouds* and *Lysistrata*, see the Prefaces to the three plays.
4. Ancient scholars knew of forty-four plays attributed to Aristophanes, but considered four of these to be possibly spurious. There

may have been others whose scripts had disappeared by the time the librarians of Hellenistic Alexandria began to collect and catalogue Aristophanes' comedies, about a century after his death.

5. From the period between AD 300 and 650 there survive some thirty-five papyrus fragments of the hundreds of comedies produced in Aristophanes' time and in the preceding generation; of these fragments, all but one (containing substantial parts of Eupolis' comedy *The Demes*) come from the eleven extant plays of Aristophanes.

6. One of them, *The Poet and the Women*, only just made it, its survival depending, probably for over two centuries, on the preservation of a single manuscript.

7. *The Poet and the Women* is often referred to by its Greek title *Thesmophoriazusae* ('Women attending the Thesmophoria festival').

8. *The Assemblywomen* is often referred to by its Greek title *Ecclesiazusae* ('Women attending the Assembly').

9. *Wealth* is sometimes referred to by its Greek title *Plutus*.

10. Such honorific crowns were usually of gold, but in 405 no gold was available for such purposes.

11. Another son, Philippus, also became a comic poet himself. Two other comic dramatists of the fourth century, Nicostratus and Philetaerus, were thought by some ancient scholars to have been sons of Aristophanes too.

12. The *Symposium* was written between 384 and 379; see Sir Kenneth Dover's introduction to his edition of the dialogue (Cambridge, 1980), p. 10.

13. We cannot tell whether this remark relates to Aristophanes' plays (which were produced at festivals of Dionysus, and in which sexual themes were usually prominent) or to his private life.

14. This is almost the only passage in classical Greek literature in which sexual orientations are spoken of in recognizably 'modern' terms. Elsewhere, and not least in Aristophanes' comedies and in other parts of the *Symposium* itself, on the one hand it is assumed that the great majority of adult males are as ready to desire and pursue a young male as a young female, and on the other hand (despite the continuing popularity of Sappho's poetry) homo-erotic desire between females is almost totally ignored. Sir Kenneth Dover's *Greek Homosexuality* (London, 1978) remains the best treatment of this whole subject.

15. To take only one example, the professional speech-writer Lysias, composing a defence speech for a client prosecuted by Cinesias (not the character in *Lysistrata*, but the lyric poet who is a character in *The Birds*), thought it would help his client's case to remind the jury of alleged acts of gross impiety which Cinesias had committed, acts which

'in ordinary circumstances it is disgraceful even to mention, but *which you hear about from the comic dramatists every year*' (Lysias, fragment 53).

16. Appointment by lot excluded a few positions (e.g. generals, ambassadors) for which it was considered vital to have the best persons available, and which were therefore filled by election.

17. The so-called 'First Peloponnesian War' (459–446 BC).

18. The wars of 431–404 are usually, following the contemporary historian Thucydides, spoken of as a single war ('the Peloponnesian War' *par excellence*). Most Athenians, however, at the time and for at least two generations afterwards, thought of them as a series of separate wars; usually they distinguished two wars against Sparta and her allies (431–421 and 414–404) plus the Sicilian war of 415–413.

19. The term 'the Thirty Tyrants' for this junta is of later origin; it was not used by Athenians at the time or for generations after.

20. Indeed, there is good reason to believe that certain features of the *Republic*'s ideal state are consciously modelled on the society created by Praxagora in *The Assemblywomen*.

21. Current criticism is represented at its best by Michael Silk's recent book, *Aristophanes and the Definition of Comedy* (Oxford, 2000).

22. Or else claims that it is pointless to inquire into these aims (or 'intentions', often printed in sneer quotes) because they cannot be known. As T. P. Wiseman has pointed out (*The Principal Thing* [Classical Association Presidential Address, 2001], p. 6), if this claim were valid, then all historical study would be impossible, as would many of the inferences and decisions we make all the time in everyday life: 'any proposition about the past is formally unknowable, since we can't go back there to find out, but meaningful statements about the past can be made, and constantly are made even by the most theoretical of us.'

23. We cannot, of course, tell with precision what proportion of the 14,000 or so in a full Theatre of Dionysus were adult male citizens, but characters and choruses certainly often address the audience as if it were identical with the citizen body. In the Assembly the quorum for certain types of business was 6,000, and it appears that the enclosure on the Pnyx hill, where meetings were held, was designed to contain just about that number; in 411 it was claimed that in practice attendance never even reached 5,000 (see Thucydides 8.72) – and though doubtless tendentious, this statement cannot have been totally out of touch with reality, since many members of the naval crews to whom it was addressed will have often attended Assembly meetings themselves.

24. For this purpose I define a right-winger as one who favours the active use of the power and institutions of the state to maintain or

extend privilege and inequality among its citizens, and a left-winger as one who favours the active use of the power of the state to reduce or eliminate such privilege and inequality. I have discussed the issues raised here more fully in my articles 'How to avoid being a *komodoumenos*' (in *Classical Quarterly* 46 [1996], pp. 327–56) and 'The theatre audience, the *demos*, and the *Suppliants* of Aeschylus' (in C. B. R. Pelling, ed., *Greek Tragedy and the Historian* [Oxford, 1997], pp. 63–79, esp. 63–71).

25. Even then it was sometimes necessary to use cautious language: Peisander, arguing before the Assembly in 411 that Athens must change her constitution or lose the war, said that what was needed 'at present' was 'not to have a democracy *of the present kind*' but 'a more sensible constitution, tending *more* to place *office* in the hands of a limited number', and that once the emergency was overcome these arrangements could be changed again (Thucydides 8.53).

26. Another frequent comic target, Pericles (who died in 429, before Aristophanes' career had begun), is also so described by fourth-century writers (Plato, *Gorgias* 515e; Aristotle, *The Athenian Constitution* 27–28).

27. Only five living male Athenians are known to have been mentioned favourably in comedy between 432/1 and 405/4: Thucydides son of Melesias, an old antagonist of Pericles; Ulius, the son of another of Pericles' opponents, Cimon; Nicias, an opponent at different times of both Cleon and Hyperbolus; Archeptolemus, a known oligarch, later executed for treason; and the tragic dramatist Sophocles, who Pericles had once said was incompetent to hold elective office, and who as a *proboulos* (see Preface to *Lysistrata*) had a significant degree of responsibility for the installation of an oligarchy in 411 (compare Aristotle, *Rhetoric* 1419a26–29).

28. The attempt sometimes made in the 1980s to draw parallels between *Lysistrata* and the activities of the 'peace women' of Greenham Common was equally misleading. Lysistrata, far from seeking to disarm Athens unilaterally, actually takes hostages (line 244) to ensure that the women from the enemy states will carry out their part of the agreed plan – even though these women, like those from Athens, have already sworn a solemn oath to do so.

29. Lysias, *Against Eratosthenes* 71–6.

30. *The Acharnians*, lines 308, 509–12; *Peace*, lines 623, 1063–8; *Lysistrata*, line 629.

31. Cratinus, fragment 342.

32. See my article 'Old Comedians on Old Comedy', *Drama* 1 (1992), pp. 14–33, esp. 27–30.

33. Athena was born from Zeus' head after he had swallowed her mother, Metis, on learning of a prophecy that if she bore a child, that child would overthrow Zeus. The sea-goddess Thetis was married to the mortal Peleus after Zeus and Poseidon, her previous suitors, had been told that Thetis was destined to bear a son mightier than his father.

34. In thinking about ancient Greek religion, nothing is more liable to put the modern mind on a wrong track than the assumption, axiomatic to all modern religions, that divinity is inherently good. It is evident from much that ancient Greeks, both real and fictitious, say or are made to say that they would have *liked* to believe that the gods were good; but only too often the gods' actions seemed to make such a hypothesis untenable. To the ancient Greek, what was axiomatic about the gods was that they were *powerful*.

35. Aristophanes in *The Acharnians* (lines 502–8) draws attention to this fact to protect himself from being again accused of 'slandering the City in the presence of foreigners'.

36. A papyrus commentary on an unknown play of Aristophanes (Oxyrhynchus Papyrus 2737) cites the comic dramatist Plato as saying that when the first play he produced in his own name (evidently at the City Dionysia) was placed only fourth, he 'was thrust back *eis tous Lēnaikous*' (which might mean 'to the Lenaean competitions' or 'into the ranks of Lenaean poets'). This implies that at any given time, there were some dramatists who were thought worthy to compete at the City Dionysia and others, including those who had recently failed there, who were considered 'second-division' talent fit only for the Lenaea.

37. It is disputed whether the programme at the City Dionysia was reduced (and the number of comedies cut from five to three) during the 'Peloponnesian War'. On the one hand, whereas the ancient note on the production of Aristophanes' *Wealth*, in 388, names four competing plays, the seven such notes we possess for comedies produced before 404 each name only two; and a passage in *The Birds* (lines 786–9) implies that in 414 tragedy and comedy could be seen on the same day, in the morning and afternoon respectively. On the other hand, we now know that at some time during this period a comedy was placed fourth (see previous note), and it has been calculated that the number of known Old Comic play-titles is too great to be accommodated in the available competition slots if it is assumed that only three plays per festival were produced between 431 and 404. It is possible to reconcile these data if we assume (i) that the production-notes for wartime plays list not all the competitors but only the prizewinners and (ii) that when

a day was divided between tragedy and comedy, there were sometimes two comedies rather than one in the afternoon.

38. For example, the making of important official proclamations (cf. *The Birds* 1072–5) or, on at least one occasion (probably in the 420s), a display of the funds currently stored in the Athenian state treasury (in the form of a procession of several hundred porters each carrying a talent of silver). On the civic significance of these ceremonies see S. D. Goldhill, 'The Great Dionysia and civic ideology', *Journal of Hellenic Studies* 107 (1987), pp. 58–76, esp. 59–64 – who, however, goes well beyond the evidence (and in some cases well beyond probability) in assuming that they were all held every year and that they were all held on the first day of the tragic competition.

39. The presence of foreigners is explicitly recognized in *The Acharnians*, line 508 – where it would have suited Dikaiopolis' argument better to have ignored them, had he been able to.

40. Many of those who attended the City Dionysia may have come from the ranks of the free courtesans (*hetairai*): they lived independently, they had few or no family and household responsibilities, they had no inhibitions about being seen in the company of men – and they would have enjoyed the bawdier aspects of comedy (and of satyr-drama too).

41. This segregation is a possible (though not the only possible) interpretation of *Peace* 962–7.

42. The number of such seats may have been close to a thousand, given that, for example, the whole Council of Five Hundred had a right to seats in a reserved block (the *bouleutikon*). Occasionally a distinguished individual was given a personal right to privileged seating (*prohedria*) in honour of some great achievement; in *The Knights* Aristophanes has much to say about the bestowal of *prohedria* on Cleon after his victory at Pylos.

43. The Archon was also called the 'eponymous' archon, because he gave his name to the year for which he held office. He was nominally the chief magistrate of the state, but had little actual executive power.

44. The title Basileus means 'king', and the Basileus, though junior in rank to the Archon, was theoretically the successor to the ancient kings of Athens. His functions were mainly connected with religion, and he presided over several of the oldest Athenian festivals.

45. See further P. J. Wilson, *The Athenian Institution of the Khoregia* (Cambridge, 2000).

46. Probably because comic production was a much more complex affair than tragic, with more bodies on stage, much more physical interaction, and rapid movements calling for precise timing.

47. *The Knights* 512–13. The question is probably put this way round to distract attention from the more interesting, and possibly embarrassing, question why Aristophanes *had* asked for a chorus in his own name for *The Knights* itself (probable answer: because Callistratus, after what had happened over *The Babylonians*, was not prepared to run the even greater risks involved in producing a play consisting almost entirely of vilification of Cleon).

48. The poet Plato was a slightly junior contemporary of Aristophanes; not to be confused with the philosopher.

49. See my discussion in 'Platon, Eupolis and the "demagogue-comedy"', in F. D. Harvey and J. Wilkins, eds., *The Rivals of Aristophanes* (London/Swansea, 2000), p. 447, note 21.

50. It is not, in fact, quite clear how an unequivocal rank order of the competitors was arrived at. Various procedures have been suggested; one which would work, and which is consistent with the evidence we have, is the following. Each judge writes down a complete rank ordering of the competitors on his tablet. Five of the tablets are drawn, and the first, second, third, etc., placings for each competitor are tallied. The winner is the competitor placed first by the greatest number of judges; if two or more competitors have the same number of first placings, the prize goes to the one with most second placings, and so on down. Lower rankings are determined on the same principle. If two competitors have identical vote profiles, a sixth tablet is read; this will *always* break the tie.

51. Aristophanes' choruses make such an appeal in *The Clouds* (lines 1115–30), *The Birds* (lines 1102–17) and *The Assemblywomen* (lines 1154–62).

52. *The Acharnians*, lines 1150–55.

53. *The Acharnians*, lines 659–64.

54. And in two successive songs earlier in the play (at lines 569–70 and 601–2) the chorus address Ether as 'our Father' (speaking as cloud-goddesses) and Athena as 'our Protectress' (speaking as Athenian citizens).

55. At least one lost comedy, Eupolis' *Maricas*, is also known to have had a divided chorus. In *The Acharnians* the chorus divides briefly into antagonistic halves at lines 557–71.

56. Even the nude female personification 'Reconciliation' in *Lysistrata* will have been played by a suitably costumed man.

57. Occasionally, both in tragedy and in comedy (where *The Assemblywomen* is the only surviving instance), the chorus was made to depart for a time and return later.

58. The available evidence on dance, mainly derived from vase-

paintings, is discussed by T. B. L. Webster, *The Greek Chorus* (London, 1970).

59. This rule was definitively proved by D. M. MacDowell, 'The number of speaking actors in Old Comedy', *Classical Quarterly* 45 (1995), pp. 325–34. Child parts, played by young boys, were in my view exempted from the limit; otherwise, since a boy would not have been able to play an adult part, a dramatist who used one in a single scene would have been forced to operate an actor short for the rest of the play.

60. Sophocles (or rather his grandson, who produced the play after his death) must have split parts in *Oedipus at Colonus*, which could not otherwise have been performed by three actors. In the comedies of Menander (342–291) part-splitting is frequently unavoidable.

61. As the text stands it seems as though Socrates has to change mask and costume in no time; but had the revised play ever been produced, this change would doubtless have been covered by a choral song. In my article 'The silence of Strepsiades and the *agon* of the first *Clouds*', in P. Thiercy and M. Menu, eds., *Aristophane: la langue, la scène, la cité* (Bari, 1997), pp. 269–82, I argue that in the original play, produced in 423, Strepsiades had not been present to hear the debate.

62. Or more likely, to change his mask and to remove the elaborate costume of the 'peacock ambassador'; the much simpler costume of Amphitheus could have been worn under the other.

63. These are the two quickest changes in Aristophanes, but there is a quicker one in Menander: in his *Dyskolos* (*Old Cantankerous*), one of two actors who exit at line 873 must re-enter in a different role at line 879.

64. A choral passage in this part of *The Acharnians* (lines 971–99) has some, but not all, of the typical features of a second *parabasis*. In *The Clouds*, where we should expect a second *parabasis* we get only a single 16-line speech by the chorus-leader (lines 1115–30); probably, had the revision of the play been completed, two songs and a further speech would have been added here.

65. *Peace*, another play on the same theme not included in this volume, likewise has no *agon*.

66. The Magistrate is made to begin the *agon*, not by making an assertion, but by asking a question; after that he makes twenty-nine further speeches in the *agon* – with an average length (in Greek) of 5.9 words per speech.

67. This sketch of the functional structure of Aristophanic comedy is based on that in the introduction to my edition of *The Acharnians* (Warminster, 1980), pp. 11–13. A much fuller analysis, applied in detail to all

eleven plays, is offered by G. M. Sifakis, 'The structure of Aristophanic comedy', *Journal of Hellenic Studies* 112 (1992), pp. 123–42.

68. I apologize for the gendered pronouns here, having been unable to find any stylistically tolerable device for avoiding them.

69. This comic concept of happiness consists essentially of 'song, dance, food, drink, sex, sleep, and good company' (Sir Kenneth Dover, *Aristophanes: Clouds* [Oxford, 1968], p. liii).

70. The only other surviving instance of such a failure is in *The Poet and the Women*, where Euripides is trying to prevent the women from taking revenge on him for slanders against them of which he admits he is guilty (lines 85, 1166–7); in the end he is forced to promise to desist from such slanders in future. In *The Birds* the hero's aim was *initially* selfish (to avoid being forced to pay his debts), but his plan of building a city of birds turns out to benefit the whole human race by liberating them from the oppressive domination of the gods.

71. The number of steps shown leading up to the platform is almost always four.

72. London F151 (Apulian, *c.* 380 BC); see O. P. Taplin, *Comic Angels and Other Approaches to Greek Drama Through Vase-Painting* (Oxford, 1993), pl. 12.6.

73. *Eisodoi* is Aristophanes' name for these passages (e.g. *The Clouds*, line 326); from the third century BC they tended to be called *parodoi*, and many modern scholars still use this term.

74. Hence the leader of the chorus was sometimes called the 'left-hand man' (Cratinus, fragment 229).

75. *Ekkyklema* (which means 'a rolling-out') was used by ancient commentators to refer, not to the device itself (whose ancient name is unknown), but to an instance of its being used.

76. Whence the term *deus ex machina*.

77. In the *parabasis* of *The Clouds*, Aristophanes claims credit for not using 'a great thick floppy red-tipped leather tool' in that play; this disavowal is phrased in very restrictive terms (a phallus that was both 'floppy' and 'red-tipped' would have to be a circumcised one, and only Egyptians, Phoenicians and certain other 'barbarians' would ever be represented as having such) and is in no way evidence that male characters in *The Clouds* did not wear visible phalli. (In any case, this *parabasis* makes numerous other assertions about low-comic features that *The Clouds* allegedly does not contain, and nearly all of them eventually prove to be false!)

78. Except those females whose sole dramatic function was that of a sex-object – such as Reconciliation in *Lysistrata*, and the two girls accompanying Dikaiopolis at the end of *The Acharnians*.

79. Or other entities such as 'dramas', 'cities' or 'new moons' (the titles of three comedies of the 420s).

80. A male who was beardless would be either very young (like Pheidippides in *The Clouds*) or of doubtful masculinity (like the two 'eunuchs' in *The Acharnians*).

81. Though a similar (but probably not identical) mask will have been worn by the Cyclops in Cratinus' *Odyssês*, most likely produced in 439 or 438.

82. Which of course leaves us wondering how Cleon (or Paphlagon, as he is called in the play) *was* represented: one plausible suggestion is that he was given a mask reminiscent of a horrific mythical monster – perhaps the hell-hound Cerberus, to whom he is compared later in *The Knights* (line 1030), in *The Wasps* (line 1031) and twice in *Peace* (lines 313, 754).

83. Since this debate is part of an educational package for which Socrates charges high fees, it is illogical that it should be presented to Pheidippides *outside* the Thinkery door, in a public place.

84. Though it is an important part of the dynamics of this scene that the audience *know* there will be no consummation: sexual intercourse, like birth, violent death, or even the slaughter of sacrificial animals, was never represented on stage in any form of Greek drama.

85. I cannot give the exact length of the word in letters, since several parts of it are textually uncertain, but it is likely to be 171 plus or minus 2.

86. A generation later 'The Saw' was one of several nicknames of a man named Mnesitheus, apparently a figure in public life, who was said to be, or to have once been, a timber-porter, and who is mentioned (under another nickname) in *The Assemblywomen* (line 77).

87. In *The Knights* Aristophanes introduces *spondai* in the even more agreeable guise of a couple of young women – and with a different pun. The peace treaty, as in *The Acharnians*, is to be for thirty years (in Greek, the *spondai* are to be *triakontoutides*); hence (i) the two girls probably have a *combined* age of thirty and (ii) Demos (the personified Athenian People) is made to ask, 'Am I allowed to *katatriakontoutisai* them?' – a word, coined for the occasion, which it just so happens could be taken to mean 'pierce them three times with a long pole from below' (from *kata*, 'down'; *tria*, 'three'; *kontos*, 'punt-pole'; and *outān*, 'to wound by thrusting').

88. Michael Silk, *Aristophanes and the Definition of Comedy* (Oxford, 2000), pp. 403–9. All italics are mine.

Further Reading

EDITIONS OF ARISTOPHANES

All the eleven comedies of Aristophanes have been edited, with translation and commentary, by A. H. Sommerstein (Warminster, 1980–2001). The final volume (*Wealth*) contains updates to all the preceding volumes.

There are excellent separate editions (Greek text and commentary) of *The Clouds* by Sir Kenneth Dover (Oxford, 1968), *Lysistrata* by Jeffrey Henderson (Oxford, 1987), and *The Acharnians* by S. Douglas Olson (Oxford, 2002).

ARISTOPHANES AND HIS WORK

K. J. Dover, *Aristophanic Comedy* (London, 1972).

K. J. Reckford, *Aristophanes' Old-and-New Comedy I: Six Essays in Perspective* (Chapel Hill, 1987).

P. A. Cartledge, *Aristophanes and his Theatre of the Absurd* (3rd edn; Bristol, 1995).

D. M. MacDowell, *Aristophanes and Athens* (Oxford, 1995).

M. S. Silk, *Aristophanes and the Definition of Comedy* (Oxford, 2000).

N. W. Slater, *Spectator Politics: Metatheater and Performance in Aristophanes* (Philadelphia, 2002).

GREEK THEATRE PRODUCTION

C. W. Dearden, *The Stage of Aristophanes* (London, 1976).

L. M. Stone, *Costume in Aristophanic Comedy* (New York, 1981).

A. W. Pickard-Cambridge, *The Dramatic Festivals of Athens* (3rd edn revised by J. Gould and D. M. Lewis; Oxford, 1988).

C. F. Russo, *Aristophanes: An Author for the Stage* (London, 1994).

E. G. Csapo and W. J. Slater, *The Context of Ancient Drama* (Ann Arbor, 1994).

J. R. Green, *Theatre in Ancient Greek Society* (London, 1995).

Translator's Note

My translation, first published in 1973, was inspired by, and modelled on, David Barrett's magnificent translation in this series of *The Wasps*, *The Poet and the Women* and *The Frogs* (1964); later (1978) I had the privilege of collaborating with him on a further volume which included the remaining five extant plays of Aristophanes. I chose to translate *The Acharnians*, *The Clouds* and *Lysistrata* basically for the simple reason that, among the plays not included in Barrett's first volume, they were the ones I liked best. They also, though, represent, between them, most of the major themes and interests found in Aristophanes' work – *The Acharnians* with its dominating hero,[1] its strongly political subject, its concern with the war/peace and town/country oppositions,[2] its connection with the feud with Cleon,[3] its exploitation of Euripidean tragedy;[4] *The Clouds* which experiments with an intellectual theme which it treats, in some respects, rather uncomically, and is the earliest surviving Aristophanic play to include the motif of the overthrow or vanquishing of Zeus;[5] and *Lysistrata*, another war/peace play in which the hero is female[6] and women's voices predominate over men's in the play as a whole.[7]

The aim in my 1973 translation was, as David Barrett's had been, to offer a reasonably faithful rendering which was also, in Barrett's words, 'both readable and actable'; and so it remains. For this new edition I have completely revised the translation, aiming to bring it closer to the original and to update it in the light of progress in scholarly understanding of the text and action, while leaving its basic style and spirit unaltered. The annotations have likewise been completely overhauled.[8]

In general, as in my 1973 translation, passages of spoken verse are translated as prose,[9] and passages of song are translated as verse; but one or two spoken passages in which the diction or metre of tragedy is imitated are rendered in blank verse, and the speeches in the *parabases* (which were probably declaimed in strict rhythm to musical accompaniment) in rhymed verse.

To give an idea of the verbal humour which, as I have said, was an essential part of Aristophanes' comic technique, I have often found it necessary to adapt his jokes, or, where even this is impossible, to compensate for their loss by adding something elsewhere. I have generally at such points given an idea in the notes of what the author wrote.

In both *The Acharnians* and *Lysistrata* characters appear who come from parts of Greece other than Athens, and Aristophanes makes use of their dialectical peculiarities for comic purposes. I have correspondingly made them speak distinctive dialects of English, in a manner which is not now as common in fiction and drama as it once was, but which is not intended to imply any disparagement of any group of English speakers who find, or may think they find, their dialect represented or misrepresented here.[10]

My stage directions, like virtually all stage directions in all translations of ancient dramatic texts, correspond to nothing in Aristophanes' Greek text,[11] and should be regarded as a guide only; in particular, directors are positively encouraged to seek in the text possibilities in the nature of farce or slapstick which I have not noticed. I have dropped the act and scene divisions which were inserted in my 1973 translation; the original production did not have any intervals, and the placing of intervals (if any) in a modern production is not something that a translator should be prescribing.

For reference purposes, line numbers (of the standard reference system used in all scholarly publications) are shown in the outside margin. Owing to differences in word and clause order between Greek and English, these can only give an approximate guide, but a reference based on them will always be correct to within two lines and usually to within one.

I ended my 1973 introduction with the following paragraph: 'I should particularly like to thank Mrs Betty Radice for being an even kinder foster-mother to this translation than the Athenian public was to Aristophanes' *The Banqueters*, and for helping to remove numerous warts that disfigured the infant. I am also grateful to David Watkinson, who read the draft of my translation over a year ago and was the first to encourage me to think it worth publishing, and above all to David Barrett, without whose example it would never have been written, and without whose co-operation once it had been written it might never have seen the light of day. To all, many thanks.'

To these three – of whom, alas, only one is with us today – I should now add Laura Barber, who invited me to make this revision and has shown extreme patience with my tardy production of it. I hope it is worthy of the confidence she has shown.

NOTES

1. As in *Peace* and *The Birds*.
2. As notably in *Peace*, though the town/country opposition features in several other plays too.
3. As in *The Knights*, *The Wasps* and (after Cleon's death) *Peace*.
4. As in *The Poet and the Women* and *The Frogs*.
5. Zeus is successfully overthrown in *The Birds* and *Wealth*, and in *Peace* his will is successfully thwarted.
6. As in *The Assemblywomen*.
7. As in *The Poet and the Women* and *The Assemblywomen*.
8. For a closer translation with much fuller annotations, the reader should consult my editions of *The Acharnians*, *The Clouds* and *Lysistrata* in the Aris & Phillips series (Warminster, 1980, 1982, 1990, respectively); extensive updates are provided in my edition of *Wealth* (Warminster, 2001), pp. 219–321.
9. Aristophanes' Greek text itself contains no prose except in a few passages where prayers, laws and other highly formal texts are quoted or parodied. There are no such passages in the three plays in this volume.
10. The jury is still out on the question of the extent, if any, to which the representation of non-Athenian dialects in Old Comedy was designed to disparage their speakers; see S. Colvin, *Dialect in Aristophanes* (Oxford, 1999).
11. Accordingly, the stage directions should *never* be quoted as if they were the work of Aristophanes!

Note on the Text

My original translations were primarily based on the texts of Sir Kenneth Dover's edition of *The Clouds* (Oxford, 1968) and of Benjamin Bickley Rogers' editions of *The Acharnians* (London, 1910) and of *Lysistrata* (London, 1911). Since then J. J. Henderson has produced a fine new edition of *Lysistrata* (Oxford, 1987), and I have also published my own editions of all Aristophanes' plays in the Aris & Phillips series (Warminster, 1980–2001). The present revised translation broadly follows my Aris & Phillips texts, but diverges from them where subsequent scholarship, or my own second or third thoughts, have convinced me that it is right to do so.

THE ACHARNIANS

Preface to *The Acharnians*

The Acharnians was produced in January or February of 425 BC. Almost annually, for six years, the Spartans and their allies had mustered at the Isthmus of Corinth in the spring, marched into Attica and ravaged portions of its territory, destroying not only any corn there might be but also vines and olive trees. On the first occasion, in 431, the devastation had been particularly thorough in the area of the large and important town of Acharnae, some eight miles north of Athens in the direction of Mount Parnes and the Boeotian border, in the hope that its inhabitants would persuade the Assembly to order the Generals to challenge the invaders to battle – a battle which the leaders on both sides knew the Athenians could not win. This gambit had failed, and this and later invasions of Attica were allowed to proceed without resistance except for cavalry raiding. Instead, after the invaders had withdrawn, the Athenians regularly revenged themselves by inflicting similar devastation upon a weaker enemy close at hand, the Megarians. Neither through these operations, nor through the other campaigns that had taken place in various parts of Greece, had either side achieved anything remotely resembling a decisive advantage – though the Thebans had had the satisfaction of seeing the destruction of the small town of Plataea in southern Boeotia, long an ally of Athens. But on the one hand the Athenian sea-empire was intact (the revolt on Lesbos having been crushed), and on the other hand nothing had happened to induce Sparta to think of abandoning her struggle for the 'liberation of Greece'. Indeed, the Spartans may well have felt that time was working in their favour. The vast financial reserves with which Athens had

entered the war were now much diminished, and could be
expected to decline further; within a few months, in an attempt
to rebuild them, Athens would be doubling or trebling the
annual tribute imposed on her subject allies, despite the risks of
increasing disaffection that this involved. And during most of
the war Athens had also been afflicted by a devastating disease
epidemic which had already killed something like one third of
her population. This plague had broken out in the spring of
430, raged for two years, died down (but not out) in 428,
and flared up again in the winter of 427/6, this second major
outbreak lasting for at least a year. That is to say, Athenians
were still dying of the disease in large numbers while Aristophanes was writing *The Acharnians*; when the play was produced, the epidemic was probably fading away again – but it
had faded away before, and had come back. The plague is never
referred to in *The Acharnians*; but then it is never referred to in
any surviving text of any kind composed for public performance,
delivery or display at Athens. No doubt it was too terrible an
experience to mention – but it was also too terrible to forget.
And few can have doubted that the plague and the war were
connected events; many, indeed, saw the plague as an act of
divine intervention by Apollo, who through the Delphic oracle
had promised the Spartans his aid in the war – and in the winter
of 426/5 the Athenians were trying to propitiate Apollo by
undertaking an ostentatious purification of his sacred island of
Delos.

Such was the situation in the war in which Athens was
engaged. Meanwhile, Aristophanes, or his producer Callistratus, or both, had also a private war of their own. The
previous year's City Dionysia had seen the production of *The
Babylonians*, with its scathing indictments of Athenian politicians and policies, both internal and external; and Cleon
had threatened one or both of those responsible for the play
with prosecution for 'slandering the City in the presence of
foreigners'. Dikaiopolis, speaking at this point in the name of
the author or producer, says (line 379) that he was 'dragged . . .
into the Council Chamber', which suggests that an attempt was
made to invoke the procedure of *eisangelia*. By this procedure,

an accusation of a serious offence against the state or the public interest could be presented to the Council, which could either dismiss the charge or order that the accused be tried by a jury-court (or possibly in some cases by the Assembly); if he was then found guilty, the jury or Assembly would decide the penalty, and the death penalty was an option if the prosecutor chose to demand it. Nothing is said in the play about the case going before the Assembly or a court, and it is therefore likely that the Council refused to commit for trial; but until that decision was made, the *Babylonians* production team had been in peril of their lives – as Dikaiopolis is in the play. This is why Aristophanes is at such pains in *The Acharnians* to point out that no such charge can be made to stick this time, since no foreigners were present at the Lenaea (lines 502–8); and, even so, emphatically ascribes the initiation of the events that caused the war to 'a bunch of good-for-nothing individuals', 'not Athens, mind you, not the City'. There is also a hint or two that he will have his revenge on Cleon shortly – as he did, in *The Knights*, the following year.

'The play is one of those that are extremely well composed, and it appeals for peace in every possible way.' So says the author of the ancient summary (*hypothesis*) which is prefixed to the play in many of the medieval manuscripts. Few have disagreed with the first part of his verdict, but over the last sixty or seventy years many have disputed the second part. It is pointed out (among other things) that Dikaiopolis breaks an important norm of Athenian society by taking political action on his own account without the consent of the community; that when he secures peace, he seems more concerned to enjoy its benefits himself than to share them with others; that his account (lines 515–39) of how the war originated out of petty, indeed scandalous, private quarrels is obvious nonsense and would be perceived as such; that making peace was not, in fact, an option for Athens in winter 426/5, except at a cost that no self-respecting Athenian would be prepared to pay; and (most persuasively) that if his aim had been to persuade his audience to support a policy of ending the war, he would not have included in his *parabasis* a prediction (lines 650–51) that the Athenians would win the war easily (if they continued to have him for an adviser!) and a recommendation (lines 652–5) that they should never accept the demand for the surrender of the island of Aegina which was one of Sparta's self-declared conditions for peace.

Most of these arguments are no more than specious. Before Dikaiopolis decides to make a private peace, both he and Amphitheus have repeatedly been silenced or ignored when they tried to raise in the Assembly the issue of whether the Athenian state should attempt to make an official one – although, according to Amphitheus, it is the will of the gods that they should (and his own miraculously rapid return from Sparta, with peace made, suggests that he was telling the truth). Dikaiopolis is acting without the consent of the community because the community – the assembled people – has never been allowed to express its views: another important norm of Athenian society was freedom of speech, and we have seen this being systematically denied. As to Dikaiopolis' alleged selfishness, in Old Comedy it is normal and expected for the hero who takes exceptional risks, as he has certainly done, to gain exceptional rewards. At the end of the play he participates, and wins a prize, in a civic celebration (the 'Pitcher Day' feast), with the blessing of civic officials like the *basileus* and the priest of Dionysus. Far from being the isolated, selfish individual ignoring the will of the city, he has successfully *given effect* to the will of the city which, in the Assembly meeting, the Executive Committee tried so hard to suppress. Whether there really was such a 'silent majority' in favour of peace is dubious but also irrelevant: in modern democracies, too, every minority agitator claims that (s)he is speaking for 'the people' whose views the political establishment is ignoring – and most of them, so far as one can tell, do so with perfect sincerity. That peace was not a practical possibility at the time, if true, is likewise irrelevant, unless one is prepared to claim that no political programme has ever been based on wishful thinking.[1] Dikaiopolis' account of the origins of the war is indeed fantastic; but an equally fantastic (though quite incompatible) account, put in the mouth of Hermes in *Peace*, was treated by the fourth-century historian Ephorus as factual, and similar allegations (against, for instance, Franklin Roosevelt and Bill Clinton) in connection with twentieth-century wars have been believed implicitly by millions.

It is another matter when a play that supposedly 'appeals for peace in every possible way' takes at one moment such an apparently hawkish line as is taken in the passages cited above from the *parabasis*. It should, however, be remembered that advocates of peace in wartime are always liable to the charge that they are really defeatists advocating surrender, and that the obvious defence to such a charge is to argue, in effect: 'Yes, if we do carry on with this war, we can win it, but we'll have to pay a heavy cost in money and lives to do so, and we don't *need* to carry on, because we could get peace terms right now that would be good enough to satisfy any reasonable patriot.' And this is just what is argued in the *parabasis*. Before the outbreak of war, the Spartans had made far-reaching demands amounting in effect to the dissolution of the Athenian empire; but they had also said that there would be no war if the 'Megarian decree' was repealed (compare lines 530–38) – and many Athenians had believed them then and went on believing them (the Megarian decree is the only event that figures both in the account of the war's origins in *The Acharnians* and in that in *Peace*). These same Athenians will likewise have believed, or wanted to believe, that the Spartan demand for Aegina was no more than a bargaining counter, and that if it was refused it would be withdrawn – particularly if the Spartans knew, as we have just been told they ought to know, that they were bound to lose the war anyway. There is no real inconsistency. In the world of *The Acharnians*, peace means happiness, and peace is possible – if (and this is crucial) we stop demonizing the Spartans.

The hero Dikaiopolis ('Honest Citizen') is at some points so closely identified with the author (or maybe the producer) that it has several times been suggested that Aristophanes actually played the part. Such an identification of an individual character with the author is, however, not unique (two years later, indeed, Aristophanes' older rival Cratinus literally made himself a character in his last play, *The Wicker Flask*, which soundly defeated *The Clouds*), and there is no good evidence

that Aristophanes ever was an actor. The ascription to Dikaiopolis of experiences which were actually the experiences of
Aristophanes or Callistratus serves by itself, without such external aid, to lend author-ity, as it were, to his other statements
and opinions – to make him seem like the voice of the poet
throughout.

The main *bête noire* of the play, Cleon, never actually appears
in it (not even in a disguised form), but two other well-known
contemporaries do, Euripides and Lamachus. We should not
read back into the treatment of Euripides in this play the stric-
tures on his technique and (above all) on his allegedly corrupting
influence on society that are made in *The Frogs*: in *The Acharnians* almost the only disparaging thing said about Euripides is
that his mother had been a greengrocer. Euripides here is primarily a highly imaginative tragic poet who is very strong in two
fields, pathos (as in his presentation of ragged or crippled heroes)
and rhetoric (as in the speech or speeches of Telephus on which
the great speech of Dikaiopolis, lines 497–556, is modelled), and
who – unknowingly, to be sure, and to some extent unwillingly –
helps the hero to gain his triumph.

The portrayal of Lamachus, on the other hand, is undoubtedly
hostile – and, on our other evidence, grossly unfair: far from
being a corrupt coward or a knee-jerk militarist, he was one of
those who in 421 swore the oaths of peace, and shortly afterwards of alliance, with Sparta; he was still a relatively poor man
when elected one of the commanders of the Sicilian expedition
in 415; and he was killed about a year later in an action of
considerable courage and initiative (and perhaps of insufficient
caution). He was, however (or at least had been and hoped
again to be), a general; he was senior to most other currently
active military figures, having commanded an expedition to the
Black Sea ten or twelve years earlier; he had a martial name[2] (it
could be taken to mean 'Great Battler') – and had named his
son after the famous mythical warrior Tydeus; and he had
recently been elected to serve on an embassy – that is, in the eyes
of the ordinary Athenian, to go to foreign parts at public expense
as a highly paid messenger-boy. So if it was desired to represent
Athenian bellicosity, of the military rather than the political

variety, in a single figure – and to suggest that it had self-interested rather than patriotic motives – he was at least as good a choice as any.

Produced, like Aristophanes' previous plays, by Callistratus, the play won first prize, defeating plays by Cratinus and Eupolis – who centuries later were to be regarded, together with Aristophanes, as the canonical trio of Old Comic dramatists (just as Aeschylus, Sophocles and Euripides were the canonical trio for tragedy). A few months later, the audience which had applauded it (or rather an Assembly meeting containing many of the same persons) found a real-life Spartan delegation in Athens with proposals for peace. By the opportunism of their general Demosthenes and his men, the Athenians had fortified the promontory of Pylos, in the south-western Peloponnese, and beaten off a naval attack; now over 400 Spartan troops were blockaded on the neighbouring island of Sphacteria, many of them full Spartan citizens – and the Spartan citizen body was not large. The terms proposed seem to have been that the men on the island should be allowed to leave unharmed, that each side should hold what it currently held (which meant, among other things, that Athens could retain Aegina – and for that matter Pylos too), and that Athens and Sparta should make an alliance.[3] These terms were far better than could realistically have been anticipated the previous winter, and they were considerably better than those which Athens was to accept four years later (after having suffered some serious setbacks, especially in the northern Aegean). But they were not good enough for most Athenians: there had, after all, been a peace rather like that (though without an alliance) in 446/5, and (as Dikaiopolis never acknowledges, though the Spartans themselves conceded it in later years) the Spartans had broken it. Better to capture the 400, use them as hostages to ensure that the Spartans did not invade Attica again, and try to regain Megara (Athenian from 460 to 446) and dominate Boeotia. Accordingly the Assembly agreed to counter-proposals drafted by Cleon which were designed to, and did, make negotiations impossible. The opportunity did not recur.

NOTES

1. In any case, Aristophanes evades the issue by making it seem (notably in Dikaiopolis' speech, lines 497–556) as though to prove that it is right to end the war, it is sufficient to prove that the war ought not to have been begun in the first place. This is, of course, totally fallacious; it is perfectly coherent, and all too often accurate, to say 'we ought not to have got ourselves into this war, but as things are now we can't get out of it'.

2. It has ingeniously been pointed out (in a recent conference paper by Andrea Ercolani, since published in A. Ercolani ed., *Spoudaiogeloion: Form und Funktion von Verspottung in der aristophanischen Komödie* [Stuttgart, 2002]) that Lamachus was at this time one of only two generals or ex-generals (that we know of) with strongly martial names; and the other, Nicostratus, was known principally for a brave but unsuccessful attempt to make *peace* between the rival factions at Corcyra in 427.

3. Thucydides 4.17.4, 4.19.1.

Characters

DIKAIOPOLIS, *an old farmer*
CRIER
AMPHITHEUS, *an immortal*
AMBASSADOR, *lately returned from the Persian Court*
PSEUDARTABAS, *the Great King's Eye*
THEORUS, *ambassador to the King of Thrace*
CHORUS *of old men of Acharnae*
DAUGHTER *to Dikaiopolis*
SERVANT *of Euripides*
EURIPIDES, *the tragic poet*
LAMACHUS, *the general*
MEGARIAN
FIRST and SECOND GIRL, *his daughters*
(disguised as pigs)
INFORMER
THEBAN
NICARCHUS, *another informer*
SLAVE *of Lamachus*
DERCETES, *a farmer*
BRIDEGROOM'S SLAVE
FIRST MESSENGER
SECOND MESSENGER
THIRD MESSENGER

Silent Characters

THE EXECUTIVE COMMITTEE
SCYTHIAN ARCHER-POLICEMEN
AMBASSADORS
TWO 'EUNUCHS', *attendant on Pseudartabas*
ODOMANTIAN SOLDIERS
WIFE *to Dikaiopolis*
PIPE BAND, *attendant on the Theban*
ISMENIAS, *the Theban's servant*
BRIDESWOMAN
TWO DANCING-GIRLS
CITIZENS, SLAVES, SOLDIERS, *etc.*

SCENE: *The orchestra at first represents the Pnyx, where the Assembly met. The stage-platform represents the speaker's platform; close to it are benches for the Executive Committee. The* skene *is at present ignored; later its doors will at various moments represent the houses of Dikaiopolis, Euripides and Lamachus.*

[DIKAIOPOLIS *arrives by a side-passage and sits on the ground, well away from the platform. He waits patiently for a minute or two, then, finding himself still alone, begins fidgeting, yawning and showing other signs of boredom; then turns to address the audience.*]

DIKAIOPOLIS: My heart has drunk deep of the cup of woe, and 'scant the joys I've known' – yes, very scant – [*counts on his fingers*] four, that's right, against countless zillions of things that gave me pain. Now, what was there that I enjoyed, that was really pleasurific? Ah yes, I remember – it really warmed   5
my heart – when Cleon coughed up his thirty grand.[1] That made me ecstatic. Knights, I love you for that; you did a good thing for Greece. But then there was something really traumatic, not to say tragic. There was I sitting there, mouth   10
open, eager for a dose of Aeschylus, and then the crier goes, 'Bring on your chorus, *Theognis*'.[2] Well, you can imagine, I nearly had heart failure. But another thing that made me really happy was when that lyre-player Moschus finished and Dexitheus came on instead to play a Boeotian number. To   15
come to this year, though – it was like being tortured to death, when Chaeris[3] stooped his way on to play the Orthian tune.[4]

But never in all the years I've . . . washed have I been so stung
by soap in the eyes as I'm feeling now. Regular meeting of the
20 Assembly, due to start at sunrise, and not a soul here on the
Pnyx! Everybody's down in the Market Square gossiping,
that is when they're not dodging the red rope.[5] Even the
Executive[6] aren't here. They'll come in the end – hours late –
all streaming in together, and push and shove and heaven
25 knows what to get the front seats. That's all they care about.
How to get peace – they don't give a damn about that. Oh,
Athens, Athens, what are you coming to? Now me, I'm always
the first to get here. So I sit down, and after a bit, when I find
30 no one else is coming, I sigh and yawn and stretch and fart
and then don't know what to do, and then doodle on the
ground or pluck my hairs or count to myself – and all the
time I'm gazing at the countryside over yonder and pining for
peace, cursing the city and yearning to get back to my village.
35 My village! Where no one said 'Buy my charcoal' or 'Buy my
vinegar' or 'Buy my oil'; we didn't even know the word 'buy',
we produced everything we needed for ourselves, we were a
sale-free zone.[7] Well, anyway, this time I've come prepared:
if any speaker dares say a word about anything except peace,
I'll shout, I'll heckle, I'll abuse, I'll – [*Enter the* CRIER, *followed by the members of the* EXECUTIVE COMMITTEE, *who
40 are attended by* SCYTHIAN ARCHER-POLICEMEN.] Ah, here
they are at last – at midday! And look at them! Just like I said
– all fighting for the best places.

CRIER [*taking his place in front of the Executive, who have
now taken their seats; addressing the 'public'*[8]]: Come forward! Come forward! Everyone within the consecrated
enclosure![9]

45 AMPHITHEUS [*arriving late and breathless; to Dikaiopolis*]:
Have they started yet?

CRIER: Who wishes to speak?[10]

AMPHITHEUS [*rising*]: I do.

CRIER: Your name?

AMPHITHEUS: Amphitheus – 'Doubly Divine'.

CRIER: Not human?

AMPHITHEUS: No, I am an Immortal. My ancestor and name-

sake was the son of Demeter and Triptolemus. He begat
Celeus, who married Phaenarete, that's my grandmother, and
begat Lycinus, who begat me; and that makes me immortal.[11]   50
And the gods have commissioned me to make peace with the
Spartans – only me. But though I am immortal, gentlemen, I
have been given no expenses. The Executive won't let me have
them!

[*The* CHAIRMAN *of the Executive makes a signal to the
Crier.*]

CRIER: Police!

[*Two of the* POLICEMEN *grab* AMPHITHEUS *by the arms
and drag him off.*]

AMPHITHEUS [*struggling*]: Triptolemus and Celeus, why do   55
you not help me?

DIKAIOPOLIS [*rising*]: Members of the Executive, the arrest of
that man was an insult to the Assembly! He only wanted to
give us peace so we could hang up our shields on the wall
where they belong.

CRIER: Silence! Sit down!

DIKAIOPOLIS: I will not, not until the Executive commit us to   60
a debate on peace.

CRIER [*ignoring him*]: The ambassadors from the Persian
Court!

DIKAIOPOLIS: Persian Court indeed! I'm sick of all these
ambassadors and their peacocks[12] and their tall tales.

CRIER: Silence!

[DIKAIOPOLIS *subsides, for the time being. Enter an*
AMBASSADOR, *followed by his colleagues, all dressed like
Persian grandees.*]

DIKAIOPOLIS [*aside*]: Whew! Holy Ecbatana,[13] what a get-up!

AMBASSADOR: You sent us, gentlemen, to the Great King, with   65
a salary of two drachmas per person per day, in the year when
Euthymenes was archon.[14]

DIKAIOPOLIS [*aside*]: Oh, god, how many drachmas is that?

AMBASSADOR: And I may say we had a very hard time of it.
We processed very slowly up the Cayster valley in shaded   70
coaches, and we actually had to lie down in them. It was sheer
murder.

DIKAIOPOLIS [*aside*]: I certainly had it good, then, sleeping among the rubbish on the city walls!

AMBASSADOR: And wherever we put up, our hosts compelled
75   us, willy-nilly, to drink sweet wine, neat, out of gold or crystal cups.

DIKAIOPOLIS [*aside*]: City of Cranaus,[15] can't you see how your envoys are making fools of you?

AMBASSADOR: Because in Asia, you know, the test of your manhood is how much you can eat and drink.

DIKAIOPOLIS [*aside*]: With us it's how many bugger you and how many you suck.

80 AMBASSADOR: After three years we reached the Persian capital; but we found the King away – he had gone with his army on an expedition to a bog, and he stayed there, shitting on the Golden Hills,[16] for eight months.

DIKAIOPOLIS [*aside*]: And how long did he take to close up his arse? Was it at the full *moon*?[17]

85 AMBASSADOR: And then he returned home. Then he gave a dinner for us, serving us whole oven-baked oxen.[18]

DIKAIOPOLIS [*aside*]: Who ever heard of oven-baked oxen? How big a liar can you get?

AMBASSADOR: And, I swear, he served us an enormous fowl, three times the size of Cleonymus; they called it a hoodwin.[19]

90 DIKAIOPOLIS [*aside*]: So that's why you've been hoodwin-king us all this time, at two drachmas a day!

AMBASSADOR: And now we have returned, bringing with us Pseudartabas, the Great King's Eye.[20]

DIKAIOPOLIS: I hope a crow knocks it out – and your ambassadorial eye with it!

CRIER: The Great King's Eye!

[*Enter* PSEUDARTABAS. *His mask has no nose or mouth, only one enormous eye set roughly where the mouth should be and partly veiled. He is attended by two 'EUNUCHS' who try to keep him on a straight course.*]

95 DIKAIOPOLIS: Heracles and all the gods, man, you look like a warship rounding a headland. This way for the docks! Is that an oar-sleeve you've got down there round your eye, or what?[21]

AMBASSADOR: Pseudartabas, will you please deliver the message that the King gave you for the people of Athens?

PSEUDARTABAS: Iyartaman exarxas apisona satra.   100

AMBASSADOR: Did you hear what he says?

DIKAIOPOLIS: Yes – what was it?

AMBASSADOR: He says the King is going to send you gold. [*To Pseudartabas*] Gold, tell them about the gold, and make it loud and clear.

PSEUDARTABAS: You not will get goldo, you wide-arse Yawonian.[22]

DIKAIOPOLIS: Good grief, that's clear enough!   105

AMBASSADOR: Why, what does he say?

DIKAIOPOLIS: What does he say? He says that us Ionians are wide-arsed idiots, that's what, if we expect to get gold from Persia.

AMBASSADOR: No, he said we were going to get gold in wide carts.[23]

DIKAIOPOLIS: Wide carts indeed! You're nothing but a great big liar. Get off with you! I'll do the interrogating myself.   110
[*The* AMBASSADOR *and his colleagues docilely leave.* DIKAIOPOLIS *confronts* PSEUDARTABAS, *raising a fist at his face.*]
Look at this and tell me the truth, or I'll paint your face Lydian purple. Is the Great King going to send us gold? [PSEUDARTABAS *indicates the answer is 'no'*.[24]] So those ambassadors were talking total and utter boloney? [PSEUD-ARTABAS *gravely nods; so do the* 'EUNUCHS'.] Strange these   115
guys should nod the way Greeks do. I verily believe they *are* Greeks! In fact [*examining one of the 'eunuchs' closely*] I seem to know this one very well indeed. Cleisthenes,[25] isn't it, the famous wrestler?[26] 'O thou that shavest close thy passionate arse!'[27] You cheating monkey – with a beard like yours,   120
you come here got up as a eunuch! And who's the other? Not Strato,[28] by any chance?

CRIER: Silence! Sit down! – The Council hereby invite the Great King's Eye to dinner in the City Mansion.[29]   125
[*Exit* PSEUDARTABAS, *attended by the* 'EUNUCHS'.]

DIKAIOPOLIS: Doesn't all this just choke you? Am I supposed to hang around here, while people like that get endless free

meals? I'm going to do something really awesome. Amphitheus! are you still there?

AMPHITHEUS [*who has slipped back in unnoticed*]: Here.

130   DIKAIOPOLIS: Look, here's eight drachmas. You go and make
peace with the Spartans – only for me and the wife and
the kids, though, right? [AMPHITHEUS *takes the money and
leaves unobtrusively.*] You [*gesturing towards the platform*]
go on playing diplomats, *you* [*gesturing towards the audience*] go on sitting gawping at them, I couldn't care less!

CRIER: Come forward, Theorus, lately returned from the court
of King Sitalces!³⁰

THEORUS [*coming to the front*]: Here I am.

135   DIKAIOPOLIS [*aside*]: Here we are – the next liar in the series!

THEORUS: My stay in Thrace would have been much shorter –

DIKAIOPOLIS [*aside*]: If you hadn't been drawing so much pay
for it.

THEORUS: – if it had not been for the blizzards which covered
the whole country and froze all its rivers, just about the time

140   that Theognis³¹ was on stage here. During that time I was . . .
drinking with Sitalces. He showed himself your sincere friend,
a true lover of Athens; so much so that he was scratching

145   graffiti on walls saying 'Athens is sexy'. And his son, whom
we'd made an Athenian citizen,³² was crazy to eat sausages at
the Festival of the Clans,³³ and was beseeching his father to
come to the aid of his fatherland. And Sitalces, he poured a
libation and swore to bring an army to help us, 'so great an

150   army', he said, 'that the Athenians will take it for a swarm of
locusts'.

DIKAIOPOLIS [*aside*]: I'll be damned if I believe a word of what
you've said, except about the locusts.

THEORUS: And now he has sent you a contingent from the
bravest tribe in Thrace.

DIKAIOPOLIS [*aside*]: Well, *that's* something concrete, anyway.

155   CRIER: Come forward, the Thracians whom Theorus has
brought with him!

[*Enter a party of* ODOMANTIAN SOLDIERS,³⁴ *savage-
looking and poorly equipped.*]

DIKAIOPOLIS: What on earth is this rabble?

THEORUS: The Odomantian army.

DIKAIOPOLIS: Odomantian army indeed! [*Examining them with curiosity*] Here, what on earth's this? Who cut the leaves off their fig-trees?[35]

THEORUS: These light infantry, for two drachmas a day,[36] will subdue the whole of Boeotia for you.

DIKAIOPOLIS: Two drachmas for that lot, with not a whole willy between them! The top-grade oarsmen who keep the City safe would moan a bit about that. [*Some of the* SOLDIERS *pounce on his lunch-basket and begin to help themselves to the contents.*] Help! Murder! The Odomantians are pillaging my vegetables! Put down that garlic, will you?

THEORUS: Keep away from them, you stupid fool! The stuff makes them fighting mad.[37]

DIKAIOPOLIS: Are the Executive going to sit by and do nothing while I'm maltreated like this by barbarians in my own country? [*No answer.*] Well, I hereby forbid you to debate the issue of hiring these Thracians. I declare to you that Zeus has sent a sign! I distinctly felt a drop of rain![38]

CRIER: The Thracians will withdraw, and attend here again the day after tomorrow. The Executive declare this Assembly closed.

[*Exeunt all but* DIKAIOPOLIS. *As the benches are cleared away, he sadly gathers up the remains of his lunch.*]

DIKAIOPOLIS: Ah, what a fine savoury mash went west there! [*He begins walking slowly towards his home. Enter* AMPH-ITHEUS, *running furiously, and carrying three large wine-skins.*] Ah, Amphitheus, back from Sparta! Had a nice day?

AMPHITHEUS: Maybe, when I can stop running! I've got to get clear of those Acharnians.

DIKAIOPOLIS: What do you mean?

AMPHITHEUS: Well, I was coming here as quickly as I could, bringing you your peace, and these old men from Acharnae smelt it. They're close-grained oak and maple, they are, hard as nails – the same as when they fought at Marathon.[39] And they all yelled at me – 'You utter villain, making peace treaties with the men who cut our vines down!' Then they started picking up stones and putting them in the folds of their cloaks

160

165

170

175

180

185   – and I started making myself scarce, and they ran after me,
        still shouting.

        DIKAIOPOLIS: Well, let them! You've got the peace terms?[40]

        AMPHITHEUS: Yes, here they are – three samples to choose
        from. This is a five-year one. Have a sip.

        DIKAIOPOLIS [*repelled by the smell of the wine before it even
        reaches his lips*]: Ugh!

        AMPHITHEUS: What's wrong?

190   DIKAIOPOLIS: It's loathsome! It reeks of pitch and ship-
        building.[41]

        AMPHITHEUS [*offering him the second, larger skin*]: Well, have
        a taste of this ten-year one.

        DIKAIOPOLIS [*again rejecting it untasted, though not quite
        so quickly*]: No, this one smells too acid. More diplomatic
        missions, I imagine; the allies must be playing for time.[42]

        AMPHITHEUS [*offering the third skin*]: Now then, *this* one is
195   for *thirty* years, by land and sea.

        DIKAIOPOLIS [*inhaling deeply what is evidently an exquisite
        aroma*]: Holy Dionysia! *This* has the scent of ambrosia and
        nectar, and of not having to listen out for the words 'three
        days' rations'.[43] [*He puts the skin to his lips.*] And in my
        mouth it says, 'Go where you please!' Yes, I'll take this one
        [*hugging it to his bosom*]; I hereby [*pouring a little of the
        wine on the ground*] make peace; and then I'll drink the lot
200   of it, and the Acharnians can do what *they* please! I'm done
        with troubles, I'm done with war, and I'm going to go inside
        and celebrate the Country Dionysia! [*He takes the skin into
        his house.*]

        AMPHITHEUS: And *I'm* going to try and get away from the
        Acharnians! [*He runs off.*]

        [*Enter, as fast as they can (which is not all that fast), the
        CHORUS OF ACHARNIANS, very old and very ferocious
        men.*]

        LEADER:
                Chase him,[44] chase him, everybody, for the traitor must
                    be found.
205   Everyone that you run into, ask them where he's gone
                    to ground.

It's our duty to the City to arrest this evil man.
[*To the audience*]
　　Where's he gone with that foul treaty? Tell us, anyone
　　　　who can!
[*But there is no answer, and no sign of anyone.*]

CHORUS:
　　Ah, our quarry has escaped us,
　　　　Gone and vanished from the scene!
　　Woe is us that we so many
　　　　Years upon the earth have been!   210

　　In my youth I'd pace Phaÿllus[45]
　　　　Laden with a sack of coal;
　　If I'd chased this fellow then, he'd   215
　　　　Not have been a happy soul!

LEADER:
　　Now our legs have all gone heavy and our calves are
　　　　stiff and sore,
　　And our dear old Lacrateides can't keep running any   220
　　　　more –
　　And he's got away. But chase him! Let him never grin
　　　　with glee
　　At outstripping the Acharnians, old and feeble though
　　　　we be!

CHORUS:
　　Zeus and all you gods, take notice!
　　　　With our foes he's made a pact,   225
　　More abhorrent now than ever
　　　　To the men whose lands they sacked.

　　They have trampled on our vineyards,
　　　　And they'll pay for all their guilt:
　　I'll not rest till, sharp and painful,   230
　　　　I have pierced them to the hilt!

LEADER:
   Search on, search on, look all the way to Peltingham,[46]
235 Chase him through all the world, if need be, till he's
   caught!
   For never could I have my fill of pelting him with rocks!
DIKAIOPOLIS [*within*]: Speak fair! Speak fair![47]
LEADER:
   Hush! Did you hear the call for holy silence?
   That is our man, about to sacrifice.
240 He's coming out, so let's get clear of him.

   [*The* CHORUS *withdraw to one side. Enter, from the house,*
   DIKAIOPOLIS *with his* CHILDREN *and* SLAVES; *his* WIFE
   remains by the door. Dikaiopolis' DAUGHTER, *who is
   bedecked with jewellery, carries on her head a basket containing the requisites for the sacrifice; two* SLAVES *carry
   between them a phallus mounted on a pole.*]

DIKAIOPOLIS: Speak fair! Speak fair! Move forward a little,
   basket-bearer. [*His* DAUGHTER *advances towards the altar.
   He turns to one of the slaves*] Xanthias, make sure that phallus
   is erect. [*To his daughter*] Put the basket down, my girl, so
   we can make the opening sacrifice.
245 DAUGHTER [*putting down the basket next to the altar and
   taking a cake out of it*]: Mum! Can you let me have the
   soup-ladle? I need it to pour the soup over this with.
   [*The* WIFE *disappears for a moment and returns with a
   ladle, which is passed to her daughter.* DIKAIOPOLIS *takes
   a pot of soup from one of the slaves and holds it for his
   daughter to ladle some of the soup on to the cake, which
   she then places on the altar. Then she takes up the basket
   again and stands in front of the slaves holding the phallus.*]
DIKAIOPOLIS: That's fine. [*Stretching his hands out towards
   the altar*] O Lord Dionysus, accept with favour this offering
   and this procession from myself and my household, and may
250 we, released from warfare, celebrate with good fortune thy
   Country Dionysia; and may the thirty years' peace I have

made be a blessing to me. – Now, my girl, carry the basket beautifully, like the beauty you are, and with a really sour look on your face.[48] My, he'll be a lucky man that marries   255 you and produces a brood of little pussycats, all as good as you at farting in the grey dawn! Step off, now, and take care of that crowd [*indicating the audience*], in case any of them snaffles your jewellery on the sly. And Xanthias, you two *must* hold your phallus erect behind the basket-bearer! I'll   260 bring up the rear and sing the phallic hymn. Wife, you watch me from the roof. [*She goes inside.*] All right, off we go.

[*Dikaiopolis'* WIFE *appears on the roof. The procession circles the altar as* DIKAIOPOLIS *sings.*]

O Phales,[49] companion of Bacchus in nocturnal revel
    and rout,
Seducer of boys and of women, I give you my greeting   265
    devout!
Six years it has been, but I've gladly come home to my
    village once more,[50]
I've made peace with the foe, and I'm finished with   270
    Lamachus, trouble and war!

O Phales, O Phales, I tell you it makes me feel vastly
    more good
When I find my old neighbour's young slave-girl in the
    act of purloining some wood,
Grip her tight by the waist, like a wrestler, and lift her
    up high off her feet,
Then throw her down back to the earth, like, and take   275
    out her grape-pip – how sweet![51]

O Phales, O Phales, come join us and quaff at our party
    tonight;
Should you be hung-over tomorrow, drink some peace
    and you'll soon be all right!
The shield that I bore in my battles will be hanging up
    over the fire –

[*Here the* CHORUS *rush at the procession, singing and shouting, and it scatters in panic, all except* DIKAIOPOLIS *fleeing indoors.*]

CHORUS:

280   That's the man,   that's the man!
            Stone him, stone him, stone him, stone him,
            Hit him hard   as you can!
            Stone him, won't you? Stone him, won't you?

DIKAIOPOLIS [*who has picked up the soup-pot to defend himself*]: For Heracles' sake, what's all this? You'll smash the pot!

CHORUS:

285   No, we'll not   smash the pot,
            But we'll smash your evil head
            As we stone – you – dead!

DIKAIOPOLIS: But, my most venerable Acharnians, what have I done wrong?

CHORUS:

            You want *us* to tell you what?
290   Did you make a peace or not?
            How dare you look us in the eye,
            You traitor of the deepest dye?

DIKAIOPOLIS: But you don't know *why* I made peace. Listen – won't you listen?

CHORUS:

295   We will never listen to you –
            Straight away to death we'll do you!
            Die beneath a heap of stones:
            They will serve to hide your bones.

DIKAIOPOLIS: Just let me say something first! Just *wait* a moment!

CHORUS:

            Wait? No, never! Not a word!
            We don't want you to be heard!
            When *your* wickedness we scan,
300   Cleon seems a virtuous man!

(We'll be doing *him* to rights –
Cut him up to shoe the Knights![52])

LEADER: We don't mean to listen to long speeches from a man who has made peace with the Spartans! We mean to punish him!

DIKAIOPOLIS: Good people, can you forget about the Spartans 305
for a minute, and just let me talk about my peace treaty? Was I right to make it? That's the question.

LEADER: *Right?!* To make a treaty with that lot – whose pledged word, whose oath, whose most solemn sacrifice, are worthless?[53]

DIKAIOPOLIS: Oh, I know we always say hard things about the Spartans, but are they really responsible for all our troubles? 310

LEADER: The Spartans not responsible? You dare to say that, bold as brass, to our face, and you expect to escape with your life?

DIKAIOPOLIS: Yes, not entirely responsible, not entirely responsible. In fact I could prove to you quite clearly that they have a good many legitimate grievances themselves.

LEADER: This is too much – it's affecting my heart! The nerve 315
of the man – addressing us as an advocate for the enemy!

DIKAIOPOLIS [*struck by a brilliant idea*]: And if the People [*indicating the audience*] don't think I have justice on my side, then – I'm willing to speak with my head over a butcher's block![54]

LEADER [*quite unimpressed*]: What are we hoarding these stones for? We should be turning[55] this man into a scarlet 320
cloak!

DIKAIOPOLIS [*who has had another brilliant idea*]: Well, well, the black embers of your wrath have blazed up all right! Now then, gentlemen of Acharnae, are you really determined not to listen to me?

LEADER: Absolutely, we will not.

DIKAIOPOLIS: You'll be being very unfair, you know.

LEADER: I'd sooner die than listen to you.

DIKAIOPOLIS: Oh, please don't do that, my dear Acharnians.

325   LEADER [*taking a stone in his hand; all the* CHORUS *do like-
         wise*]: Your life is about to terminate!

      DIKAIOPOLIS [*mysteriously*]: I can bite you too! If you try any
         such thing, I will kill your nearest and dearest. I am holding
         them as hostages, and I will execute them if necessary. [*He
         goes into the house.*]

      LEADER [*to his colleagues*]: You got any idea what he means –
         these threats he's making against us? He doesn't maybe have
330   one of our children locked up in there? What's he so confident
         about?

      DIKAIOPOLIS [*emerging triumphantly, carrying in one hand a
         knife and in the other a basket full of coals*]: All right, stone
         me, whenever you want to. Only if you do, I'll kill this one.[56]
         We'll soon see which of you really loves his . . . coals.

      LEADER: No, no! That basket is one of our own! Don't do it!
         Don't, don't, don't!

335   DIKAIOPOLIS: Yes, I will. Shout away; I'm not going to listen.

      CHORUS:
               Will you make my age-mate perish,
               Whom all charcoal-burners cherish?

      DIKAIOPOLIS: You wouldn't listen to me, and I'm not going to
         listen to you. [*He raises his knife.*]

      CHORUS:
               All right, you can tell us, and tell us right now,
                  Why you reckon the Spartan a friend:
340   My dear little coal-basket I'll not betray,
                  But be faithful right up to the end!

      DIKAIOPOLIS: First of all you've got to drop those stones.

      CHORUS [*dropping the stones in their hands*]:
               There you are: now for you,
               You must drop   your sword[57] too.

      DIKAIOPOLIS: I'm sure you've still got some stones sitting in
         those cloaks.

      CHORUS [*shaking the stones out of their clothes as they
         dance*]:
               Look, how can you doubt that we've shaken them out?
                  Our missiles all lie on the floor.

Now no more excuses, but put down that blade –   345
     We'll be done if *these* [*indicating their phalli*] shake
          any more!
[DIKAIOPOLIS *lays down the knife.*]
DIKAIOPOLIS [*reflectively*]: I *thought* I'd manage to quieten
you down in the end. But it very nearly cost the life of some
innocent coals from Mount Parnes, and all because of the
silliness of their fellow-townsmen. [*Putting down the basket,
and inspecting his sooty clothes*] And that basket was so   350
frightened, it made a thick black mess on me as if it was a
cuttlefish! But really, it's not right that people should have a
temper like sour grapes, and want to yell and throw stones,
and refuse someone a fair hearing. I know I want to speak in   355
defence of the Spartans, but I did say I was willing to speak
with my head over a block. And don't think I don't love my
own life, either.

CHORUS:
     Then why don't you get on with it? Bring out the block,
          And let's see how your argument goes.   360
     We're consumed with desire to know what you intend
          To say on behalf of our foes.

[DIKAIOPOLIS, *who has gone inside taking basket and
knife with him, now returns with an enormous butcher's
block.*]

LEADER:
     You offered of your own accord to stand your trial this way;
     So set it down, and let us hear just what you've got to say.   365

DIKAIOPOLIS [*putting down the block, front end facing the
audience*]: There you are. There's the block, and here's little
me ready to speak. Don't worry, I'm not going to wrap myself
up in fancy words, just speak my mind in defence of Sparta. I   370
know I've good cause to be afraid. I know what country
people are like. They just love it when some fast talker flatters
them and Athens, true or false, it doesn't matter. They can be
bought and sold, and never know a thing about it. And the   375
senior citizens, who serve on juries – I know what they're like
too: they never think of anything except who's to be stung

next.[58] I've personal experience now, after what Cleon did to
me on account of last year's play.[59] He dragged me into the
380   Council Chamber, made all sorts of trumped-up charges,
spewed out a torrent of sewage – I very nearly perished in the
flood of filth. So this time [*to the Chorus*] could you please,
before I speak, let me dress up to look really wretched and
downtrodden.[60]

CHORUS:
385   What's the point of this scheming, these time- wasting
                       tricks,
                   This wriggling this way and that?
                We don't mind if you use Hieronymus' hair
390   For an invisibility hat![61]

LEADER:
I'm sure your speech has all the tricks from Sisyphus's
       store[62] –
So come, let's hear it! We don't want excuses any more!
       [*The* CHORUS *withdraw to one side, waiting until* DIKAI-
       OPOLIS *is ready.*]
DIKAIOPOLIS: 'Now is the hour to have a steadfast heart' – [*He
is struck by another brilliant idea.*] I think I should go and see
395   Euripides. [*He goes up to Euripides' house and knocks.*] Boy!
Boy!
SERVANT[63] [*opening the door*]: Who is this?
DIKAIOPOLIS: Is Euripides at home?
SERVANT: He is and is not, if you understand.
DIKAIOPOLIS: He is and is not ... what does that mean,
please?
SERVANT: Very simple. His *mind* is not at home, it's out gather-
ing flower...y phrases; but he himself *is* at home, with his feet
400   up, writing a play.
DIKAIOPOLIS: Happy Euripides, to have a slave who gives such
clever answers! Can you call him here?
SERVANT: Sorry, it's not possible.
DIKAIOPOLIS: Do it anyway. [*The* SERVANT'*s answer is to shut
the door in his face.*] I'm not going to go away, I'll just keep

on knocking. [*He knocks loudly and repeatedly, calling out
at the same time.*] Euripides! Sweet Euripides![64] If e'er you   405
answered mortal's prayer, answer me now. It's Dikaiopolis
from Cholleidae[65] calling you – that's me.

EURIPIDES [*inside*]: Sorry, I'm busy.

DIKAIOPOLIS: Then have yourself wheeled out.[66]

EURIPIDES: Sorry, it's not possible.

DIKAIOPOLIS: Do it anyway.

EURIPIDES: Very well. I'll have myself wheeled out; I'm too
busy to get down.

> [*A trolley is wheeled out of the door. On it,* EURIPIDES *is
> seen reclining on a couch, with his* SERVANT *in attend-
> ance. On the couch are scattered numerous ragged or
> patched costumes; more are seen in an open cupboard
> behind.*]

DIKAIOPOLIS: Euripides –   410

EURIPIDES: What sayest thou?

DIKAIOPOLIS: Now I know why you put so many cripples in
your plays. *You've* renounced the use of your legs.[67] And all
these tragic rags, sorry, 'piteous garb'? No wonder you create
beggars! But [*touching Euripides' knees like a tragic suppliant*] I beg of you by these knees, could you give me a rag or   415
so out of that old play of yours?[68] I've got to make a long
speech to the chorus very shortly, and if I do it badly, it means
death.

> [*During the following dialogue, as each tragic character is
> referred to,* EURIPIDES *takes that character's costume from
> the couch and displays it to Dikaiopolis.*]

EURIPIDES:
Which ragged raiment? Is it this, perchance,
In which ill-starred old Oeneus[69] once appeared?

DIKAIOPOLIS: No, not Oeneus. Someone in even worse misery.   420

EURIPIDES:
Then these, blind Phoenix's?[70]

DIKAIOPOLIS: No, not Phoenix. There was another one worse
off than Phoenix.

EURIPIDES [*to himself*]:
Whose tattered vesture doth the fellow seek?

[*To Dikaiopolis*]
Meanest thou then the beggar Philoctetes?[71]

425 DIKAIOPOLIS: No, someone much, much more beggarly than
         him.

EURIPIDES:
         Is this, mayhap, the squalid garb thou seek'st,
         Which once was born by lame Bellerophon?[72]

DIKAIOPOLIS: No, not Bellerophon. The man I'm after, though,
         he was lame too – *and* a beggar – and a very glib, very clever
         speaker.

EURIPIDES:
430   I know the man: 'tis Mysian[73] Telephus.

DIKAIOPOLIS: Yes, that's right, Telephus. Could you, I beg
         you, give me his wrappings?

EURIPIDES [*to his servant*]:
         Give him the ragments, boy, of Telephus.
         They lie below the rags of Ino, and
         Above those of Thyestes.[74]

SERVANT [*taking the Telephus costume from the cupboard;
         it consists chiefly of holes*]: Here, take it. [*He hands it to
         Dikaiopolis.*]

435 DIKAIOPOLIS [*inspecting the costume*]: 'O Zeus who seest
         through and under all!' [*As he begins to put it on*] Euripides,
         since you have been so kind with this, could you possibly give
         me those other things that go with the outfit? The Mysian felt
         cap for my head, for example?

440   'For I this day must seem to be a beggar –
         Be who I am, but not *appear* to be.'[75]
         That is, the *audience* have got to know who I am, but the
         chorus have got to be totally fooled, so I can screw them good
         and proper with my neat little phrases.

EURIPIDES:
445   I'll give it thee; for densely dost thou weave
         The finely spun contrivings of thy mind.
         [*The* SERVANT *gives the cap to* DIKAIOPOLIS, *who puts it
         on at once.*]

DIKAIOPOLIS:
         'O be thou blest; and as for Telephus,

May he get all that I desire for him!'[76]

That's good, the way I'm filling up with poetic phrases
already! Now, to be a real beggar, I still need a walking-stick.

EURIPIDES [*who is getting exasperated*]:

Take this, and straightway quit these marble halls.

[DIKAIOPOLIS *is given a gnarled walking-stick.*]

DIKAIOPOLIS:

Seest thou, my soul, how I am thrust away,   450
Still needing lots more props?

I've got to be a really clingy, wheedling beggar. Euripides,
give me a little wicker basket – one that's had a hole burnt in
it by a lamp.

EURIPIDES:

Why needest thou that wicker, thou poor wretch?

DIKAIOPOLIS:

Need have I none, yet I desire to have it.   455

EURIPIDES [*passing it to him*]:

Know thou annoyest me, and go from hence.

DIKAIOPOLIS [*in satisfaction*]: Ah!
'O be thou blest' – as once your mother was![77]

EURIPIDES:

Now, pray, begone.

DIKAIOPOLIS: No, no, just give me one thing more – a little
drinking cup, chipped at the rim.

EURIPIDES [*almost throwing it at him*]:

Take it and vanish, vexer of our house!   460

DIKAIOPOLIS [*aside*]: Vexer! *You're* a fine one to talk![78] –
Darling Euripides, just one thing more: give me a little cooking
pot, with a hole in it, stuffed with sponge.

EURIPIDES:

Thou'lt rob me of the whole damn tragedy!
Take this, and go!   465

DIKAIOPOLIS [*trying to find a spare pair of fingers to hold the
pot*]: I'm going, I'm going. – No, no, what do I mean? I
still need one thing more, otherwise I'm done for. – Listen,
Euripides darling. If you give me this, I'll go away and
never come back: some cast-off lettuce leaves to put in my
basket.

EURIPIDES:

470   You'll be the death of me! [*Giving him lettuce leaves*]
         Here you are. [*Lamenting*] I've lost my life's work!

DIKAIOPOLIS: No, no, that's all. I'm going. I can see I've upset
you –

         'Yet thought I not the kings would hate me so.'[79]
         [*And this time he really is going – but suddenly he stops and
         slaps his head.*] Heaven help me, I'm done for! I forgot the

475   one thing that's absolutely vital! Sweet Euripides – darling,
         beloved Euripides – may I be struck dead if I ever ask you for
         anything again – except just one thing, just this, only this:
         give me some chervil, 'inherited from her who gave thee birth'.

EURIPIDES:

         The man insulteth us. Make fast the house.
         [*The trolley is rolled back inside.*]

DIKAIOPOLIS:

480   So we must march forth chervil-less, my soul!
         [*He begins to move back towards the block, but with much
         hesitation.*]
         Do you know what a trial you've let yourself in for, by
         undertaking to make a speech in defence of Sparta? Forward,
         my soul; you see the starting line! [*But his feet stay put.*]
         What's wrong? Go on, *move* – you're full of Euripides, after

485   all! [*He takes a step or two.*] Congratulations! Come on now,
         my heart, old thing, go over there. Say what you want to say,
         and then if they want your head, they can have it. Be brave –
         come on – move! [*He rushes over to the block and stands
         behind it.*] Well done, heart.

CHORUS:

         What will you do? What will you say?

490   We marvel at your gall,
         Who dare to risk your neck and speak
             Alone against us all.
         He does not tremble at the task –
             So to it, man, we say.

495   It's by your choice you're doing this:
             Go on, then, speak away!

DIKAIOPOLIS:

   'O hold it not against me,' you spectators,

   'If, though a beggar, I make bold to speak'[80] –

before the Athenian people about matters of state – and that
when I'm a comic poet.[81] Even comedy knows something   500
about truth and justice; and what I'm going to say may be
unpalatable, but it's the truth. At least this time Cleon can't
smear me with the charge of slandering the City in the presence of foreigners. This time we're all by ourselves; it's only
the Lenaea, and there aren't any foreigners here yet – no   505
delegations bringing tribute, no allied troops, no one. We're
all by ourselves, all grain, no husk (I count the immigrants[82]
as the bran of the body politic). Now I hate the Spartans
tremendously. I hope Poseidon on Mount Taenarum sends   510
another earthquake[83] and brings all their houses down on
their heads. I've had vines of mine chopped down as well. But
after all – we're all friends talking together here – why do we
blame it all on the Spartans? It was some Athenians who   515
started it – *some* Athenians, mind you, not Athens, remember
that, not the City – but a bunch of good-for-nothing individuals, worthless counterfeit foreigners, bad coin through
and through. They kept denouncing Megarians – first of all
their woollen cloaks, and soon, whenever they saw a cucum-   520
ber or a young hare or a piglet or some garlic or some
rock-salt, 'Megarian goods!' they'd say, and had them confiscated and auctioned the same day.[84] Well, that was a minor
thing, just normal Athenian behaviour;[85] but then some young
roisterers got drunk, went to Megara and kidnapped their   525
tart Simaetha; and this raised the Megarians' hackles, and
they stole two of Aspasia's tarts[86] in retaliation. And that was
the reason why this war erupted throughout the Greek world:
it was on account of three whores.[87] Because when it hap-   530
pened, Pericles – Pericles the Olympian[88] – sent out thunder
and lightning and threw Greece into turmoil, passing laws
written like drinking songs –

   'No Megarian shall be

   On the land or the sea;

Let our market henceforth be Megarian-free!'[89]

535   Well, after that the Megarians were starving by slow degrees,
        and they asked the Spartans to get the decree of the three
        whores reversed. And *they* asked, several times, but we
540   refused – and then came the clashing of shields. Someone will
        say, 'They shouldn't have done that.' Tell me, then, what
        should they have done? Suppose some Spartan had 'sailed
        forth his bark'[90] and had denounced and sold a puppy-dog
        belonging to the Seriphians[91] –
             'Would you have sat within your halls? Far from it!'
545   You'd have launched a fleet of three hundred instantly, and
        every ear in the City would have been full of military noises
        – shouting crowds around ships' captains, pay being distribu-
        ted, figureheads of Athena being gilded, the Peiraeus corn
        market groaning[92] as rations were measured out, people buy-
550   ing leathers and rowlock thongs and jars, or garlic and olives
        and nets of onions, garlands and anchovies and flute-girls and
        black eyes;[93] and down at the docks, the sound of planing
        spars for oars, hammering in dowels, boring oar-holes, of
555   reed-pipes and pan-pipes and boatswains and warblings.[94] I
        know very well that's what you'd have done;
             'And do we think that Telephus would not?'[95]
        If we do, then we really *are* stupid.
             [*He lays his head on the block. Half the* CHORUS *ad-
             vance menacingly upon him; the other half move to stop
             them.*]

FIRST SEMICHORUS:
        You filthy beggar, do you dare to say such things of us?
        Suppose there *was* the odd denouncer, what's the great big
             fuss?
SECOND SEMICHORUS [*forming a ring to protect Dikaiopolis*]:
560   So may the great Poseidon help me, I declare that I
        Thought all he said was true and right, without a single
             lie.
FIRST SEMICHORUS [*trying to break through*]:
        Well, true or false, what business did *he* have to say it
             here?
        He'll find that his audacity is going to cost him dear!

SECOND SEMICHORUS:

   Where do you think you're going, mate? No further! If you
      dare
   To strike this man, you'll quickly find your feet are in the   565
      air!

    [*After a short fight the* SECOND SEMICHORUS *have the*
    FIRST *pinned down.*]

FIRST SEMICHORUS [*trying to free themselves*]:

      Lamachus of the lightning glance, he of the fearsome
         crest,
      Our tribal champion,[96] come quickly, thy friends are
         sore distressed!
      And every general or colonel who ever has stormed a   570
         wall,
      Make haste to come to our rescue, and do not ignore
         our call!

    [LAMACHUS *bursts on to the scene. He is accoutred in full
    armour, his shield bearing a horrific Gorgon-head, and
    wears a helmet with an enormous triple crest and two
    gigantic feathers. He is followed by a company of soldiers.
    The* SECOND SEMICHORUS, *dumbfounded, let go of their
    prisoners.*]

LAMACHUS [*bombastically*]:

   Whence came the cry of battle that I heard?
   Whom must I aid, and where my havoc wreak?
   Who has aroused my Gorgon from her case?[97]

DIKAIOPOLIS [*in mock adoration*]: O mighty hero Lamachus!   575
   What crests, what cohorts!

LEADER OF FIRST SEMICHORUS [*indicating Dikaiopolis*]:
   Lamachus, don't you know that this man has been persistently
   slandering the City?

LAMACHUS [*in a rage worthy of a hero*]: How dare you say
   such things, you, a beggar?

DIKAIOPOLIS [*grovelling*]: O mighty hero Lamachus, do pardon me, if I spoke a bit more freely than a beggar ought to!

LAMACHUS: What did you say about us? Out with it!   580

DIKAIOPOLIS: I – don't remember at the moment. It's that terrifying armour of yours, it makes me all giddy. Please take away that horrid face!

LAMACHUS [*reversing his shield to hide the Gorgon-head*]: There you are.

DIKAIOPOLIS: No – put it on the ground, face down, in front of me.

LAMACHUS [*complying*]: There.

DIKAIOPOLIS: Now if you could give me that plume off your helmet?

585 LAMACHUS [*taking a large feather from his helmet*]: Here's a baby feather for you.

DIKAIOPOLIS [*bending over the shield*]: Right. Now could you take hold of my head, so that I can be sick? It's those crests of yours that do it!

LAMACHUS [*furious*]: What the hell do you think you're doing, using my baby feather to help you vomit?

DIKAIOPOLIS: Your *baby* feather? For heaven's sake, what bird does it come from? A *boastard*, perhaps?

590 LAMACHUS [*trying to throttle him*]: Why, you –. I'll murder you!

DIKAIOPOLIS [*wriggling free again*]: No, no, Lamachus! We're not having a trial of strength here. Though [*coming close to him; in a seductive voice*] if you *are* so strong, why don't you give me a bit of a thrill?[98] You're well enough equipped!

LAMACHUS: How dare you talk to a general like that, you, a beggar?

DIKAIOPOLIS: A beggar? I'm no beggar.

LAMACHUS: What are you, then?

595 DIKAIOPOLIS: What am I? A decent citizen. I've never run for office, and ever since the war started I've been in the front line. And *you*, ever since the war started you've been in the pay queue![99]

LAMACHUS: I was democratically elected –

DIKAIOPOLIS: Yes, by three cuckoos.[100] That's the sort of thing

600 that nauseated me, and that's why I made peace – when I saw grey-headed men serving in the ranks while strong young fellows like you[101] skived off and got sent to Thrace on three

drachmas a day, like Teisamenus and Phaenippus and that
swine Hipparchides, and another lot going to Chares,[102] and
another lot in Chaonia[103] – Geres, Theodorus and that brag-   605
ging liar from Diomeia[104] – and more in Sicily, in Camarina
and Gela and Gelaughatus[105] –

LAMACHUS: They were democratically elected too.

DIKAIOPOLIS: Then how comes it that you lot are always on
paid missions somewhere or other, and none of *these* people
[*indicating the Chorus*] ever is? Tell me, Marilades, you've   610
been grey for many years; have you ever been an ambassador?
[MARILADES *indicates 'no'.*] He hasn't, you see, although
he's a decent, hard-working man. How about you, Dracyllus?
or you, Euphorides? Or you, Prinides? Any of you ever been
to Ecbatana or Chaonia? [*All indicate 'no'.*] None of them,
you see. But Coesyra's boy,[106] and Lamachus here, *they* have!
And yet only the other day they were so much in arrears with   615
repayments on loans from their friends that they were warned
to 'stay clear', like people say when they're emptying slops
into the street of an evening.[107]

LAMACHUS: Goddess of Democracy, this is intolerable!

DIKAIOPOLIS: Nothing's tolerable to you, unless you're drawing pay for it.

LAMACHUS: Well, come what may, I shall never stop making   620
war on the Peloponnesians, all of them, and harry them
everywhere, by sea and by land, to the utmost of my power.
[*He departs with his men.*]

DIKAIOPOLIS: And I proclaim to the Peloponnesians, all of
them, and the Megarians and Boeotians too, to come and   625
trade with me – but not with Lamachus. [*He goes inside; the
CHORUS, now united again, come forward and address the
audience.*]

CHORUS:
            He's defended his peace with triumphant success
                And converted you all[108] to his view.
            Now let's strip for the dance, for it's time to embark
                On the section where *we* talk to you.
            [*They remove their outer garments.*]

LEADER:

Since our producer[109] started writing comedies, he's never
Made use of his Parabasis to say that he is clever.

630 But since (in Athens, always quick to swallow slanderous lies)
He's been accused by enemies of writing comedies
Which with insults to the City and the People did abound,
He wants to answer them (in Athens, quick to turn around).
He says that all the good he's done deserves some
        recognition:
For now you do not gawp at every diplomatic mission
That comes from foreign parts with lies to flatter and
        entreat you,

635 Nor feel delight when grovelled to, nor ever let them cheat
        you!
It used to be they only had to call you 'violet-crowned'[110]
And you sat up so, your little rumps were almost off the
        ground.

640 And when they called your city 'rich and shining', you were
        hooked
By an epithet that properly describes sardines well cooked!
And that's not all he's done: he's also tried to demonstrate
Exactly what 'democracy' means in a subject state.[111]
That's why, next time the tribute's due, your allies all will be
Eager to come and bring it here, because they'll want to see

645 This splendid, valiant poet, whom danger could not fright
Out of telling the Athenians what was true and fair and
        right.
His courage now is famed the whole world over – they
        report
That when the Spartans sent their envoys to the Persian
        court,
The King, who questioned them about the progress of the
        war,
First asked about the rival fleets: 'In ships, which side has
        more?'
And then he asked about this poet: 'Would you say his mind
To speak harsh words of Athens or of you was more
        inclined?

He makes much better people of whoever he reviles;   650
If they keep him as adviser, they will win the war by
    miles.'
That's why the peace proposals made by Sparta never lack
A clause that stipulates that we must give Aegina back.
It's not the island that they want; they'd willingly forgo it,
Only it offers them a chance to take away this poet.[112]
Be sure, though, and hold on to him. He'll wield the comic   655
    sword
Of truth and justice, speaking many a good, instructive
    word,
And make you wiser, happier men. There won't be any
    diddling,
Nor flattery, nor promises of covert bribes, nor fiddling,
Nor will he praise you till you drown in floods of fulsome
    goo:
His job's to teach you what is best, and that is what he'll do.
So let Cleon contrive
    What he will against me![113]   660
Both justice and right
    Are my allies, you see,
And I'll never be known
    (As *he* is, far and near)
As a cowardly fag
    Who's promiscuously queer!

CHORUS:
    O come, Acharnian Muse, inspire   665
    Us with thy power of ardent fire.[114]
    As from the coal the sparks arise
    When fanned, as on the embers fries   670
    A dish of sprats, while servants shake
    The gleaming Thasian sauce, and make
    The barley-cakes, so come thou, bring
    A lusty song for us to sing,
    A stirring song of rustic cheer,
    For us, thy fellow-townsmen here.   675

LEADER:

We old men think the City does us wrong.
Time after time we've toiled both hard and long
In naval battles, and that ought to earn
Support in our old age as fair return –
But what d'you do? You let the younger sort
On fearful charges haul us into court,

680   Young orators who mock us left and right,
Knowing *our* vocal strength's exhausted quite.
'Poseidon sees your footing slippeth not':[115]
A stick's the sole Poseidon that *we've* got!
Mumbling, dim-eyed, we stand there, and can trace
Only the faintest outline of the case.

685   The youth who's schemed to get himself the brief
Slings at us hard round words without relief,
Then questions us, with traps all set to spring,
Tears us to pieces, leaves us yammering.

690   So off we go convicted; and we sob
And weep, and tell our friends: 'That last few bob
I'd saved to buy a coffin – it must go,
Thanks to this trial, to pay the fine I owe!'[116]

CHORUS:

It's a scandal and a shame to dishonour and defame,
    As he stands beside the water-clock in court,
695   One who's snowy-headed now, but whose sweat
        flowed down his brow
    When for hearth and home at Marathon he fought.

For at Marathon – ah, then we were proved courageous
        men,
    As hotly we pursued our fleeing foes;
700   Now it's *us* that get pursued by these wicked men and
        lewd
    (Or prosecuted, as the expression goes).[117]

And then when the talking's done, there's no need to
        ask who's won –
    It will always be a 'guilty', every day:

Just let Grabber,[118] if he dare, try and argue that is
    fair –
I don't think that he will find a word to say.

LEADER:
Can it be right that someone old and bending,
Like poor Thucydides,[119] should be contending
Against that 'Scythian wilderness', the young
Son of Cephisodemus,[120] glib of tongue?   705
I pitied him, I wiped the tear-drops back,
To see that archer harry him to wrack.
When he was younger, he'd have been defiant,
He'd not have stood such insults from a giant![121]
No, ten times he'd have wrestled down[122] that fellow,   710
Silenced three thousand Scythians with his bellow,
And proved himself a better archer than
Cephisodemus' son and all his clan.
Look, if on trying old folk you insist,
Then put their names upon a separate list.
For old defendants it would be astuter   715
To choose an old and toothless prosecutor,
And keep for young accused the subtleties
Of smart young queers like Alcibiades:[123]
As in the proverb, make the rule to hold
That young men drive out young, and old men old.[124]

> [Enter DIKAIOPOLIS *from his house, carrying three leather*
> *straps and a number of boundary stones, which he begins*
> *to set out in a large circle.*]

DIKAIOPOLIS: Right then, there's the boundaries for my
market. Within these limits the Peloponnesians may trade, all   720
of them, and the Megarians and Boeotians too, but only if
they trade with me – and not with Lamachus. An election by
lot has been held for the office of Market Commissioners,
and I declare these three straps from Lepri elected.[125] No   725
informers will be admitted, nor any other bird of that
feather.[126] [*He hangs the straps from pegs on his wall.*] But
I'd better go and get my inscribed copy of the peace treaty

and put it on display here in my market-place. [*He goes inside.*]

> [*Enter a* MEGARIAN *with his two little* GIRLS. *All three are very emaciated. The father carries a sack containing various bits and pieces whose nature and purpose will be clear from what follows.*]

MEGARIAN: Weel, hullo, Athenian market. We Megarians lo'
730   ye dearly, and we've longed for ye, I sweir by the god of friendship, as though ye were our ain mither. Ye twa puir bairns, listen to yer wretched auld father: go up there [*pointing towards the house*] and see can ye find anything to eat anywhere aroond. [*The* GIRLS *climb the steps to the platform, but can find nothing edible there. Meanwhile their father has taken his paraphernalia out of the sack.*] Listen, then, and dinna let yer bellies – I mean yer minds wander. Which wuid ye rather – be sold as slaves, or starve tae death?

735 GIRLS: Be sold, be sold!

MEGARIAN: I go along wi' that. But wha's sae far gone in his mind that wuid buy ye? He'd be makking a sheer loss! Och, weel, I've a guid Megarian trick to play. I'll kit ye oot and say
740   I've brought porkers[127] to sell. So first of a', pit on these trotters, and do try and luik like ye had a guid sow for a mither. For Hermes knows, if ye come hame again unsold, ye'll ken for real what starvation is. Pit on these snoots too,
745   that's recht, and then get into this sack here. [*The two* GIRLS, *by now trottered and snouted, burrow into the sack.*] Mak sure ye let oot some guid grunts – oink, oink – like the wee porkers do at the Mysteries doon at Eleusis.[128] And I'll call and see if Dikaiopolis is hereaboot. Dikaiopolis! wad ye like tae buy some porkers?

750 DIKAIOPOLIS [*within*]: What's the matter? [*Opening the door*] Why, a Megarian!

MEGARIAN: We're come tae do business.

DIKAIOPOLIS: How are you getting on, back there?

MEGARIAN: We sit by the fire and shrink.

DIKAIOPOLIS [*misunderstanding him*]: Very agreeable too it must be, especially if there's also music.[129] How are things going at Megara otherwise?

MEGARIAN: Och, so-so. When I left tae come here, the govern- 755
ment was doing all it could tae see we attained speedy and
complete disaster.

DIKAIOPOLIS: Then you'll soon have nothing more to worry
about.

MEGARIAN: Exactly.

DIKAIOPOLIS: What else is up in Megara? What's the price of
corn like?

MEGARIAN: *That's* up high eneugh – as high as the gods in
heaven!

DIKAIOPOLIS: Well, anyway, what have you got to sell? Salt? 760

MEGARIAN: Ye've takken that awa, have ye no?

DIKAIOPOLIS: Garlic, then?

MEGARIAN: What garlic? Every time ye raid oor country, ye
uproot them[130] a', as if ye were fieldmice!

DIKAIOPOLIS: Well, then, what do you have?

MEGARIAN: I hae some porkers for the Mysteries.

DIKAIOPOLIS: That's nice. Let's see them. 765

MEGARIAN: Och, but they're pretty. Tak one oot, if ye like.
[DIKAIOPOLIS *takes one of the girls out of the sack.*] How
pretty and plump she is!

DIKAIOPOLIS: What on earth is this?

MEGARIAN: Why, a porker.

DIKAIOPOLIS: What do you mean? What breed of porker is this?

MEGARIAN: A Megarian one. Ye're not saying it's no a porker?

DIKAIOPOLIS: Doesn't look like one to me.

MEGARIAN: Can ye believe it? Luik! Why will this mon no trust 770
me? He says this is no a porker. Well and guid: if ye're willing,
I'll bet ye a block o' salt flavoured wi' thyme that *this* [*lifting
up the girl's dress and pointing to what lies beneath*] is what
a' Greeks call pork.

DIKAIOPOLIS: Yes – *human* pork.

MEGARIAN: Weel, holy Diocles,[131] of course – it's mine! Wha' 775
did ye think it was? Wad ye like to hear its voice?

DIKAIOPOLIS: I certainly would.

MEGARIAN: A' right. [*To the girl*] Let's hear it from ye noo,
piggie. [*No answer.*] Ye willna? Grunt, confound ye! [*Quietly
in her ear*] As Hermes is my witness, I'll tak ye back hame!

780 FIRST GIRL [*terrified at this prospect*]: Oink, oink!

MEGARIAN: Satisfied? Is that a porker or no?

DIKAIOPOLIS: It may look like that now, but it'll grow up to be a beaver![132]

MEGARIAN: Aye, give her five years and she'll luik just like her mither.

DIKAIOPOLIS: But this one I can't even sacrifice.

785 MEGARIAN: And why not, pray? What's wrong wi' it?

DIKAIOPOLIS: It hasn't got a tail.

MEGARIAN: Och, it's young yet. When it grows up it'll have[133] a lang thick red one. [*He brings the second girl out of the sack.*] Do ye want tae rear them? This one is pretty, is she no?

DIKAIOPOLIS [*lifting her dress*]: She's got one just like the other's!

790 MEGARIAN: Aye, they're fu' sisters. Ye ken, when they thicken up and grow a bit o' hair, a porker maks the perrfect sacrifice to Aphrodite.

DIKAIOPOLIS: But you can't sacrifice pigs to Aphrodite.[134]

MEGARIAN: Pork to Aphrodite? She's the ainly one it *is* offered
795 to. And ye ken, if ye skewer them on a spit, their flesh is delicious.

DIKAIOPOLIS: Can they eat yet without their mother?

MEGARIAN: Aye, and withoot their father forby.

DIKAIOPOLIS: What do they like having?

800 MEGARIAN: Whatever ye gie them. Ask them yersel'.

DIKAIOPOLIS [*to First Girl*]: Piggy-piggy!

FIRST GIRL: Oink, oink!

DIKAIOPOLIS: Do you like chickpeas?

FIRST GIRL [*half-heartedly*]: Oink, oink . . . oink.

DIKAIOPOLIS: How about dried Phibalian figs?

FIRST GIRL [*greedily*]: Oink, *oink!*

DIKAIOPOLIS [*to Second Girl*]: What about you? Do you like them too?

SECOND GIRL: Oink, oink, *oink!*

DIKAIOPOLIS: That word 'figs' sure makes them hit the high
805 notes! [*Calling into the house*] Someone bring out some of our dried figs for these piglets. [*A* SLAVE *brings figs, which are scattered in front of the girls.*] I wonder if they'll eat them?

[*The* GIRLS *fall on the figs as if they had eaten nothing for weeks.*] Whew! The sound of those jaws! Mighty Heracles! Where do they come from? Eat-olia,[135] by the look of it!

MEGARIAN: Weel, they've no eaten a' the figs. I did pick up this ane for mesel' [*displaying a fig*].   810

DIKAIOPOLIS: Quite a nice pair of beasts, certainly. Tell me how much you're asking for them.

MEGARIAN: For this one, a bunch o' garlic, and for the ither, if ye wuid, twa pints o' salt.[136]

DIKAIOPOLIS: It's a deal. Just wait a moment, could you, please? [*He goes into his house.*]   815

MEGARIAN: Very weel. – O Hermes, god o' marketing, if I cuid ainly sell my wife and my mither as easily!

[*Enter an* INFORMER.]

INFORMER: You, state your place of origin.

MEGARIAN: Megara. I'm here tae sell pigs.

INFORMER [*laying hold on the sack, in which the two girls have hidden themselves*]: In that case I denounce these piglets as contraband of war, and I also denounce you.   820

MEGARIAN: Here we are agin, back where the whole sair tale began!

INFORMER: I'll teach you to talk, Megarian! Let go of that sack!

MEGARIAN [*holding desperately on to it*]: Help, help! Dikaiopolis! I'm being informerized!

DIKAIOPOLIS [*coming out*]: Who by? Who is it trying to denounce you? [*Taking down his three straps from their pegs*] Come on, Market Commissioners, it's your job to get rid of   825 these informers. [*To the informer*] What do you think you're up to, pretending to throw light on murky dealings, when you haven't even got a wick?[137]

INFORMER: I've got a right to expose enemy aliens!

DIKAIOPOLIS: You'll be squealing if you try. Go off and do your denouncing somewhere else.

[*Exit* INFORMER, *with some assistance from the straps.*]

MEGARIAN: What a plague o' them ye have here in Athens!

DIKAIOPOLIS: Never mind them, my Megarian friend. Look,   830 here's what you wanted for the pigs: take the garlic, and the salt. Goodbye, and the best of luck.

MEGARIAN: It's no the custom to have that at Megara.

DIKAIOPOLIS: Well, I wouldn't want to interfere in your ways,
so on my own head be it!

MEGARIAN [*to the girls*]: Weel, my wee porkers, dinna forget
835   to swallow yer cake wi' salt, if ye get any.

[*He leaves with the garlic and salt;* DIKAIOPOLIS *takes the
girls into his house.*]

CHORUS:

Do you hear how brilliantly success upon this man has
shined?

In the deed he planned much profit and much blessing
he will find,

840   And he'll quickly give old Ctesias a pain in his behind
If he tries to play informer in this market.

He need never fight to buy things in the public Market
Square,

Nor get his cloak all dirty jostling with the shoppers
there,

845   Like Cleonymus[138] and Prepis, like the fatso and the
queer,
Nor be summonsed by Hyperbolus[139] in the market.

He will never meet Cratinus, whose coiffure looks so
unchaste,[140]

850   That literary reprobate who writes with frantic haste
And whose life you'd think had all been spent in seas of
human waste
From the way that he smells in the market.[141]

From the jokes of wretched Pauson[142] he at last has got
relief,

855   From Lysistratus[143] as well, who's always bathing deep
in grief,
Whom you'll see far gone with hunger and shivering
like a leaf
Forty days every month in the market.

[*Enter a* THEBAN *with an enormous and very heavy sack of wares, attended by a slave,* ISMENIAS – *who is carrying, very carefully, a single plant – and followed by a* BAND OF PIPERS.]

THEBAN [*setting down his load*]: Ar, boi Heracles, this shoulder 860 o' moine be sore. Here, Ismenias, be gentle when you put down that pennyroyal plant. And you, my Theban poipers, take your bone-poipes and let's hear 'The Dog's Arse'.

[*They play raucous music, which quickly brings an angry* DIKAIOPOLIS *out of the house.*]

DIKAIOPOLIS: Stop that din, damn you! Must I have these wasps buzzing all round my house? Where did all these blasted 865 bumble-bees come from? Who are they, the Chaeris clan?[144]

[*Drives the* PIPERS *away.*]

THEBAN: Boi Iolaus,[145] sir, that be a great favour you just done me. They've been blowing moi ears off all the way from Thebes, and they've blown the blooms off moi pennyroyal plant too. Would you care to buy any of my wares, with two 870 wings or four?[146]

DIKAIOPOLIS: Welcome, my bap-eating Boeotian friend! What have you got with you?

THEBAN: Every one of the good things Boeotia produces. Marjoram, pennyroyal, doormats, lamp-wicks, ducks, jackdaws, 875 francolins, coots, wrens, dabchicks –

DIKAIOPOLIS: Gale warning: this man has brought fowl weather to our market!

THEBAN: And also geese, hares, foxes, moles, hedgehogs, cats, badgers, martens, otters, eels from Lake Copais. 880

DIKAIOPOLIS: The most delicious thing man ever sliced! You've brought eels? Let me greet them!

THEBAN: 'O eldest of Copais' fifty daughters',[147] come out here and pay your respects to the gentleman. [*He brings an eel out of the sack.*]

DIKAIOPOLIS [*to the eel*]:
My love, long lost, long yearned for, thou hast come! 885
What joy among the comic choruses,
What joy for gastronomes,[148] at thy return!
Ho, varlets, bring my brazier and its fan!

[*Two* SLAVES *bring out these utensils, which* DIKAIOPOLIS
now addresses.]

Look, children, on this noblest of all eels,

890   After six years of absence hither come,

Long pined for. Greet her kindly, little ones;

I'll give you coal in honour of her visit.

Go, take her in: for nor alive nor dead

May I be parted from my beet-wrapped love![149]

[*The eel and cooking appliances are solemnly removed.*]

895   THEBAN: Ahem – may oi expect to be paid for this, sir?

DIKAIOPOLIS: No, I'm taking that in lieu of market tax. Is there
anything else you're interested in selling, though?

THEBAN: The lot, sir, the lot.

DIKAIOPOLIS: How much for? Or would you prefer to swap
them for some goods to take back home?

900   THEBAN: Boi all means. Some local product of yourn that can't
be obtained in Boeotia.

DIKAIOPOLIS: So you'll want some Phalerum whitebait, or
some Attic pottery?

THEBAN: Whitebait? Pottery? We've got those.[150] No – something that we don't have at all, and that you produce lots of.

DIKAIOPOLIS [*as by a stroke of inspiration*]: I know, an

905   informer! Pack one up – like a pot, with care – and take him
home with you.

THEBAN: Ar, by the Two Gods,[151] if I took one I could make
a heap of money. Full of tricks, he'd be, as clever as a
monkey.

DIKAIOPOLIS: And look, here comes Nicarchus, in search of
someone to denounce.

THEBAN [*looking at* NICARCHUS, *who is just coming on*]: Bit
on the small side, isn't he?

DIKAIOPOLIS: But such bad quality!

910   NICARCHUS [*pointing at the sack*]: Who do these goods belong
to?

THEBAN: They're moine. Oi brought them from Thebes, as Zeus
is my witness.

NICARCHUS: In that case I hereby denounce them as contraband
of war.

THEBAN: What's with you, fighting a war against little dicky-
birds?

NICARCHUS: And I intend to denounce you also.

THEBAN: Why, what wrong have oi done to you?

NICARCHUS: For the sake of these bystanders [*with a vague*   915
gesture which might take in the Chorus and/or the audience],
I had better explain. [*Displaying a wick which he has taken
from the sack*] You are attempting to import enemy-made
lamp-wicks.

DIKAIOPOLIS: You're denouncing him for the sake of a
lamp-wick?

NICARCHUS: This could be used to set fire to the Docks.

DIKAIOPOLIS: A lamp-wick? Set fire to the Docks?

NICARCHUS: I believe it could.

DIKAIOPOLIS: How?

NICARCHUS: All it would take would be for a Boeotian to put   920
one into a small unmanned boat, wait for a northerly gale,
set it alight, and launch it down a drain leading to the Docks
– then if once any of the ships caught fire, they'd all be ablaze
in no time.[152]

DIKAIOPOLIS: Set ablaze by a wick sent down a drain? I'll wick   925
you! [*He beats Nicarchus with one of his straps.*]

NICARCHUS: Help! Assault! [*He is seized and overpowered by*
DIKAIOPOLIS, *the* THEBAN *and* ISMENIAS.]

DIKAIOPOLIS [*to the Theban*]: Shut his mouth, will you? [*The*
THEBAN *holds Nicarchus firmly by the head and chin.* DIKAI-
OPOLIS *addresses a slave who has come outside on hearing
the noise*] Give me some shavings. I want to pack him up like
china, so he won't get broken en route.

[*During the following song* SLAVES *bring out shavings,
rope, etc., and together with* ISMENIAS *they pack up the
screaming Nicarchus under Dikaiopolis' direction.*]

LEADER:

Be careful how you pack the goods
   For this good Theban's sake,   930
To ensure that while he takes them home
   They do not go and break.

DIKAIOPOLIS:
    I'm being careful; after all,
       This pot is not first-rate.
  [*Striking Nicarchus repeatedly, and listening critically to his screams*]
    It doesn't have an honest ring;
    I think it's cracked – a poor-class thing,
       An earthen reprobate!

LEADER:
935   What is there one can use it for?
DIKAIOPOLIS:
    It serves for many needs:
    A bowl, a mortar, or a cup
    To mix or pound or stir things up
       While bent on shady deeds;

    Or you could light a lamp in it
       To scan officials' files –
LEADER:
940   But is it really safe to use?
    All these ear-splitting sounds it spews –
       You'd hear them all for miles!

DIKAIOPOLIS:
    No, it's a strong and robust thing,
       I'm sure it will not shatter;
    Even if you hung him by the heels
945   Head down, it wouldn't matter.
  [*By now* NICARCHUS *is packed and trussed up.*]

LEADER:
    That's got it fine.
THEBAN [*exultant*]:
               I'll make a mint!
LEADER:
    I truly hope you do, sir;
    Now take him home: whatever task

(In the informing line) you ask,   950
    He'll serve you bad and true, sir.

DIKAIOPOLIS: The blighter was a devil to tie up. There's your
    pot, old chap, all ready to go.
THEBAN: Get your shoulder under it, then, Ismenias.
    [ISMENIAS *picks up Nicarchus, and they set off, with*
    Nicarchus slung over Ismenias' shoulder.]
DIKAIOPOLIS [*calling after them*]: Mind how you carry him. I   955
    know he's low-grade stuff, but all the same. If you make a
    profit on these goods, you'll have achieved the feat of getting
    an informer to make you happy!
    [*As the* THEBAN *departs at one side, enter from the other,*
    running, a SLAVE *of Lamachus.*]
SLAVE: Dikaiopolis!
DIKAIOPOLIS: Who is it? What are you calling me about?
SLAVE: Lamachus wants to buy some of your stuff for the   960
    Festival of Pitchers.[153] Here's a drachma he'll pay for some of
    your thrushes, and three he'll give for a Copaic eel.
DIKAIOPOLIS: Lamachus wanting an eel? And who may Lam-
    achus be?
SLAVE:
    The dreaded warrior with the oxhide shield,
    Bearing the Gorgon's head, who brandishes   965
    Three mighty crests that cast a fearful shade.[154]
DIKAIOPOLIS: Him? I wouldn't sell him anything if he gave me
    his shield! Let him shake his crests at the salt-fish vendors![155]
    And if he complains, I'll set my Market Commissioners on to
    him. [*Exit* SLAVE, *hastily, as* DIKAIOPOLIS *shakes a strap at*
    him.] This consignment is for *me*! Inside I go, 'to the beat of 970
    thrushes' and blackbirds' wings'! [*He goes inside, dragging*
    the sack.]

CHORUS:
    Citizens, see the reward of his wisdom,
        How peace wins him many a fine business deal,
    Cheap access to valuable household possessions   975
        And things that, served warm, are just right for a meal!

Into his house all good things come unbidden! –
   One bad thing never will come into mine:
Never will War be a guest at my parties,
980   Never will he on my couches recline.
For when he's drunk he's a creature of violence:
   When we were happy, he crashed through our door,
Then went amok, started fights, upset vessels,
   And left the wine running all over the floor.
985   'Lie down,' said I, 'drink, and let's all be friends here!'
   He wouldn't listen, but took to his heels,
Went to our vineyards, chopped vines, burnt up
    vine-props,
   And left the wine running all over the fields.

[*Pointing to fallen feathers lying in front of Dikaiopolis'
door*]
He's ready for dinner and proud of his triumph:
   See there the proof of his prosperous life! –
Friend of the Love-goddess, friend of the Graces,
   O Reconciliation, the cure of all strife,
990   How lovely your face is, and I never knew it!
   I wish that young Eros could join us in one,
Just like in the picture,[156] with garlands of flowers!
   D'you think I'm too old and my vigour all gone?
With *you* I could still manage three close encounters:
995   Vines, fig-trees, more vines, I would plant in your
    soil,
And all round your field olive-trees in a circle,
   To anoint you and me, each New Moon, with their
    oil.[157]

[*Re-enter* CRIER.]
1000 CRIER: Hear ye, hear ye! When the trumpet sounds, all shall
    drink from their pitchers,[158] according to ancient custom;
    and whoever is the first to empty his will win a skinful of
    Ctesiphon![159]

    [*A platform is rolled out, on which are* DIKAIOPOLIS *and
    a couple of* SLAVES, *frenziedly engaged in cooking.*]

DIKAIOPOLIS [*calling over his shoulder*]: Boys! Women! What
are you doing? Didn't you hear the proclamation? Get the   1005
water to the boil – get the spit turning – roast the hare and
take it off – quick! Get those garlands strung! Pass me the
skewers to put the thrushes on!
[*He is given a pair of skewers, on each of which he impales
a thrush, and sets them to roast over the fire.*]

CHORUS:
       How wise you are and how fine your feast!
       My eyes with envy burn.   1010
DIKAIOPOLIS:
       What will you say when you see the thrush
       Roasted and done to a turn?
CHORUS:
       I fancy there you have a point!
DIKAIOPOLIS:
       Here, someone, poke the fire!
CHORUS:
       He's as skilled as any professional cook –   1015
       A *cordon bleu* DIY-er!

[*Enter* DERCETES, *weeping and sobbing.*]
DERCETES: Help me! Help me!
DIKAIOPOLIS: Heracles save us, who's this?
DERCETES: A man that fate has ruined.
DIKAIOPOLIS: Well, don't sneeze on *me*, then.
DERCETES: My dear friend, I know that you and only you   1020
possess peace. [*Holding out a hollow reed*] Measure some
out for me – even five years would do.
DIKAIOPOLIS: Why, what's happened to you?
DERCETES: I've lost my two oxen! I'm *ruined*!
DIKAIOPOLIS: How did you lose them?
DERCETES: Boeotian raiders carried them off from Phyle.[160]
DIKAIOPOLIS: How appalling! I'm surprised you're not dressed
in black.
DERCETES: And the pair of them had always kept my life in   1025
such good ordure!

DIKAIOPOLIS: Well, what do you want now?

DERCETES: I've wept for them till I cried my eyes out. Please, if you care for poor Dercetes[161] of Phyle, rub some peace on my eyes, quickly.

1030 DIKAIOPOLIS: I'm very sorry for you, but I don't happen to be the public physician.

DERCETES: No, please! – if I can only get my oxen back –

DIKAIOPOLIS: No go. Sob off to Pittalus and Co.[162]

DERCETES: Couldn't you just drip one little drop of peace into my reed-stalk?

1035 DIKAIOPOLIS: No, not so much as a smear! *Will* you go away and moan somewhere else?

DERCETES [*departing*]: Oh, my poor, poor dear ploughing oxen!

[DIKAIOPOLIS *returns to his cooking.*]

CHORUS:
          He's found he really likes this peace:
          To share it he does not wish.

DIKAIOPOLIS:
1040   Now pour some honey over the tripe
          And brown the cuttlefish.

CHORUS:
          Just listen to those stirring cries!

DIKAIOPOLIS:
          Now turn the eel about!

CHORUS:
1045   The neighbours will die of envy when
          They smell it and hear you shout!

DIKAIOPOLIS [*handing some more meat to the slaves*]: Roast these, will you, nice and brown?

[*Enter a* BRIDEGROOM'S SLAVE, *carrying several slices of meat, accompanied by the* BRIDESWOMAN.][163]

BRIDEGROOM'S SLAVE: Dikaiopolis!

DIKAIOPOLIS: Who's this?

1050 BRIDEGROOM'S SLAVE: I've come from a wedding. The bridegroom sends you these [*showing him the meat*].

DIKAIOPOLIS: Very kind of him, whoever he is.

BRIDEGROOM'S SLAVE: And in return he wants you to give him just one ladleful of peace, in this flask,[164] so he won't need to go to the war but can stay at home and fuck.

DIKAIOPOLIS [*with a gesture of rejection*]: Take the meat away; I don't want any of it. I wouldn't give you any of this for a thousand drachmas. [*Noticing the brideswoman*] Here, who's she? 1055

BRIDEGROOM'S SLAVE: She's the brideswoman, and she's got a request from the bride to make in your private ear.

DIKAIOPOLIS [*to the brideswoman*]: All right, what have you got to say? [*He bends down to let her whisper to him; then he laughs uproariously.*] Gods in heaven! Do you know what the bride's message was? 'I would like you very much to make sure that my bridegroom's prick stays at home for me.' Very well; [*to a slave*] bring the treaty here. I'll give her some specially. She's a woman, and she wasn't responsible for the war. [*The wine-skin embodying the peace treaty is brought to him.*] Put the flask to the spout, lady. [*He pours a little wine into the flask.*] Now do you know what to do with it? Tell the bride this: any time they're preparing the army lists, just rub this on to your bridegroom's prick at night. [*To his slave, as the* BRIDEGROOM'S SLAVE *and the* BRIDESWOMAN *joyfully leave*] Take the treaty away and bring me the wine ladle, so I can take some wine and pour it into my pitcher. 1060 1065

LEADER: But look, here comes someone in a hurry – bringing bad news, by the frown on his face. 1070

[*Enter* FIRST MESSENGER, *running towards Lamachus' house.*]

FIRST MESSENGER: O War, O Battle, O Lamachus!

LAMACHUS [*coming to the door, without his armour*]: Who is it knocks without these brazen halls?

FIRST MESSENGER: Orders from the Generals, sir. You're to go immediately, with all your troops and all your crests, take up position in the snow and keep a look-out for enemy raiders. There's been a report that the Boeotians may take advantage of the Pitcher and Pot Feasts[165] to do a spot of rustling. 1075

LAMACHUS: O High Command, more numerous than kind! – Isn't it dreadful that I don't get time off even for a festival?

1080 DIKAIOPOLIS [mockingly]: Ho for the Lamachobellicose Expeditionary Force!

LAMACHUS [indignantly]: Really, do you have to laugh at me as well?

DIKAIOPOLIS: You want a fight, do you, you dreadful four-plumed monster?[166]

LAMACHUS: Alack, what news have I received this day?

DIKAIOPOLIS [seeing another MESSENGER approaching]: Alack, what's this fellow coming to tell me?

1085 SECOND MESSENGER [running up to Dikaiopolis]: Dikaiopolis!

DIKAIOPOLIS: Yes?

SECOND MESSENGER: Message from the Priest of Dionysus, sir. You're to come to dinner as quickly as possible. Bring a boxful of food, and your pitcher. Hurry up, you're keeping

1090 everyone else waiting. He's got everything ready: couches, tables, cushions, covers, garlands, unguents; the nuts and raisins are there, so are the tarts, and sponge-cakes and flat-cakes and sesame-cakes and wafer-cakes and – oh yes, and lovely dancing-girls, 'Harmodius' beloved',[167] so to speak. Come on, hurry!

LAMACHUS: Oh, woe is me! What great misfortunes do encompass me!

1095 DIKAIOPOLIS: Well, what do you expect when you choose that great big Gorgon for a patron? [To his slave] Close up the house. [The platform is rolled back inside. DIKAIOPOLIS calls into the house] And get my dinner ready to take, someone.

[In the ensuing scene, slaves of both Lamachus and Dikaiopolis are kept busy carrying out their masters' instructions.]

LAMACHUS: Boy! bring me out my ration-bag.

DIKAIOPOLIS [mimicking him – as often hereafter]: Boy! Bring me out my dinner box.

LAMACHUS: Bring some salt flavoured with thyme, and some onions.

1100 DIKAIOPOLIS: I'm fed up with onions; bring me some slices of fish.

LAMACHUS: Now some salt fish in a fig-leaf – stale, please.

DIKAIOPOLIS: Yes, a fig-leaf of pork fat[168] would be nice. I'll cook it when I get there.

LAMACHUS: Bring me the two plumes for my helmet.

DIKAIOPOLIS: Bring me the pigeon and thrush.

LAMACHUS: This ostrich feather is lovely and white.   1105

DIKAIOPOLIS: This pigeon's meat is lovely and brown.

LAMACHUS [*turning haughtily to Dikaiopolis*]: Would you please, my man, not make fun of my equipment?

DIKAIOPOLIS: Would you please, my man, not look hungrily   1108
at my thrush?

LAMACHUS: Would you please, my man, not presume to speak   1113
to me?

DIKAIOPOLIS: It's just that my boy and I have a little argument going. [*To his slave*] Let's make a bet of it, and let Lamachus be the judge: which is nicer to eat, locusts or thrushes?

LAMACHUS: Damn your insolence!

DIKAIOPOLIS: He'd much rather have the locusts, obviously!   1117

LAMACHUS: Bring me out the crest-case with my triple crest.   1109

DIKAIOPOLIS: And could I have my bowl of hare's meat?

LAMACHUS [*inspecting his crest*]: Don't say the moths have been eating it!

DIKAIOPOLIS: Don't say I'm going to be eating this before   1112
dinner even begins!

LAMACHUS: Boy! Take my spear off the peg and bring it to me.   1118

DIKAIOPOLIS: Boy! Take my sausages off the fire and bring them to me.

LAMACHUS: Let me pull the cover off the spear. Hold the other   1120
end, boy. [*His* SLAVE *holds the spear while he pulls off the cover.*]

DIKAIOPOLIS: And you, boy, hold on to this. [*His* SLAVE *holds the spit while he pulls the sausages off.*]

LAMACHUS: Bring me the stand for my round shield.

DIKAIOPOLIS: Bring me the oven-baked loaves for my round tummy.

LAMACHUS: Now bring me the Gorgon-faced shield itself.

DIKAIOPOLIS: And bring me a cheese-faced flat-cake.   1125

LAMACHUS: This is flat mockery in anyone's book!

DIKAIOPOLIS: This is delicious cake in anyone's book!

LAMACHUS: Pour on the oil, boy. [*The* SLAVE *does so, and begins to polish the shield.*] Reflected in the bronze I spy . . . the face of an old man who's going to be prosecuted for cowardice.

1130 DIKAIOPOLIS: Pour on the honey. Reflected on the cake I spy . . . the face of an old man who's telling Lamachus Fitz-Gorgon to get stuffed!

LAMACHUS: Bring me my martial corslet.

DIKAIOPOLIS: Bring me my martial pitcher.

LAMACHUS: This will fortify me stoutly against the enemy.

1135 DIKAIOPOLIS: *This* will fortify me stoutly to meet my fellow-diners.

LAMACHUS: Tie my bedding to the shield, boy –

DIKAIOPOLIS: Tie my dinner up in the box, boy –

LAMACHUS: – and I'll carry the ration-box myself.

DIKAIOPOLIS: – and I'll take my coat and go.

1140 LAMACHUS: All right, boy, take the shield and let's be off. Brr! It's snowing. Wintry outlook!

DIKAIOPOLIS: Take my dinner, boy. It's a party outlook!

[*Exeunt, on one side,* LAMACHUS *and his* SLAVE; *on the other,* DIKAIOPOLIS *and his* SLAVE, *each pair laden as described.*]

CHORUS:

Go your ways, and may fortune go with you!
  How different the paths that you tread!
1145 One leads to the wine and the garlands,
  One leads to cold bivouacs instead –
And just guess which ends up with a bimbo
  Massaging his whatsit in bed!

LEADER:

1150 As for Antimachus, the son of Splutter,
I hope Zeus visits him with ruin utter.
Not just because his lyrics show no skill:
Though mean his verse, the author's meaner still.
Last time he sponsored a Lenaean chorus
1155 He didn't deign to hold a dinner for us!

May I behold him longing for a dish
Of lovely, well-cooked, sizzling cuttlefish;
Let it be lying shipshape on the table,
Be placed before him – but, before he's able
To put his hand out or to pick it up,   1160
Let a dog grab it, run away and sup!
Here is another malediction grim
I hope and pray may come by night on him:
When coming home from riding, flushed and red,   1165
May drunk Orestes[169] smash his agued head!
Then may he find the stone he stoops to take
Is nothing but a turd of recent make!   1170
Then let him wildly throw his lump of shit
And – hit Cratinus in the face with it.

[*Enter, breathless, a* THIRD MESSENGER, *running up to
Lamachus' house.*]

THIRD MESSENGER [*in tragic tones, with occasional lapses*]:
Ye varlets in the house of Lamachus,
Heat water, water, in a little pipkin!   1175
Get lint and wax-salve and some greasy wool,
To make a bandage for his injured ankle!
The man's been wounded by a pointed stake
When crossing o'er a ditch; he dislocated
His ankle, broke his head upon a stone,   1180
And wakened up the Gorgon on his shield,
And dropped the boastard-plume from off his helm
Upon the rocks, which seeing, he lamented:
'My glorious treasure, now I leave thee, never
To see thee more, O light of all my life!   1185
I am no more.' So said he, having fallen
Into the ditch; then to his feet he rose,
And stayed his fleeing troops, and then pursued
The fleeing raiders with his trusty spear.
Now here he cometh: open wide the door!

[*Enter* LAMACHUS, *wounded, supported by two* SOL-
DIERS.]

LAMACHUS:

1190   Ah me, ah me,
          Hateful and gory woes!
              Sorry my lot,
          Stricken by furious foes!
1195   But worst of all
          If that old peasant should see
              My wretched fate,
          And then should mock at me!

[*Enter* DIKAIOPOLIS, *drunk, garlanded, waving an empty pitcher, and with a* DANCING-GIRL *on each arm.*][170]

DIKAIOPOLIS:

              Oh my, oh my!
          What lovely bouncy tit!
1200   Kiss me, my pets
          (And put some tongue in it!)
              To celebrate
          My victory – for I
              Am first in town
          To drink my pitcher dry!

LAMACHUS:

          O culmination dire of all my woes!
1205   O wounds of dismal pain!

DIKAIOPOLIS:

          Lammie![171] hello again!

LAMACHUS:

          Ah, ah, my wretched plight!

DIKAIOPOLIS [*to the girls*]:

          I said to kiss, not bite!

LAMACHUS:

1210   O dreadful, fatal charge –

DIKAIOPOLIS [*speaking*]: What, you've been *charged* for your entertainment on Pitcher Day?

LAMACHUS:

          O save me, Paean,[172] save –

DIKAIOPOLIS [*speaking*]: It's not *his* feast today, you fool.

LAMACHUS:
> Friends, hold my leg with kindly hands –
> Ah, ah, it hurts, take care!   1215

DIKAIOPOLIS:
> Girls, hold my prick between you both –
> Hold tight, my darlings – there!

LAMACHUS:
> That stone has shaken up my brains:
> How dizzy is my head!

DIKAIOPOLIS:
> Well, as for me, I'm all tooled up   1220
> And keen to go to bed.

LAMACHUS:
> Take me to Doctor Pittalus
> As gently as you can.

DIKAIOPOLIS:
> Where are you, judges? Where's the King?[173]
> Give me that wine-skin, man!   1225

LAMACHUS [*as he is carried off*]:
> A direful hostile spear has pierced my bones![174]

DIKAIOPOLIS [*to the (real) Basileus in his front-row seat*]:
> Behold my empty jug, and hail me champion!

LEADER:
> Since, friend, you ask us to –

CHORUS:
> > *Hail to the champion!*[175]

DIKAIOPOLIS:
> I poured it neat, and drank it at a draught!

[*A spectator, placed and primed for the purpose, runs up
with a full wine-skin and presses it into Dikaiopolis' hands.*]

LEADER:
> Once more, you noble soul –   1230

CHORUS:
> > *Hail to the champion!*

LEADER:

> Now off we go, and take the skin with you.

[DIKAIOPOLIS *prepares to move off, still flanked by the* DANCING-GIRLS, *and followed by the* CHORUS.]

DIKAIOPOLIS:

> Yes, follow on and sing with lusty glee
> 'Hail to our splendid champion' – that's me!

CHORUS:

> Yes, for your sake we'll gladly follow you:
> Hail to our champion – and his wine-skin too!
>   Hail to the champion!!!

THE CLOUDS

Preface to *The Clouds*

In the 420s BC Greece, and in particular Athens, was in an intellectual ferment. New forms of education were being developed; fundamental questions were being asked about ethics and values; teachers of rhetoric were training their pupils to argue for and against the same thesis with equal persuasiveness; scientific explanations of natural phenomena were challenging traditional assumptions that they were the acts of gods; the very existence of the gods and the possibility of objective knowledge were being called into doubt. Inevitably it was in general the young and impressionable who were most likely to take up the new thinking with enthusiasm. Their fathers, brought up in the old ways, might reject the new ideas simply because they were new, or might very rationally fear that a society not built on a firm foundation of accepted values would lack cohesion and could easily slide into anarchy or despotism – or be defeated, and possibly destroyed, by its external enemies, who, being Spartan, would certainly not be obliging enough to handicap themselves in the same way. And who were these men who made a living as teachers of this new learning – the sophists, as they were called?[1] What were they, some felt, but quacks and spongers, taking money from the gullible for corrupting them intellectually and morally?

Aristophanes was himself a man of the new generation, and at least one of his rivals saw him as being strongly influenced by the new learning (see Introduction, p. xxi); but in this respect, as in others, his comedies take the traditionalist point of view. In his very first play, *The Banqueters*, he had dramatized a contrast, and a contest, between two brothers, one with a traditional and the other with a sophistic education; and in *The Clouds*, produced at the City Dionysia of 423, he returns to this theme, as a rustic father and his cityfied son come into contact with the new learning in all its major aspects – natural science, rhetoric, the new morality and the new irreligion.

It made good dramatic sense for all these tendencies to be embodied in a single individual. Aristophanes could have created, if he had wanted to, a fictitious composite of the leading 'sophists' of the day – Protagoras, Antiphon, Diogenes of Apollonia, and others. Many, indeed, would argue that that was precisely what he did. But the tradition of Old Comedy was that major satirical targets should be given the identities, and usually the names, of actual contemporaries (like Lamachus in *The Acharnians* and Cleon ['Paphlagon'] in *The Knights*); and Aristophanes gave his fictitious composite the identity and the name of Socrates.

Socrates is now widely thought of as the father of Western philosophy, a status he owes principally to the literary, dramatic and intellectual genius of his follower Plato. There is no evidence that his contemporaries in general regarded him as a man of any exceptional merit at all. He was known to be interested in ethical issues; he was a tireless interrogator who would not let any assertion pass unquestioned, no matter how widely believed it might be; he showed a striking disregard for the accepted comforts and pleasures of life, to the extent that he must often have been fairly smelly (Plato confirms, what we might otherwise have supposed to be a comic slander, that he rarely bathed or wore shoes). He had attracted to himself a significant number of young men of wealthy families who discussed intellectual questions with him and each other, listened to his conversations and sometimes tried to imitate his methods themselves. In late 424 he had come to public notice in another way, by having behaved with notable courage during the Athenian retreat after the battle of Delium – typically not noticing or caring if his confident bearing was interpreted by his comrades as evidence of a disdainful attitude towards them. If for this reason he was particularly unpopular in the winter of 424/3, it may help to explain why he was made a significant figure in *two* of the comedies produced the following spring (the other was *Connus*, by Ameipsias). On the other hand, there is no good evidence that he questioned the existence or power of the gods, or neglected (or encouraged others to neglect) their traditional worship,[2] nor that he taught rhetoric, nor that he propounded specific doctrines about natural phenomena as he is made to do in *The Clouds*. Why then does Aristophanes in this play attribute to him all those characteristics of *other* intellectuals that were widely regarded as subversive?

In the first place, once he had decided to have a single major sophist as a central figure in his play, and to identify him with an actual person, Socrates was the obvious choice. Most of the (other) leading sophists[3] were not Athenians, and even those who were (like Antiphon), taught mainly in private and had public reputations based more on hearsay (or, for the minority who read books, on their writings) than on first-hand knowledge. Socrates was always in public places; his lifestyle was in certain respects unconventional, as we have noted; and (if we are to believe Plato) his appearance had something of the comically ugly about it. In the second place, while *questioning* received wisdom is a very different thing from *denying* it, there were undoubtedly many in Socrates' time, as there are now, who did not understand the difference – and who assumed, furthermore, that anyone who questioned/denied *some* traditional beliefs probably rejected *all* of them. And (if, again, we are to trust Plato) Socrates, while constantly questioning the beliefs of others, generally avoided any explicit statement of his own beliefs. It could plausibly be argued that of all the intellectuals of the late fifth century, he would seem to the outsider to be the one who excelled in negative criticism but had least to offer in the way of constructive ideas.

On the face of it, *The Clouds* might well seem to be, in the words of Sir Kenneth Dover, 'an invitation to violence or repressive legislation' against Socrates and other sophists. In fact it is unlikely that Aristophanes or anyone else, in 423, dreamed that it might have such consequences. Euripides too was portrayed in comedy as an atheist and a subverter of morality, but he never seems to have had any difficulty in getting a chorus for the City Dionysia when he wanted one. When, twenty-four years later, Socrates was prosecuted for 'corrupting the young' and for 'not believing in the City's gods but in other strange deities', it is likely that the prosecution was in reality a political one. Several of Socrates' close associates had been among the thirty-man junta who had tyrannized over Athens in 404/3, among them the junta's most extremist leader, Critias; and the many traditional practices which he had been known to question had apparently included the Athenian democratic practice of appointing most magistrates by lot. But to question a specific political institution was not an offence; and even if a jury could have been persuaded that Socrates had incited Critias and others to overthrow the democracy in 404, such a pro-secution would have been barred by the amnesty to which every citizen had sworn when democracy was restored. Accordingly a charge was laid under the conveniently vague rubric of 'impiety' – and backed by exploiting, among other things, the jurors' recollections of *The Clouds* and other comedies. The object was probably no more than to frighten Socrates into leaving Athens; the main author of Socrates' death was Socrates himself.[4] And if this was true in 399, certainly in 423 no one could have imagined that this man, tiresome and useless ec-centric though he was, would one day be put to death for it.[5]

In any case, Socrates is hardly the only unsympathetic charac-ter in this play – even leaving aside the figure of Wrong,[6] the personification of the immoralism allegedly taught in his school. The initial predicament of the play's central character, Strepsi-ades (whose name means 'Twister'), may be more his misfortune than his fault (though it was proverbially foolish to marry a wife accustomed to a lifestyle beyond the husband's resources), but he is ready and indeed eager to evade the payment of just debts by dishonest means (the chorus twice describe him as 'in love' with wickedness). His son Pheidippides is no model of sonship or piety even before he goes to Socrates' school; in the very first scene of the play we see him not only disobeying his father but breaking an oath,[7] and we already know that his extravagance has been a major cause of his father's financial plight.[8] Wrong's antagonist, Right, the champion of the old education, has an erotic interest in young boys which is overdone even for fifth-century Athens, particularly in the case of one who holds himself out as a teacher.[9] And the Clouds, as they in the end admit, act as *agents provocateurs*: perceiving that Strepsiades and Socrates are minded to follow the path of vice, they positively and explicitly encourage them both to stay on that path, in order that they may fall over the cliff at the end of it, as they duly do. That, to be sure, is for fifth-century Greeks a recognized pattern of divine behaviour; but it is a tragic, not a comic, pattern.[10] Indeed, the plot of *The Clouds* as a whole is tragic in basic structure, though not of course in its detailed execution: two criminal enterprises (Strepsiades' plan to practise dishonesty, and Socrates' to teach it) interact in such a fashion that, partly through divine action, they recoil on their originators – though others (notably the innocent if rather ludicrous Creditors) also suffer along the way.

The Clouds, in fact, is an unusually dark comedy, and it was apparently too dark for its original audience. When it was produced at the City Dionysia of 423, it proved a flop.[11] The winner was Cratinus, who had been ridiculed in *The Acharnians* and *The Knights* as a senile, smelly, incontinent drunkard, but who now triumphed with *The Wicker Flask*, a brilliant satire on . . . himself. As we can see from the parabasis of *The Wasps* (lines 1016–17, 1043–50), Aristophanes bitterly resented this failure, and in or about 419 he set to work revising the play, apparently with a view to a second production. The revision, however, was never completed, possibly because the Archon refused to grant a chorus for what was, after all, not a new play; the revised play was never produced in Athens, and indeed the script as we have it could not have been staged under the rules of the Athenian comic competition[12] and contains passages that are inconsistent with each other,[13] though the inconsistencies do not affect the plot. There survive about a dozen quotations from the 'first' *Clouds* (two of which are identical with passages in the surviving text),[14] and they tend to support the statement in one of the play's ancient headnotes (hypotheses) that while there were many minor differences between the two versions,[15] the only passages to have undergone fundamental change are

(i) the speech in the parabasis (lines 518–62) in which the failure of the original production is discussed, (ii) the debate between Right and Wrong (or more probably some part of it), and (iii) the ending ('where the school of Socrates is burned' – it is not clear how early this section is to be taken as commencing).[16] In a modern production, it can safely be assumed that the various rough edges will not be noticed.

NOTES

1. The word *sophistes* originally meant merely an actual or professed expert; but since every field of traditional expertise already had a specific designation, this non-specific term came to designate those who claimed to be expert not in any traditional field but in the new intellectual pursuits. By the 420s it had already acquired a derogatory tone (see, e.g., line 331).

2. He may well have questioned the truth of certain *myths* (for example, those telling of conflicts among the gods), but there was nothing improper about this: no two poets narrating or dramatizing a myth ever did so in quite the same way, and Pindar, that arch-praiser of traditional aristocratic virtues, more than once explicitly condemns a well-established myth as immoral.

3. There is little reason to doubt that most of Socrates' contemporaries, if asked whether he was a sophist, would have replied that he was; over half a century after his death a speaker in an Athenian court refers offhandedly to 'Socrates the sophist' (Aeschines, *Against Timarchus* 173).

4. He could have saved himself by leaving Athens before his trial; or by taking a more conciliatory attitude towards the jury during it, especially when arguing against the prosecution's demand for the death penalty; or by escaping from prison during the interval of a month between his conviction and execution.

5. The only person known to have been sentenced to death in classical Athens purely for religious unorthodoxy is Diagoras of Melos (alluded to in line 830), who seems to have gone beyond theoretical arguments and attacked specific religious observances, notably the Eleusinian Mysteries.

6. I use Dover's names Right and Wrong for the two characters who in the Greek text are called, literally, 'the Superior Argument' and 'the Inferior Argument'.

7. Not every oath in the dialogue of Greek comedy is necessarily to be taken at its full value, but we are surely meant to notice the contradiction when Pheidippides first promises, with an oath 'by Dionysus', to do whatever it is his father wants him to do (lines 90–91), and then, seventeen lines later, having heard what his father's request is, says, with an oath 'by Dionysus', that he will not comply at any price.

8. Note that a man who had squandered his inherited property was disqualified from speaking in the Assembly (like, e.g., those who had assaulted a parent, thrown away their shield in battle, or engaged in male prostitution). Pheidippides' offence is in one way even worse, since he is squandering property which he has *not* yet inherited!

9. That Athenians were concerned about the possibility of sexual exploitation of boys by their teachers is evident from the existence in the fourth century of a law forbidding teachers to open their schools before sunrise or keep them open after sunset (Aeschines, *Against Timarchus* 10).

10. Given lapidary expression by the ghost of Darius in Aeschylus' *Persians* (line 742), in reference to the disaster that has befallen his son Xerxes: 'When a man is eager for something, the god lends him a hand.'

11. How bad a flop we do not know for sure, since it is uncertain how many comedies were produced at this festival (see Introduction, note 37). If there were three, *The Clouds* finished third; if there were five, it may well have come fourth or fifth.

12. In lines 885–92, as the text stands, five actors are required (for Socrates, Strepsiades, Right, Wrong and Pheidippides). Had the revised play ever been produced, there would doubtless have been a choral song between what are now lines 888 and 889.

13. In the *parabasis*, one speech (lines 575–94) urges the Athenians to punish Cleon, with reference to events of 425 and 424, while in another (lines 553–9) mention is made of several plays of which the earliest, Eupolis' *Maricas*, is known to have been produced after Cleon's death. Outside the *parabasis*, however, the surviving text contains nothing that needs to be taken as a reference or allusion to any event later than spring 423.

14. The remaining ten have a combined length of thirty-five Greek words.

15. In particular, one or two self-contained passages such as choral songs seem to have been deleted and had not yet been replaced by new material at the time work on the revision was abandoned. What was probably once a complete second *parabasis*, comprising two songs and two speeches, is now represented by a minute snatch of lyric and a single speech (lines 1113–30).

16. I have argued elsewhere (P. Thiercy and M. Menu, *Aristophane: la langue, la scène, la cité* [Bari, 1997], pp. 280–81) that of the ten quotations ascribed to the first *Clouds* which do not appear in the second, five probably come, in view of their metre, from the sections labelled (i) or (ii) above, two have content (a reference to punishment, a threat of violence) that suits the conclusion of the play, one may well come from one of the deleted choral songs – and one of the other two has previously been suspected, on independent grounds, of being wrongly attributed to the play.

Characters

STREPSIADES, *an elderly farmer*
PHEIDIPPIDES, *his son*
SLAVE
STUDENT *at Socrates' school*
SOCRATES, *the philosopher*
CHORUS *of Cloud-Goddesses*
RIGHT, *or the Superior Argument*
WRONG, *or the Inferior Argument*
FIRST CREDITOR
SECOND CREDITOR
CHAEREPHON, *a friend of Socrates*

Silent Characters

STUDENTS *at the school*
WITNESS, *brought by First Creditor*
XANTHIAS *and other slaves of Strepsiades*

SCENE: *For the time being, an indeterminate space, possibly to be thought of as the courtyard of Strepsiades' house. Two men are lying asleep – or rather, one, Pheidippides, is sleeping soundly under an enormous weight of blankets, while his father Strepsiades is restlessly tossing and turning. Finally he abandons all attempts at sleep, and sits up.*

STREPSIADES: O Lord Zeus, how long the night is! Will it never end? When will it be day? Come to think of it, I heard the cock crow ages ago. And the servants are still snoring! They'd 5 never have dared to in the old days. Damn this war! One can't even discipline one's own slaves.[1] And what about this dutiful son of mine? *He* never wakes up before sunrise either; just farts merrily away wrapped up in five or six blankets. Well, 10 there's nothing for it: let's cover up and snore too. [*He lies down again and tries to sleep, but soon gives up.*] It's no good, I can't. I'm being bitten all over. Not by bugs – by horses and bills and debts, on account of this son of mine, him and his long hair[2] and his riding and his chariot and pair. Even his 15 dreams are all about horses. Result, every time the date gets past the twentieth, I'm fairly dying with fear as the interest gets ready to take another step up.[3] [*Calling through the door behind him*] Boy! [*A* SLAVE *appears.*] Light a lamp and bring my accounts here. I want to see how many people I owe 20 money to and how much the interest comes to.

[*The* SLAVE *goes out, and presently returns with a lamp and a number of waxed tablets. He gives* STREPSIADES

the tablets, and stays holding the lamp for him to read by.]
Let me see now, what have we got? To Pasias, twelve hundred
drachmas.[4] What was that for? Why did I borrow it? Oh yes,
when I bought the koppa-bred horse. Heavens, I might just
as well have copped it right then and there![5]

25   PHEIDIPPIDES [*in his sleep*]: Watch it, Philon, you're cheating.
Stop cutting across me.

STREPSIADES: You see? That's what's ruined me. Even in his
sleep it's racing, racing, racing.

PHEIDIPPIDES: How many laps is the war-chariot race?

STREPSIADES: Not as many bends as you've driven your father
30   round! [*Looking at his accounts again*] Now what was the
next one after Pasias? Mm – three hundred for a small foot-
board and a pair of wheels.

PHEIDIPPIDES: Let the horse have a roll, groom, and take him
home.

STREPSIADES: A roll! *You've* been rolling all right – in *my*
money! I've already got court judgments against me, and
35   there are creditors threatening to seize my goods in lieu of
interest! [STREPSIADES' *voice has now risen so much that it
wakes his son up.*]

PHEIDIPPIDES: Really, dad, what's wrong with you, tossing
and twisting about all night long?

STREPSIADES: I'm getting bitten by a bailiff, or something, in
the bedclothes.

PHEIDIPPIDES: With all respect, could you let me get a bit of
sleep? [*He lies down as before.*]

STREPSIADES: Fine, you do that. But just remember that all my
40   debts will be yours one day! Gods, I wish I could strangle the
matchmaker who put the idea in my head of marrying your
mother! I had a marvellous life in the country, not caring
45   about etiquette or tidiness or washing, rich in bees and sheep
and olives. And then I married this city girl, the niece of
Megacles the son of Megacles, no less, a stuck-up, spoilt little
Coesyra of a woman![6] On our wedding night, I went to bed
50   smelling of new wine, drying-racks, fleeces and affluence –
and she of perfume, saffron, french kisses, spending, over-
eating and erotic rituals. Don't get the idea she was idle,

though. She did work at clothes-making – got through a great
deal of wool – until I showed her this cloak of mine and said   55
[*holding up his threadbare cloak – under which he has been
sleeping – and revealing a distinctly flaccid phallus*], 'Missus,
you're wearing away my resources!'[7]

[*The lamp held by the slave goes out.*]

SLAVE: The lamp's out of oil, sir.

STREPSIADES: Well, did I ask you to use the thirsty one? Come
here – I'll make you regret it.

SLAVE [*evading him*]: Why should I? [*He disappears through
the door.*]

STREPSIADES [*calling after him*]: Because you put in such a fat
wick, that's why. [*During the next few lines he is getting up
and putting on the cloak.*] Well, when me and my [*with heavy   60
sarcasm*] good lady had this boy, we had a great row about
what to call him. She insisted on getting a horse into the
name, something ending in *-hippus* or the like – Xanthippus,
Chaerippus, Callippides[8] – while I wanted to name him Phei-   65
donides after his grandad. Well, we argued for quite some
time, but in the end we came to terms and settled for Pheidippides.[9] Then she used to hold him in her arms and say, 'When
you're a big boy and drive in procession to the Acropolis in
your chariot, wearing a lovely smooth robe, like your Uncle   70
Megacles . . .', until I took him and said, 'When you drive the
goats home from the fells, like your daddy did before you,
wearing a leather smock . . .' But it was no good. He never
took any notice of anything I said, and now he's brought the
family fortunes down with *galloping consumption*.[10] Well,   75
anyway, I've been hunting all night for a way out, and I've
found one – a narrow path, but a marvellous one. It'll lead
me out of the wood, if I can only get that boy to help. But I
need to wake him up first. Now what's the sweetest way to
wake him up? Hmm . . . [*Bending over* PHEIDIPPIDES; *in
sugary tones*] Phei*dip*pides! Phei*dip*pides, darling!   80

PHEIDIPPIDES [*waking up, and sluggishly rising*]: Whar-
risiddad?

STREPSIADES: I want you to kiss me and put your right hand
in mine.[11]

PHEIDIPPIDES [*doing so*]: There you are. What's up?

STREPSIADES: Tell me, do you love me?

PHEIDIPPIDES [*pointing to a statue near the door*]: Yes, by Poseidon here, the Lord of horses.

85 STREPSIADES: No Lord of horses, *please!* He's the god that's brought all this trouble on me. Well, my boy, if you really love me from your heart, will you do something for me?

PHEIDIPPIDES: What do you want me to do for you?

STREPSIADES: To change your ways, right now, and go and take the course of study I'm going to suggest.

90 PHEIDIPPIDES: Come on, now, what are you *asking* for?

STREPSIADES: You'll do it?

PHEIDIPPIDES: I will, by Dionysus.

[*By now the remaining bedclothes have been removed, and the two men are out in the orchestra. We can imagine them, therefore, as being in the street. Behind them, we now perceive, are two houses. One is their home.* STREPSIADES *points to the other.*]

STREPSIADES: Look over this way. You see that nice little door and that nice little house?

PHEIDIPPIDES: Yes. What is it, actually, father?

95 STREPSIADES: It is a Thinkery for intellectual souls.[12] That's where the people live who try to prove that the sky is like a baking-pot all round us, and we're the charcoal inside it.[13] And if you pay them well, they can teach you how to win a case whether you're in the right or not.

100 PHEIDIPPIDES: Who are these people?

STREPSIADES: I don't quite remember their name. They're very fine reflective intellectuals.

PHEIDIPPIDES: Yecch! I know the villains. You mean those pale-faced bare-footed quacks such as that wretched Socrates and Chaerephon.

105 STREPSIADES: Now, now, quiet there, don't talk so childishly! If [*emotionally*] you care at all whether your father gets his daily bread, do please forget about racing and go and join them.

PHEIDIPPIDES: By Dionysus, no, not if you gave me all Leogoras' pheasants.[14]

STREPSIADES [*desperately*]: My most beloved son – I beg of 110
you – do go and study with them!

PHEIDIPPIDES: What do you want me to learn?

STREPSIADES: They say they have two Arguments in there –
Right and Wrong, they call them – and one of them, Wrong,
can always win its case even when justice is against it. Well, 115
if you can learn this Wrongful Argument, then of all these
debts I've run into because of you, I needn't pay anyone an
obol[15] of them ever.

PHEIDIPPIDES: I'm not going to do it. How could I ever look
my cavalry friends in the eye again, with a face looking as 120
though all the colour had been scraped off it?

STREPSIADES: Then, holy Demeter! you'll never eat anything
of mine again, not you nor any of your damn thoroughbreds.[16]
I'll throw you out of my house and you can go to hell.

PHEIDIPPIDES: No, to Uncle Megacles, if necessary. *He* won't
leave me horseless. But actually, *this* is where I'm going 125
[*pointing towards his own house*], and I couldn't care less
what you say! [*He goes inside.*]

STREPSIADES [*to himself*]: That was a hard knock, but I'm not
going to take it lying down. So may it please the gods, I shall
go to the Thinkery and get taught there myself. [*Hesitating*]
But how can I? I'm old and slow and forgetful; how can I
study all this logic-chopping and hair-splitting? [*Emboldened* 130
again] But I've got to. No more dilly-dallying; let me knock.
[*He knocks on the school door, and calls in sugary tones*]
Boy! Boyeee!

STUDENT [*from inside*]: Go to blazes! [*Opening the door*]
Who's been making all that racket?

STREPSIADES: Strepsiades is my name, son of Pheidon, from
Cicynna.[17]

STUDENT: What kind of fool are you? Do you realize that by 135
your violent and unphilosophical kicking of the door[18] you
have rendered an important discovery totally abortive?

STREPSIADES: Do forgive me; I live a long way off in the
country. But do tell me, what was it that aborted?

STUDENT [*mysteriously*]: It is not permitted to divulge it to 140
non-members of the institute.

STREPSIADES: Well, that's all right, you can tell me. I've come to the Thinkery in order to *be* a member.

STUDENT [*coming out and closing the door*]: Very well, but you must treat this as a holy secret.[19] Socrates, a moment ago,
145   asked Chaerephon how many of its own feet a flea could jump. One of them had just bitten Chaerephon's eyebrow and jumped over on to Socrates' head.

STREPSIADES: And how did he measure it?

150 STUDENT: In a very elegant way. He melted some wax and put the flea's feet into it, so that when it set the flea had a stylish pair of slippers on. And then he took the slippers off and used them to measure out the distance [*illustrating by taking a step or two, toe touching heel*].

STREPSIADES: Lord Zeus, what a subtle intellect!

STUDENT: Like to hear about another of Socrates' clever
155   ideas?

STREPSIADES: I beg you, yes, please tell me.

STUDENT: Chaerephon of Sphettus[20] once asked Socrates whether he was of the opinion that gnats produced their hum by way of the mouth or the rear end.

STREPSIADES: So what was his opinion about the gnat?

160 STUDENT: 'The intestinal passage of the gnat', he said, 'is very narrow, and consequently the wind is forced to go straight through to the rear end. And then the arsehole, being an orifice forming the exit from this narrow passage, makes a noise owing to the force of this wind.'

165 STREPSIADES: So a gnat's arsehole is like a trumpet. How gutterly marvellous! I can see that defending a lawsuit successfully is going to be dead easy for someone who has such precise knowledge of the guts of gnats.

STUDENT: Then the day before yesterday he was robbed of a
170   great thought by a lizard.

STREPSIADES: How on earth did that happen?

STUDENT: Well, he was doing some research on the movements and revolutions of the moon, gazing upwards, open-mouthed, and then this gecko shat on him from the ceiling[21] in the dark.

STREPSIADES [*laughing heartily*]: Oh, I liked that one – a gecko shitting in Socrates' face!

STUDENT: And then yesterday we found we had nothing to eat   175
at dinner time.

STREPSIADES: Well then, what trick did he pull off?

STUDENT: He sprinkled a little ash on the table, bent a skewer
to make a pair of compasses, and then . . . nicked somebody's
cloak while he was in the gym wrestling.[22]

STREPSIADES: And we still admire old Thales?[23] Come on,   180
hurry up, open the door, and let me see Socrates right away!
I'm bursting to learn! Open the door!

[*The* STUDENT *opens the school door. A wheeled platform
is rolled out, on which are a number of other* STUDENTS,
*thin, pale and sickly looking, all motionless in attitudes
presently to be described, as if utterly absorbed in scientific
thought.*]

STREPSIADES: In Heracles' name, where did you catch these
creatures?

STUDENT: What are you so surprised about? What did you   185
think they were?

STREPSIADES: Spartan prisoners from Pylos,[24] if you ask me.
Why on earth are those ones [*pointing to one group of students*] staring at the ground?

STUDENT: They are doing research on things that are under the
earth.

STREPSIADES: Oh, looking for edible bulbs, you mean! Well,
you don't need to search for them any more; I know where   190
you can find lovely big ones. But what are that lot up to
[*pointing*]? They're completely doubled up!

STUDENT: They are investigating the lowest reaches of the
underworld.

STREPSIADES: So why is their arsehole looking at the sky?

STUDENT: It's learning to do astronomy all by itself. [*To the
other students*] Go inside; what'll *he* say if he sees you out 195
here?

STREPSIADES: No, not yet! Can't they stay a bit? I want to tell
them about a little problem I have.

STUDENT: Can't do that. Mustn't stay too long outside in the
fresh air.

[*The other* STUDENTS *go inside. At the rear of the platform*

[*can now be seen a map and a number of mathematical and scientific instruments.*]

200 STREPSIADES [*examining some of the instruments*]: What on earth are these things?

STUDENT: This is for astronomy.

STREPSIADES: And this?

STUDENT: Geometry.

STREPSIADES: Geometry? What's that useful for?

STUDENT: Well, measuring out land,[25] for instance.

STREPSIADES: You mean in an overseas settlement?[26]

STUDENT: Any land you want.

205 STREPSIADES: What a marvellous idea! A really democratic, beneficial invention!

STUDENT: And this, you see, is a map of the whole world. Look, here's Athens.

STREPSIADES [*inspecting the map*]: How do you make that out? Doesn't look like Athens to me; I can't see any jurymen on their benches.

STUDENT: No, really, this area is Attica all right.

210 STREPSIADES: Then where is my village, Cicynna?

STUDENT: It's there.[27] And look, here's the island of Euboea, lying stretched out opposite us, all along here.

STREPSIADES: Yes, we stretched it flat all right, me and Pericles and the rest of us.[28] Where's Sparta?

STUDENT [*pointing*]: Right here.

215 STREPSIADES: Too near, too near! You'd better have another thought or two about that – get it to be a *very* long way away from us.

STUDENT: It's not possible.

STREPSIADES [*raising his stick*]: Isn't it? Then take that! [*But before he can strike the Student,* SOCRATES *swings into view, airborne, like a god in tragedy, standing on a board suspended by four cords from the jib of a crane.*] Who in heaven's name is that man hanging from the meathook?

STUDENT: It's *him*!

STREPSIADES: Him? Who's him?

STUDENT: Socrates.

STREPSIADES [*reverentially*]: Socrates! Could you give him a good shout, please?

STUDENT: No, I haven't got time, you do it yourself. [*Exit hastily and fearfully into the school.*] 220

STREPSIADES [*gazing up at Socrates; in sugary tones*]: Socrates! Socrates, darling!

SOCRATES [*godlike*]: Why call'st thou me, O creature of a day?

STREPSIADES: Well, for a start, I'd very much like to know what you're doing up there.

SOCRATES: I am walking upon air and attacking the mystery of 225 the sun.

STREPSIADES: Well, if you *must* attack the Mysteries[29] of the gods, why can't you do so on the ground?

SOCRATES: Why, for accurate investigation of meteorological phenomena it is indispensable to get one's thoughts into a state of *suspension* and mix its minute particles into the air 230 which they so closely resemble. If I had remained on the ground and investigated the upper regions from there, I would never have made any discoveries – the earth exercises too powerful an attraction upon the moisture contained in thought. The same thing occurs in the case of cress.[30]

STREPSIADES [*baffled*]: I don't know what you mean, all this 235 about thought attracting moisture to cress. Do come down to me, Socrates darling, so you can teach me what I've come to learn.

SOCRATES [*as he is lowered to ground level*]: And what *have* you come to learn?

STREPSIADES: I want to be made an orator. Interest bills and 240 heartless creditors are laying me waste with fire, the sword and distress warrants.

SOCRATES: How did you manage to get so much in debt, unawares?

STREPSIADES: I was laid low by a vicious attack of horse-fever. But anyway, I want you to teach me one of your two Arguments – the one that always pays off and never pays up. It 245 doesn't matter what fees you charge; I'm prepared to swear by the gods that I'll pay them.

SOCRATES: What do you mean, swear by the gods? The first thing you'll have to learn is that with us the gods are no longer current.

STREPSIADES [*confused*]: Then what *is* the currency you swear by? Iron coins like they have at Byzantium?

250 SOCRATES: Do you want to learn for yourself the real, plain truth about religion?

STREPSIADES: Why, yes, if that's possible.

SOCRATES: And to talk face to face with *our* divinities, the Clouds?

STREPSIADES: Definitely.

SOCRATES [*motioning him towards the vacant platform*]: Then please sit on the sacred bed.

255 STREPSIADES [*doing so*]: There you are.

SOCRATES [*giving him a wreath of unattractive-looking vegetation*]: Now put this on your head.

STREPSIADES [*alarmed*]: What's this for? Socrates, please, don't go and make a sacrifice of me, like that Athamas.[31]

SOCRATES: No, this is just part of our normal initiation ceremony.

STREPSIADES: But what good will it do me?

260 SOCRATES [*picking up a bag*]: You'll become a really smooth, smarmy talker – the finest flower in the oratorical garden. Now don't move. [*He sprinkles flour from the bag over Strepsiades.*]

STREPSIADES: Did you say *become* fine flour, or be *plastered* with it?!

SOCRATES:
      Keep silence now, and hear my prayer.
      O Lord, O King, O boundless Air,
      On whom the earth supported rides,
265   O Ether bright, and you besides
      Who make the thunder roar so loud,
      You awesome Goddesses of Cloud,
      O hearken to your Thinker here:
      Arise and in the sky appear!

STREPSIADES [*hastily pulling his cloak over his head*]:
>   Not yet, not yet, don't let them soak
>   Me till I'm covered with my cloak.
>   Why was I such a silly chap
>   That I left home without a cap?

SOCRATES:
>   Come, glorious Clouds, display your power.
> [*Turning successively to the four points of the compass*][32]
>   Whether in father Ocean's bower
>   You join the Nymphs in sacred rites,
>   Or on Olympus' snow-swept heights   270
>   You sit, or draw with pails of gold
>   From Egypt's streams, or brave the cold
>   Of Mimas' peak (if there you be)
>   Or round Maeotis' inland sea:
>   Where'er you be, my prayer hear,
>   Accept my offering, and appear!
> [*He pours a little incense on the altar in front of his door,
> and sets light to it. After a short silence, the* CHORUS *are
> heard singing in the distance.*]

CHORUS:
>   Let us rise, we Clouds eternal,   275
>   Shining bright with radiant dew,
>   From the roaring Ocean's bosom
>   To the sky,[33] the world to view.

>   Let us see the distant mountains   280
>   And the holy earth below,
>   Where we irrigate the tillage
>   And the babbling rivers flow,

>   While far off the breakers thunder [*roll of thunder*]
>   'Neath the sun's unwearied rays: 285
>   Shake the rainy mist from off you
>   And to earth direct your gaze.   290

SOCRATES: Almighty Clouds, you heard my prayer indeed. [*To Strepsiades*] Did you hear their voice, and the awe-inspiring bellow of thunder that accompanied it?

STREPSIADES: Yes, and I revere them immensely– so much that in response to that thunder I'm wanting to make a great big
295   noise down below,[34] they make me shake so with fear. If it's lawful – well, actually, even if it's not – *I need a crap!*

SOCRATES: No buffoonery, please; you're not acting in a comedy now! Keep silence; there is a great swarm of divinities in musical movement.

CHORUS [*nearer*]:
    Maids of Rain, come now where Pallas
300   Rules the loveliest land on earth,
    Rich and shining land of Cecrops
        Full of men of valiant worth;

    Where the initiated worship
        At the great Eleusis shrine,
    Through its opened gates beholding
        Secrets of the world divine;

305   Where stand lofty, beauteous temples
        Full of gifts beyond all price;
    Where no season lacks its share of
310   Feast, procession, sacrifice;

    Where they hold to Dionysus
        Joyous feast at start of spring,
    Hear the pipes and hear the chorus
        In melodious contest sing.[35]

STREPSIADES: Do tell me, Socrates, who are these ladies who
315   sing so majestically? They're not some kind of female heroes, are they?[36]

SOCRATES: No, indeed. They are the celestial Clouds, the patron goddesses of the layabout. From them we get our intelligence,

our dialectic, our reason, our fantasy and all our argumenta-
tive talents.

STREPSIADES: No wonder that when I hear their voice, my soul
feels it could fly! I want to be a quibbler! I want to split hairs!   320
I want to be able to deflate my opponent with a pointed little
sound-bite and bring arguments to undermine his! If there's
any way to do it, I do so want to see them face to face!

[*At this point the first of the* CHORUS *begin to appear at
the top of the auditorium; during the following dialogue
they file down silently along the gangways, form up at the
bottom, and enter the orchestra. They have the faces of
young women; only their costumes suggest anything
cloudlike.*][37]

SOCRATES [*pointing towards the top of the auditorium*]: Look
over there, towards Mount Parnes.[38] I can see them coming
quietly down now.

STREPSIADES: Where, where? Show me.

SOCRATES [*pointing lower and to his left*]: Yes, here they come,
a whole host of them, through the glens and the woods –   325
[*noticing that* STREPSIADES *is staring at the empty sky*] no,
here, a bit to the side.

STREPSIADES [*looking in the indicated direction, but too late
to see the Chorus*]: What are you talking about? I can't see a
thing.

SOCRATES [*pointing to where the* CHORUS *are forming up in
ranks*]: There in the entryway!

STREPSIADES: Ah yes, I can just see them now.

SOCRATES: So you should, unless you've got pumpkins where
your eyes should be.

STREPSIADES: Yes, I do – and how wonderful! The whole place
is full of them.

SOCRATES: And you mean you never knew, never thought, that
they were goddesses?

STREPSIADES: Heavens, no – I thought they were mist, dew,   330
vapour, that sort of thing.

SOCRATES: You're obviously not aware that they give susten-
ance to a vast tribe of sophists, high-powered prophets,[39]

teachers of medicine, long-haired idlers with fancy signet-rings – and especially the airy quacks who write those convoluted dithyrambs. They're very happy to sustain *them* in idleness, because they bring clouds so much into their poetry.

335 STREPSIADES: Ah, that accounts for all that about 'the fearsome advance of watery clouds edged with twists of radiance' and 'locks of the hundred-headed Typhon' and 'conflagrating squalls' and 'crook-taloned air-floating birds of the airy sea' and 'showers of moisture from the dewy clouds'. And for that rubbish they get feasted[40] on gorgeous slices of barracuda and the avian flesh of thrushes!

340 SOCRATES: All thanks to these ladies, and quite right too.

STREPSIADES: Tell me, though, if they really are clouds, how come they look so human, so much like women? The other clouds – I mean the real ones – don't look like that at all.

SOCRATES: Oh, how *do* they look?

STREPSIADES: Well, it's hard to say exactly, but they sort of look like fleeces laid out to dry, and certainly not in the least like women. I mean, *these* ones have *noses*!

345 SOCRATES: Well, can I ask you a question or two?

STREPSIADES: Go right ahead.

SOCRATES: You've looked at the sky sometimes, haven't you, and seen a cloud shaped like a centaur, or a leopard, or a wolf, or a bull?

STREPSIADES: Yes; so what?

SOCRATES: They can take any shape they fancy. So if they see one of those shaggy long-haired savages like the son

350 of Xenophantus,[41] they make fun of his mania by turning themselves into centaurs.

STREPSIADES: And if they catch sight of someone who helps himself to public money, like Simon,[42] what do they do?

SOCRATES: They expose him by turning into wolves.

STREPSIADES: Ah, now I understand why they looked like deer yesterday! They must have seen that great coward Cleonymus, the one who dropped his shield!

355 SOCRATES: That's right; and now, you see, they've just seen Cleisthenes,[43] so they've turned into women!

STREPSIADES [*to the Chorus*]: Then hail to you, mighty Ladies; could you – if you ever do, do this – could you, Queens of the Universe, show me the power of your heavenly voices?

CHORUS:
> Hail, grey-headed seeker for language artistic,
>> And you, our high priest of fine twaddle!
> For although, among specialists cosmologistic,   360
>> Old Prodicus[44] has the best noddle,
> Still we favour you greatly, because of the way
>> You swagger and glance with disdain,[45]
> Endure much derision, go barefoot all day,
>> And on our account act really vain.

STREPSIADES: Holy Earth, *what* a voice! How divine, how awesome, how fantastic!

SOCRATES: Yes, you know, these are the only real divinities; all   365
the rest is bunkum.

STREPSIADES: What on earth do you mean? You don't think Olympian Zeus is a god?

SOCRATES: Zeus? Who's Zeus? What rubbish you talk! There *is* no Zeus!

STREPSIADES: What do you mean? Who makes the rain, then? That's the first thing I want to know.

SOCRATES [*indicating the Chorus*]: *They* do, of course, and I'll prove it to you very clearly. Have you ever seen it raining   370
when the sky was blue? Surely Zeus, if it *was* him, would be able to send rain even when the Clouds were out of town!

STREPSIADES: You've certainly got a good point there – though I really did think before that rain was just Zeus pissing through a sieve. But tell me too, who makes the thunder that sends shivers up my spine?

SOCRATES: *They* do too, when they roll about.   375

STREPSIADES: You'll stop at nothing. How do you mean?

SOCRATES: When they are suspended in the sky, filled with a large quantity of water, they are necessarily compelled to move while full of rain, collide with each other, and owing to their weight they burst open with a crash.

STREPSIADES: Ah, but who compels them to move? *That's* got
to be Zeus!

380 SOCRATES: No, it's a celestial vortex.

STREPSIADES: Vortex? I never knew that before. So Zeus is
dead, and Vortex has taken his place on the throne! But you
still haven't explained to me what causes the thunder.

SOCRATES: Didn't you hear? I said that it occurs when water-
filled clouds collide with each other and owing to their density
this makes a noise.

385 STREPSIADES: Who's going to believe that?

SOCRATES: You yourself are a living proof of it. You have, no
doubt – say at the Panathenaea[46] – had a bit too much soup
and got an upset stomach, and then suddenly a bit of wind
has set it all rumbling?

STREPSIADES: That's just right. It makes a great nuisance of
itself right away, and the soup crashes around and roars

390 fearfully just like thunder. First quite quietly, 'prrrr prrrr',
then it takes a step up, '*prrrr prrrr*', and then when I crap,
it really is a thundercrap, '*prrrrrrrrrrrr!*', just like they do
[*indicating the Chorus*].

SOCRATES: Well, if a little tummy like yours can create a fart
like that, is it surprising that from an infinity of air you can
get a mighty roll of thunder?

STREPSIADES: I see; so *that's* why we talk about a 'thunderous

395 fart'![47] But how about the fiery thunder*bolt*? Where does it
come from, to strike us and burn us to a cinder, or maybe
singe us alive? Obviously that's Zeus' weapon against people
who perjure themselves.

SOCRATES: You stupid, antiquated relic! If Zeus strikes down

400 perjurers, why hasn't he burned up Simon, Cleonymus and
Theorus? They're perjurers if anyone is! Instead of which, he
strikes his own temple, and the holy headland of Sunium,[48]
not to mention any number of his own sacred oak trees – or
would you say *they* were guilty of perjury?

STREPSIADES: I don't know, but what you say does seem to
make sense. What *is* the thunderbolt, in that case?

SOCRATES: When a dry wind rises to high altitude and is trapped

405 inside a cloud, it blows the cloud up from within like a bladder

and so necessarily bursts it and rushes out with very high
momentum owing to its density, which together with the
accompanying friction causes it to self-ignite.

STREPSIADES: Why, that's exactly what happened to me once
at the Diasia.[49] I was roasting a haggis for the family, I forgot
to slit it, and it puffed itself up and then went off with a bang,   410
spitting blood right in my eyes and giving me burns in the
face.   411

SOCRATES: I assume, then, that in future you will recognize   423
only the gods that we believe in, that is, Chaos, the Clouds
and the Tongue?

STREPSIADES: I will never sacrifice or pour libation or burn
incense to any other god. And if I met one in the street I
wouldn't speak to him.[50]   426

CHORUS:
>   O you who desire our high wisdom to learn,   412
>   What kudos in Athens and Greece you will earn –
>   If you're ready to toil, if your memory's good,
>   If you've got the ability to think,
>   If standing and walking don't tire you, nor   415
>   Deprivation of warmth, food and drink,
>   If exercise, wine and all follies you shun,
>   If your values are those of the smart,
>   Who worship success both in counsel and deed
>   And in deft oratorical art!

STREPSIADES: Well, I'm tough all right, and I do a lot of   420
thinking – mostly of a sleepless night – and my digestion is
used to strict economy and quite ready to dine off nothing
but herbs; so have no fear – I meet your qualifications – here
I am – get to work on me!   422

LEADER: Just tell us, then, what you want us to do for you. As   427
a worshipper of ours and a seeker after wisdom, you will
never come to grief.

STREPSIADES: It's only just one tiny little thing I want, holy
Clouds: to be the best orator in Greece, by at least a hundred   430
miles.

LEADER: No problem. In future there will be nobody who carries more resolutions in the Assembly than you do.

STREPSIADES: Not big political speeches, that's not what I'm after. I just want to be able to twist and turn my way through the thickets of the law and give my creditors the slip.

435 LEADER: Well, that's certainly not much to ask. We'll see you get it. Just put yourself confidently in the hands of our ministers here.

STREPSIADES: I'll trust you, and do it. I'm *necessarily compelled* to do it, by pedigree horses and a blasted pedigree wife!

440
So I give myself entirely to the school – I'll let them beat me,
Starve me, freeze me, parch me, flay me, I don't care
how they ill-treat me,
If they teach me how to dodge my debts and get the
reputation
Of the cleverest, slyest fox that ever baffled litigation.

445
Let men call me glib, audacious, rash, a liar bold and
nimble,
Lawcourt veteran, walking statute-book, a pest, a
tinkling cymbal,
Loathsome supple rogue, dissembler, sticky customer
and bragger,

450
Villain, whipping-post and twister, or a logic-chopping
nagger –
Let them call me any name they choose, and over and
above it
Let them chase me through each court, and I assure you
that I'll love it!
If the Thinkery can make of me a real forensic winner,

455
I don't mind if they take out my guts and serve them up
for dinner!

CHORUS:
We can see you're not a coward, and you've got the
disposition

460
To become, if taught by us, a great and famous
rhetorician,

With an enviable lifestyle –

STREPSIADES:

Can I credit what you're telling?   465

CHORUS:

Yes, they'll sit all night with patience at the entrance to
    your dwelling
To consult you and to pick your brains and learn a   470
    method shifty
To escape from paying damages of forty grand or fifty;
And by hiring out your intellect you'll gain a reputation   475
That will reach right up to heaven and resound in every
    nation![51]

LEADER [to Socrates]: Time to take your pupil through the pre-
liminaries. You must stir up his mind a bit, test his intelligence.

SOCRATES: Tell me, what kind of a mind do you have? I must
know that in order to bring my latest artillery to bear on you. 480

STREPSIADES: Pardon? Are you planning to lay siege to me or
something?

SOCRATES: No, only to ask you a few questions. Do you have
a good memory?

STREPSIADES: Yes and no. Very good if somebody owes me
something – very bad if I owe it to someone else.   485

SOCRATES: I see. Do you think you're a natural speaker?

STREPSIADES: A natural speaker, no. A natural swindler, yes.

SOCRATES: Well, how on earth do you expect to learn anything?

STREPSIADES: I'll manage.

SOCRATES: Very well, if I set a choice morsel of cosmology in
front of you, you must make sure you snap it up.   490

STREPSIADES: I'm not going to be fed learning like a dog!

SOCRATES [aside]: Do Greeks come this stupid?[52] [To Strepsi-
ades] I fear, old sir, that in the course of your education
physical punishment may be necessary. [An anxiety strikes
him] Tell me, what do you do if someone hits you?

STREPSIADES: After getting hit I wait a short time, then raise a   495
cry of assault, then wait a very short time, and then go to law.

SOCRATES: All right; take off your cloak, please. [He lays his
hand on Strepsiades' cloak.]

STREPSIADES [*resisting, evidently on the assumption that he is about to be beaten*]: Why, what have I done wrong?

SOCRATES: Nothing; only the rule here is, no outer garments in the inner sanctum.

STREPSIADES [*still clinging to the garment*]: What do you think I'm planning to do? Plant something inside and then accuse you of stealing it?[53]

500   SOCRATES: Do stop talking nonsense and take it off! [STREPSIADES *reluctantly complies, leaving the cloak on the ground.*]

STREPSIADES: Tell me, Socrates, if I'm a really keen and hard-working student, which of your other pupils will I most resemble?

SOCRATES: Nobody will be able to tell you from Chaerephon.

STREPSIADES: I'll be one of the walking dead!

SOCRATES [*going to the school door, picking up Strepsiades'*
505   *cloak on the way*]: Will you stop blethering and hurry up and come in here with me?

STREPSIADES: I will if you give me a honey-cake to feed the serpents with. I'm frightened of going down into that cave![54]

[STREPSIADES *moves gingerly towards the door. On reaching it, he hesitates to cross the threshold, fearfully eyeing the floor within.*]

SOCRATES: What are you peering down like that for? Get a move on!

[STREPSIADES *goes inside, followed by* SOCRATES.]

CHORUS:
510   Go in, brave pilgrim, and be sure
                That Fortune will be gracious,
          And blessing in profusion pour
                On your attempt audacious,
          Because, though far advanced in years,
515   You do not find it scary
          To get a tincture of ideas
                Quite revolutionary!

LEADER [*addressing the audience*]:[55]

I swear by Dionysus, him who nurtured me in youth,
Athenians, that I'll tell you now the frank and simple truth.
So may I be victorious and men think well of me,   520
I thought that you an audience intelligent would be,
And also thought I'd never written any play so witty
As this – and that is why I first produced it in this city.
A lot of toil went into it – and yet my play retreated
By vulgar works of vulgar men unworthily defeated.   525
For your sake I took all these pains, and this was all your
    gratitude!
But even so, I promise I will never take that attitude
To you, or ever let you down. For since I earned the
    attention
And praise of certain men (whom it's a pleasure just to
    mention)
With *Model Son and Pansy Boy*,[56] which, like an unwed   530
    mother,
I left outdoors in hopes it would be picked up by another
(It was; she brought it home to you,[57] and you with kindness
    great
Adopted it and made it yours to rear and educate) –
Since then, I say, I have from you a pledge as good as sworn
To look with favour on all plays that might of me be born.
So here's my latest, like Electra looking here and there   535
To find an audience that's a lock cut from her brother's
    hair.[58]
And what a modest girl she is![59] She doesn't play the fool
By bringing on a great thick floppy red-tipped leather tool[60]
To give the kids a laugh, or making fun of men who're   540
    bald;[61]
Requests to dance a cordax[62] simply leave the lass appalled,
And no old man with walking-stick beats up some tiresome
    pest
In hopes to drown the groaning at another feeble jest.
No torches, yelps, or violence, or other weak distraction:
She comes before you trusting in her words and in her
    action.

545   I'm like that too: I'm not stuck up, nor yet a smooth-faced
                cheat
        Who pretends a play is new when it is really a repeat:[63]
        I always think up new ideas, not one of which is ever
        The same as those that went before, and all of them are
                clever.
        I went for Cleon, hard and low, when he was in his pomp,
550   But never would I have the flat effrontery to stomp
        Upon him, once I'd floored him – quite unlike these tedious
                others
        Harping upon Hyperbolus,[64] his failings and his mother's!
        The first of them was Eupolis, the stinking thief, who
                bashed
        Hyperbolus in *Maricas*,[65] which was my *Knights* rehashed
555   (He also plundered Phrynichus, though on a smaller scale:
        A cordax-dancing drunk old woman,[66] gobbled by a whale.)
        Hermippus then and all the rest on one another's heels
        Attacked Hyperbolus – and stole my image of the eels![67]
560   If anyone still laughs at them, well, I can't say I mind
        If fools like that to humour such as I provide are blind;
        But if my comic novelties receive your approbation,
        Posterity will praise the wisdom of this generation.

CHORUS:
                Zeus, thou almighty Ruler[68] of the heavens,
565   Thee first we call to join our dance today;
                Thou too who wield'st the stern and savage trident,
                    Lord of the Earthquake, come to us, we pray.
                Father renowned who nourishest all creatures,
570   Ether, most holy, thee we also call;
                And him who drives the fiery solar chariot,
                    Whose brilliant rays pervade earth, sky and all.

LEADER:
575   We Clouds, my dear spectators, feel we must
                Say that the way you treat us is unjust.
                More blessings than all other gods we bring
                To you; yet you make us no offering,

Not even a libation. Just reflect
What care we take your city to protect.
If you send troops out on a foolish mission,   580
Our rain or thunder stops the expedition.[69]
Then, before you with high command invested
That Paphlagonian tanner,[70] we protested:
With knitted brow we thundered, lightning flared,
The moon forsook her path,[71] the sun declared
That, if that villain won, he'd quench his flame.[72]   585
And you elected Cleon just the same!
Athenians *always* make the wrong decision
The first time round; we gods, though, make provision
To see you get a second opportunity
To rectify your blunders with impunity.
We'll tell you how to do so this time too.   590
Get Cleon charged with theft, that's what to do,
And bribery, convict him, shove his head
Into the stocks, and then, just like we said,
Whatever errors you have made before,
You'll get back all you lost by them, and more!

CHORUS:

Thou who art throned on Cynthus' rocky summit,[73]   595
    Graciously hear us, Phoebus, Delian Lord;
Thou too, blest Maid,[74] who dwell'st in the Ephesians'
    Temple of gold, by Lydian maids adored.   600
Thou our Protectress,[75] wielder of the aegis,
    Athens' own goddess, Pallas, hear our song;
Last him whose torches blaze on Mount Parnassus,
    Bacchus, we call, amid his revel-throng.   605

LEADER:

Before we started on our journey here
We met the Moon, who said she wished good cheer
To Athens and to all her allies true,
But had a bone or two to pick with you.   610
She says you wrong her, seeing she has blessed
You always in a way that's manifest.

For instance, each of you, each month, can save
A drachma, which you'd have to give a slave
For torches, when you're going out at night:

615   So much, and more, you profit by her light.
But for all this, she says, your thanks are scurvy –
You've turned the calendar all topsy-turvy.[76]
The gods turn up for meals and have to wait
Because you've sacrificed a day too late,

620   Then blame and threaten *her* – and meanwhile you,
Instead of feasting, torture, rack and sue.[77]
And when we mourn some hero of the past[78] –
Memnon, Sarpedon – keeping solemn fast,
Too often, down on earth, we see you revel.
Some of our wrath we vented on that devil,
This year's chief envoy to Thermopylae,[79]

625   Hyperbolus: we took his wreath away,[80]
In hopes that he would realize, late or soon,
That days are rightly reckoned by the Moon!

[SOCRATES *comes out of the school, looking exasperated.*]
SOCRATES: In the name of Respiration and Chaos and Air and
all that's holy, I've never met such a clueless stupid forgetful

630   bumpkin in all my life! The most trifling little thing I teach
him, he forgets before he's even learnt it! Never mind, I'll
bring him out here in the daylight and see if that helps.
[*Calling towards the door*] Strepsiades! Where are you? Can
you bring your bed out here?

STREPSIADES [*coming out, dragging a bed*]: If the bugs will let
me.

635   SOCRATES: Come on, lay it down there, and then pay attention.
STREPSIADES [*doing so*]: All right.
SOCRATES: Now what do you want to be taught first, that you
haven't ever been taught before? Come on now. Words?
Rhythms? Measures?[81]
STREPSIADES [*eagerly*]: Measures is what *I* want to know more

640   about! Only the other day a corn-dealer cheated me out of
two whole quarts.
SOCRATES [*impatiently*]: That's not what I'm talking about.

What measure do you consider the most aesthetically attractive – the three-measure or the four-measure?[82]

STREPSIADES [*confidently*]: I think nothing beats the gallon.

SOCRATES: What on earth are you wittering about?

STREPSIADES: You want to bet that there aren't four measures   645
in a gallon?[83]

SOCRATES: Oh, to hell with you, you stupid peasant! Let's try
rhythms, perhaps you'll understand those better.

STREPSIADES: I will if they'll help me feed my family.

SOCRATES: It'll do wonders for you in social conversation, if
you understand what kind of rhythm is armamental and what   650
kind is digital.[84]

STREPSIADES: Digital? But I know all about that already.

SOCRATES: Tell me what you know.

STREPSIADES: Ever since I was a boy, it's meant *this* [*sticking
out his middle finger*[85]].

SOCRATES: You rustic moron!   655

STREPSIADES: But dammit, I don't *want* to learn any of this
kind of stuff.

SOCRATES: What *do* you want to learn, then?

STREPSIADES: That – that argument, the one you call Wrong!

SOCRATES: Ah, there are many other things you have to learn
first. For instance, which animals are truly masculine?

STREPSIADES: Well, I know *that*, if I haven't gone potty. Ram,   660
billygoat, bull, dog, fowl.

SOCRATES: And feminine?

STREPSIADES: Ewe, nannygoat, cow, bitch, fowl.[86]

SOCRATES: See what you're doing? You're calling the male and
female by the same name 'fowl'.

STREPSIADES: How do you mean?

SOCRATES: How do I mean? 'Fowl' – 'fowl'.

STREPSIADES [*after some thought*]: Ah, I get you! What ought   665
I to call them?

SOCRATES: 'Fowless', and for the male 'fowler'.[87]

STREPSIADES: Fowless? Holy Air, that's brilliant! Just for telling me that I'll fill your kneading-trough with barley meal.

SOCRATES: Hold it again. You called it a trough. Much too   670
masculine a name for such a feminine object.[88]

STREPSIADES: What do you mean, a masculine name for a
   feminine object?

SOCRATES: In the same way as Cleonymus is.[89]

STREPSIADES: I don't understand.

SOCRATES: 'Trough' is parallel to 'Cleonymus'.

675 STREPSIADES: But Cleonymus never had a trough to his name
   – he did his *kneading* in a round mortar[90] [*he illustrates his
   meaning with the help of his phallus*]. Well, what *should* I
   call it from now on?

SOCRATES: 'Trough-ena', like you say 'Ath-ena'.

STREPSIADES: Troughena, that's feminine?

SOCRATES: That's right.

680 STREPSIADES: So I should have said 'Cleonymena never had a
   troughena'?

SOCRATES: But you've still got to learn about names, which of
   them are masculine and which are feminine.

STREPSIADES: No, I know which are feminine.

SOCRATES: Which?

STREPSIADES: Lysilla, Philinna, Cleitagora, Demetria.

685 SOCRATES: And which are masculine?

STREPSIADES: Lots. [*Thinks hard*] Philoxenus . . . Melesias . . .
   Amynias[91] . . .

SOCRATES: Silly, those aren't masculine.

STREPSIADES: You don't think they are?

SOCRATES: Not a bit. If you met Amynias, what would be the
   first thing you'd say to him?

690 STREPSIADES: I'd say – I'd say 'Hello, Minnie!'

SOCRATES: There you are; you've called *her* a woman.

STREPSIADES: And rightly too – the way *she* manages to dodge
   the call-up. But what's the point of my learning all these
   things? Everybody knows them already.

SOCRATES: Never mind that. Just lie down there [*indicating the
   bed*] –

STREPSIADES: And?

695 SOCRATES: And try and think out one of your own problems.

STREPSIADES: Not there, I beg you! If that's what you want me
   to do, can't I do it lying on the ground?

SOCRATES: That is not an option.

STREPSIADES [*taking off his shoes, lying on the bed and pulling the covers over him*]: God help me, I've really been thrown to the bugs now!

[SOCRATES *goes into the school, taking Strepsiades' shoes with him.*]

CHORUS:
> Think closely, follow every track,   700
> And twist and turn and double back,
>   And when you don't know how
> To come to a conclusion true,
> Jump to another point of view,
>   And banish sleep –   705

STREPSIADES:
> Yow-ow!!

CHORUS:
> What ails thee, friend? Why criest so?

STREPSIADES:
> I'm being ravaged by a foe,
>   These buggers[92] from the bed;   710
> They gnaw my ribs, they drain my soul,
> Pull out my balls and probe my hole [*indicating his anus*] –
>   They'll quickly have me dead!   715

CHORUS:
> Nay, bear it not so grievously.

STREPSIADES:
> That's fine advice to offer me,
>   The state I'm in right now!
> No cash, no tan, no shoes, no blood,
> Just whistling in the dark and mud,   720
>   And all but done for – yoww!

[*He returns to his private agony.* SOCRATES *puts his head out of an upstairs window.*]

SOCRATES: Hey, you, what are you up to? Thinking, I trust?

STREPSIADES: Yes, very much so.

SOCRATES: And what thoughts have you had?

725 STREPSIADES: Mainly about whether there'll be any of me left when the bugs have finished!

SOCRATES: Oh, go to blazes! [*He disappears from the window.*]

STREPSIADES [*shouting in his general direction*]: I'm there already, mate! [*He moves as if intending to get out of bed.*]

LEADER: Now, now, don't be a softie; cover yourself up well. You've got to find some really juicy ideas to cheat your creditors.

STREPSIADES [*meekly retreating under the bedclothes*]: I only 730 wish someone *would* throw a juicy, sexy . . . idea or two over me, instead of these!

SOCRATES [*coming out, and going up to Strepsiades*]: Let's have a look and see what this fellow is doing. [*Kicking Strepsiades through the bedclothes*] Here, are you asleep?

STREPSIADES [*uncovering his head*]: No, I'm not.

SOCRATES: Well, have you got hold of anything yet?

STREPSIADES: No.

SOCRATES: What, nothing?

STREPSIADES [*throwing off the bedclothes with his left hand*]: Only one thing – *my* thing – I've got hold of that!

735 SOCRATES [*throwing the bedclothes back over him*]: Cover up, will you, and get thinking, right away!

STREPSIADES: What about? Do tell me, Socrates.

SOCRATES: No, *you* tell *me* what you want to discover first.

STREPSIADES: If I've told you once I've told you a thousand times. About interest – how not to pay it.

740 SOCRATES: All right; cover yourself up, open out your thinking, refine it, and explore the matter in detail, making sure you draw the correct analytical distinctions.

STREPSIADES [*obeying*]: Yoww! They're at me again!

SOCRATES: Keep still. And if one of your ideas seems to have reached a dead end, let go of it, withdraw for a bit, and then 745 get your mind at work on it again, shifting it around and weighing it up.

STREPSIADES [*getting eagerly and thankfully out of bed*]: Socrates! My beloved Socrates!

SOCRATES: Yes, old man?

STREPSIADES: I've got an evasive idea for dealing with interest.

SOCRATES: Present it to me.

STREPSIADES: Tell me –

SOCRATES: Yes?

STREPSIADES: Suppose I bought a woman slave from Thessaly, a witch, and got her to draw down the moon one night, and then put it in a big round box, like they do mirrors, and kept a close watch on it. 750

SOCRATES: What good would that do you?

STREPSIADES: Why, if the moon never rose, I'd never pay any interest. 755

SOCRATES: Why not?

STREPSIADES: Why not? Because it's reckoned by the month, of course.

SOCRATES: Very good. Let me give you another one. Someone sues you for 30,000 drachmas. How do you get rid of the case? 760

STREPSIADES: How – how – I don't know. Let me work it out.

SOCRATES [*as* STREPSIADES *cogitates*]: Don't keep your thought penned up inside you all the time. Try letting it out into the air for a bit, dangling it on a string like a pet beetle.

STREPSIADES: I've found a marvellous way of stopping that lawsuit. I fancy you'll think so too. 765

SOCRATES: Like what?

STREPSIADES: Have you seen that stone the druggists sell – the beautiful transparent one you can light fires with?

SOCRATES: You mean glass?[93]

STREPSIADES: That's right. Well, suppose when the clerk was entering the case on his tablet, I stood like this with the glass between him and the sun and melted the wax where the entry for my case was? 770

SOCRATES: Nice one, by the Graces!

STREPSIADES: Whew, I'm glad I managed to strike that 30,000-drachma case off the list!

SOCRATES: See if you can get this one. 775

STREPSIADES: Yes?

SOCRATES: You're a defendant, you've got no witnesses, you've nearly lost the case – how would you avoid conviction?

STREPSIADES: That's child's play.

SOCRATES: Go on.

STREPSIADES: Like this. When there was still one case to be
780   heard before mine was called – I'd run off and hang myself.

SOCRATES: That's no good.

STREPSIADES: Why not? Once I'm dead, I can't be put on trial!

SOCRATES: You're talking twaddle. Get out. I'm not going to
teach you any more.

STREPSIADES: Oh, why? Do, please, Socrates, for the gods'
sake.

785   SOCRATES: But anything you do learn, you forget straight away.
For instance, tell me now, what was the first thing I taught
you?

STREPSIADES: Let me see now, what came first? First, what was
first? Something we were kneading barley meal in – help,
what was it?

790   SOCRATES: Oh, to hell with you, you amnesiac old fool! [*He
turns his back on Strepsiades, but remains within earshot.*]

STREPSIADES [*in despair*]: Help, what will become of me now?
If I can't learn tongue-wrestling, I'm done for. Holy Clouds,
can you give me any advice?

795   LEADER: Well, what we advise is this: if you have a grown-up
son, send him here to be a student instead of you.

STREPSIADES: Yes, I've a son, [*sarcastically*] a fine fellow. What
am I to do, though? He doesn't *want* to study.

LEADER: And you can't make him?

800   STREPSIADES: No. He's too strong to bully, and he comes from
a long line of stinking rich women.[94] Never mind, though, I'll
go for him; and if he won't come, make no mistake, I'll throw
him out of my house. [*To Socrates*] Go inside and wait till I
come back; I won't be long. [*He moves towards his own
house.*]

CHORUS [*addressing Strepsiades as he goes into his house*]:
            How greatly blest you soon will be,
805   Only through our aid!
            Your lightest wish this man will see
                Swiftly is obeyed.

[*Turning to Socrates as he goes into the school*]
      You see how high his heart's uplifted –   810
        Make your profit fast!
      For favouring winds ere now have shifted –
        Luck don't always last.

[STREPSIADES, *very angry, comes out of his house, driving a bewildered* PHEIDIPPIDES *before him.*]

STREPSIADES: In the name of Mist, leave this house at once. Go 815
and nibble at Megacles' pillared portico.

PHEIDIPPIDES: What on earth's happened to you, dad? Why,
Zeus in heaven, you act as though you were out of your mind!

STREPSIADES: 'Zeus in heaven' – ha! How stupid can you get?
Believing in Zeus – a big boy like you? [*He laughs heartily.*]

PHEIDIPPIDES: What's so funny about that? 820

STREPSIADES: That you could be such a baby and have such
primitive ideas. Never mind. Come to daddy and he'll tell you
something that a grown-up needs to know. [PHEIDIPPIDES
comes over, and STREPSIADES *whispers, audibly, in his ear.*]
Promise you'll never tell this to anyone?

PHEIDIPPIDES [*giving his right hand in pledge*]: Promise. 825
What's the secret?

STREPSIADES: You were swearing by Zeus just now, weren't
you?

PHEIDIPPIDES: Yes.

STREPSIADES: Well now, isn't education a wonderful thing?
Pheidippides – there *is* no Zeus.

PHEIDIPPIDES: Then who's taken over?

STREPSIADES: Vortex is king now; he's driven Zeus from
power.

PHEIDIPPIDES: What on earth are you blethering about?

STREPSIADES: I assure you, it's perfectly true.

PHEIDIPPIDES: Who says so, anyway? 830

STREPSIADES: Socrates of Melos,[95] and Chaerephon, you know,
the expert on fleas' feet.

PHEIDIPPIDES: And you believe nutters like that? You must be
totally off your head.

STREPSIADES: Hush! Don't talk rudely about them. They're

835   brilliant men, and so sensible too – they live so economically:
       they never get their hair cut, never oil themselves, never pay
       for a wash in the public baths – whereas *you* go there so often,
       you've washed away my estate, as if I were dead and it was
       yours to squander! Now you go to them, right away, and let
       them teach you instead of me.

840   PHEIDIPPIDES: Huh! What can that lot teach that's any use?

      STREPSIADES: What a thing to ask! They teach you everything
       that's worth knowing. They'll soon teach *you* how dense and
       stupid you are. Here, just wait a moment, will you? [*He goes
       into his house.*]

      PHEIDIPPIDES [*to himself*]: Gods help me, my father really is
845   mad. What am I to do? Get the court to certify him, or just
       drop a word about it to the undertaker?
         [*His reflections are interrupted by the return of* STREPSI-
         ADES, *followed by a* SLAVE *who carries two wicker cages
         containing, respectively, a cock and a hen.*]

      STREPSIADES [*pointing to the cock*]: Tell me now, what do you
       call this?

      PHEIDIPPIDES: A fowl.

      STREPSIADES: That's very good. And this one?

      PHEIDIPPIDES: A fowl.

      STREPSIADES: What, both the same? You *are* making yourself
850   a laughing-stock! You'd better not do it again. In future call
       this one a fowless and the other one a fowler.

      PHEIDIPPIDES: Fowless? Was that the kind of bright idea you
       were taught while you were with those sons of the soil?[96]

      STREPSIADES: Yes, and a great deal more too; but every time I
855   was taught anything I forgot it straight away – I'm just too
       old for that sort of thing.

      PHEIDIPPIDES: I suppose that's how you came to lose your
       cloak?

      STREPSIADES: I didn't lose it, I – I invested it in education.

      PHEIDIPPIDES: And your shoes? What did you do with them,
       you old fool?

      STREPSIADES: I lost them 'for essential purposes', as Pericles
860   once said.[97] Come on now, let's go. If you think you're doing
       wrong, remember you're doing what I asked you. I remember

[*emotionally*] that I was already doing what *you* were asking me when you were a babbling six year old. I spent my very first obol of jury pay to get you a little toy cart for the Diasia!

PHEIDIPPIDES: I swear you'll be sorry for this one day. [*But he reluctantly follows* STREPSIADES *over to the door of the Thinkery.*] 865

STREPSIADES: Good for you, my boy! Socrates! Come out and see what I've got here! [SOCRATES *comes out.*] Here's my son. He didn't want to come, but I managed to persuade him.

SOCRATES: I dare say he's immature and doesn't yet know the ropes here.

PHEIDIPPIDES [*aside*]: I'd like to see you tied up with some, and getting a good lashing![98] 870

STREPSIADES: Damn you, how dare you curse your teacher?

SOCRATES: Did you hear his slack pronunciation – the drawl, the sagging lips? It's not going to be easy to teach him to win cases and master the technicalities and make good, empty debating points. And yet it's true that for six grand, Hyperbolus did manage to learn it. 875

STREPSIADES: Don't worry, you can teach him. He's always been precocious. Do you know, when he was a little boy only that high [*indicating with his hand*], he was building toy houses at home, and making model boats, and little carts of figwood, and – can you imagine? – frogs out of pomegranate peel! Well, anyway, make sure he learns your two Arguments – Right, or whatever you call it, and Wrong, the one that takes a bad case and defeats Right with it. If he can't manage both, then at least Wrong – that's essential. 880 885

SOCRATES: He'll be taught by the Arguments in person; I won't be there.[99]

STREPSIADES [*as* SOCRATES *goes inside*]: Don't forget, he's got to be able to argue against any kind of justified claim at all.[100]

[*Enter, from the school,* RIGHT, *a distinguished-looking old man dressed in the style thought to be typical of Athenian aristocrats of the Persian War period. He is followed by the smirking figure of* WRONG, *a young man of about Pheidippides' age but of much less healthy appearance – except for his large phallus.*]

890 RIGHT: This way. Let the audience see you. You're always bold as brass, anyway.

WRONG: Sure, go wherever you like. The more of an audience we have, the more soundly I'll trounce you.

RIGHT: Trounce me? What do you think you are?

WRONG: An Argument, like you.

RIGHT: Yes, a *wrong* Argument.

895 WRONG: Maybe, but I'll still beat you, Right though you call yourself.

RIGHT: How d'you think you'll contrive to do that?

WRONG: Just by thinking out a few novel ideas.

RIGHT: Yes, they're in fashion now, aren't they – because of those morons out there [*indicating the audience*].

WRONG: Morons indeed! They're extremely intelligent.

RIGHT: Anyway, I'll thrash you.

900 WRONG [*unconcerned*]: Oh, how?

RIGHT: Simply by presenting the case for justice.

WRONG: It'll crumble as soon as I open my mouth. My position is that there isn't any such *thing* as Justice.

RIGHT: No such thing?!

WRONG: Well, if there is, where is it to be found?

RIGHT: With the gods, of course.

905 WRONG: Very well; in that case, why hasn't Zeus been destroyed for putting his father in chains?[101]

RIGHT: Ugh, you make me want to puke. Fetch me a basin, somebody!

WRONG: You're just a fogbound out-of-tune old windbag.

RIGHT: And you're just a shameless out-of-condition young pansy.

910 WRONG: I'm terribly flattered.

RIGHT: And an irresponsible, flippant verbalizer.

WRONG: More of these bouquets!

RIGHT: And you beat your father.

WRONG: Do you know you're spangling me with gold?

RIGHT: Lead, more like, or so they'd have said in *my* time.

WRONG: Well, in *our* time these are all exquisite compliments.

915 RIGHT: Your shameless audacity is beyond belief.

WRONG: *You* are just *history*.

RIGHT: You're the one that encourages our adolescents to drop out of school.[102] One day Athens will wake up to what you've been doing to these young people who don't know any better.

WRONG [*sniffing*]: Do you ever wash?   920

RIGHT: *You're* not doing so badly, are you? Considering that you used to be a beggar, pretending to be that Mysian Telephus[103] and living on little scraps of ideas you got from your alms-bag or stole from Pandeletus.[104]

WRONG: Yes, wasn't I clever?   925

RIGHT: Yes, weren't you barmy? And barmier still the community that pays you to corrupt its young people.

WRONG: You don't mean to be this boy's teacher, do you, you ancient relic?

RIGHT: Yes, I do, if he wants to have a decent life and know   930
how to do something besides talking.

WRONG [*beckoning Pheidippides*]: Come here and leave him to rant.

RIGHT: Lay a hand on him and you'll regret it!

LEADER [*intervening between them*]: No more fighting and wrangling, please. You [*to Right*] explain the way you taught   935
the boys in the olden days, and you [*to Wrong*] explain the New Education, and then he can hear both of you, make up his mind, and choose which will be his teacher.

RIGHT: I agree.

WRONG: And so do I.

LEADER: All right, which of you will speak first?   940

WRONG: I'm happy to let him start;[105] and then whatever he says, I'll shoot him down with clever new phrases and ideas. By the end, if he so much as utters a sound, I'll destroy him   945
with verbal hornet-stings all over his face and eyes!

CHORUS:

As you battle with words and with thoughts of the   950
    mind,
We'll soon see who's victorious and who lags behind.
For our friends[106] a great issue hangs on this debate –   955
Education's whole future and Culture's whole fate.

LEADER [to Right]:
Now, you who fostered by your education
The glorious ancient virtues of our nation,
960   Deploy for us the voice you love to use,
Explain your personality and views.

RIGHT: I'll tell you about the way boys were brought up in the
old days – the days when I was all the rage and it was actually
fashionable to be decent. First of all, children were supposed
to be seen and not heard – not a sound. Then, all the boys of
the district were expected to walk together through the streets
965   to their music-master's, quietly and with decorum, and without cloaks, even if it was snowing confetti – and they did.
And when they got there he would make them learn some of
the old songs by heart – like 'Pallas, great sacker of cities' or
'Let the glad strain sound afar' – singing them to the traditional tunes their fathers handed down, and on *no* account
pressing their thighs together. And if any of them did anything
disreputable, tying up the melody in knots with changes of
970   mode and rhythm – the sort of thing Phrynis[107] introduced,
which they all do now – why, he was given a sound thrashing
for insulting the Muses. Then in the gymnasium, when they
sat down, they were expected to keep their legs well up, so as
975   not to – so as not to torment us with desire; and when they
got up, they had to smooth down the sand, so as not to leave
any marks on it for their admirers to feast their eyes on.
What's more, [*sternly*] they never oiled themselves below the
belt, [*dreamily*] and their privates looked like peaches, all
velvety and dewy; and you wouldn't see a boy being his own
980   pimp, walking along making eyes at his lovers and putting on
a soft tender voice, oh no! They weren't allowed to take so
much as a radish head at dinner, or any of the dill or celery if
their elders wanted it; they never ate posh fish, they never
giggled, they never stood with their legs crossed –

WRONG [*mockingly*]: How thoroughly quaint! How redolent
985   of cicada brooches,[108] oxslaughter trials[109] and Cedeides![110]

RIGHT: Be that as it may, that's the sort of discipline that I used
to rear the men who fought at Marathon. What does *your*

kind do for our young men? You teach them to wrap themselves in cloaks up to the eyebrows. And when I saw one of
them dancing at the Panathenaea,[111] and he let his shield drop
to his haunches, why, I nearly choked – the insult to our
beloved goddess! [*To Pheidippides*] So choose Right, my lad,   990
choose me, and have no fear. Keep away from the Market
Square, and the public baths too. If ever you do something
shameful, show you're ashamed. If someone makes fun of
you, flare up. If you're sitting down and an older person
approaches, stand up. Don't show disrespect for your parents,
or do anything disgraceful that would defile the face of Mod-   995
esty.[112] Don't run after dancing-girls; you never know what
may happen – suppose some little whore chucks an apple at
you as a come-and-get-me?[113] your reputation's gone in an
instant. Don't ever contradict your father or call him an
antediluvian;[114] of course he's older than you, that's how he
was able to bring you up before you could fly on your own,
so you shouldn't insult him with it.

WRONG: Don't listen to him, lad – otherwise, by Dionysus,   1000
you'll end up just like the sons of Hippocrates and be called
a boring little baby.[115]

RIGHT: What matters is that you'll be spending your time in the
gymnasium, getting sleek and healthy, not like these people
who are always chattering away in the Market Square about
some abstruse topic or other, or being dragged into court over
some piffling quibbling filthy little dispute. No, you'll go   1005
down to Academe's Park[116] and take a training run under the
sacred olive trees, a wreath of white reeds on your head, with
a nice decent companion of your own age; in autumn you'll
share the fragrance of leafy poplar and carefree convolvulus,
and you'll take delight in the spring when the plane tree
whispers to the elm!

If my sound advice you heed, if you follow where I lead,   1010
    You'll be healthy, you'll be strong and you'll be sleek;
You'll have muscles that are thick and a pretty little prick –
    You'll be proud of your appearance and physique.

1015   If contrariwise you spurn my society and turn
              To these modern ways, you'll have a pale complexion,
        And with two exceptions, all of your limbs will be too
                    small –
              The exceptions are the tongue and the e-lection;[117]

1020   You will sing the trendy song 'To be virtuous is wrong,
              And every kind of wickedness is right',
        And you'll catch the current craze for Antimachus's
                    ways –
              That is, for getting buggered every night.

CHORUS:
1025   O how sweet are your words and how modest your
                    thought,
                    You noble and glorious sage!
              How we envy the happiness of those whom you
                    taught –
                    They lived in a real Golden Age!

        [*To Wrong*]
1030   He's impressed us tremendously, and we advise
                    That you should be careful to choose
              Some real novel arguments, sure to surprise,
                    And to showcase your sexiest Muse.

LEADER:
        It looks as though you'll need the newest weapons of your
              school
1035   In order to defeat your foe and not face ridicule.
        WRONG: As a matter of fact, right through his speech I've been
        positively bursting with eagerness to refute it and smash it to
        smithereens. That's why the people at the Thinkery call me
1040   Wrong: I was the one who invented ways of proving anything
        wrong, established laws, soundly based accusations, you
        name it. Isn't that worth millions – to be able to have a
        really bad case and yet win? Well, let's have a look at this
        educational system he's so proud of. He says, for example,

[*turning to Pheidippides*] that he won't let you have any hot
baths. [*To Right*] On what principle do you object to them?   1045
RIGHT: Hot baths are *bad*. They make a man a coward.
WRONG: Hold it! I've scored one there, right away, and there's
no way you can wriggle out of it. Tell me, of the sons of Zeus,
who would you say was the bravest man and performed the
greatest number of labours?
RIGHT: The best of them was unquestionably Heracles.   1050
WRONG: And have you ever heard of Heracles having a *cold*
bath?[118] [RIGHT *is speechless*.] Well, was he the bravest of
them all, or wasn't he?
RIGHT [*spluttering*]: That – that – that's just the sort of clever
stuff that you hear the young lads coming out with all day! So
they flock to the public baths and leave the wrestling-schools
empty.
WRONG: Then you object to their hanging around the Market   1055
Square. I see nothing wrong with it at all; quite the contrary.
If it was such a bad thing, Homer would never have described
all his sages, such as Nestor, as 'marketeers'.[119] To consider
next the tongue. He says it's bad for the young to exercise it
too much; well, I say it's good. And then he talks about   1060
modesty or decency or something – another pernicious evil!
Come on, prove me wrong: tell me of anyone who's been
done any good by being modest and decent.
RIGHT: Many people. For example, that was how Peleus came
to be given a knife.[120]
WRONG: A knife! Well, well! What a rich haul, I must say! Even
Hyperbolus from the lamp market – now *he's* made a mint   1065
by being wicked, but he never got a knife!
RIGHT: And it was also because of Peleus' virtue that he got
Thetis as his wife.[121]
WRONG: Yes, and that was why she deserted him as well.[122] If
he'd been a little less virtuous he might have been a more
satisfactory performer under the covers. Women do *like* some   1070
disrespectful handling in bed, you know, you hulking old
ruin! [*To Pheidippides*] Listen to all the things that virtue
can't do for you, my lad – all the pleasures you won't be able
to have. No boys. No women. No gambling. No fancy food.

No booze. No belly laughs. Will your life be worth living, without all these? [PHEIDIPPIDES *indicates the answer is*
'no'.[123]] I thought not. Let me turn now to – to the demands of Nature. Let us say you've fallen in love with a married woman – had a bit of an affair – and then got caught in the act. As you are now, without arguing skills, you're done for. But if you come and learn from me, then you can do what you like and get away with it – indulge your desires, laugh and play, have no shame. And then suppose you do get caught with somebody's wife, you can say to him, straight out, 'I've done nothing wrong. Just look at Zeus; isn't he always a slave to erotic desire? And do you expect a mere mortal like me to be stronger than a god?'

RIGHT: And suppose your advice doesn't work? Suppose he gets radish-buggered and ash-plucked?[124] Then he'll have the arsehole of a faggot for the rest of his life. Argue yourself out of *that* one!

WRONG: So if he does have the arsehole of a faggot, what's wrong with that?

RIGHT: You mean, what could be *worse* than that?

WRONG: What will you say if I prove you wrong about this?

RIGHT: I'll have nothing to say after that.

WRONG: Very well then. From what class of persons are prosecution advocates drawn?

RIGHT: From the faggots.

WRONG: I agree with you. And our actors – I mean, of course, the tragic ones?

RIGHT: From the faggots.

WRONG: Right again. And from what class do we get our politicians?

RIGHT: From the faggots.[125]

WRONG: Then don't you see you were talking nonsense? Why, look at the audience; what do you think most of *them* are?

RIGHT: I'm looking.

WRONG: And what do you see?

RIGHT: Good gods, the faggots have it by a street! At least, I

know *he's* one [*pointing*], and him, and him there with the   1100
long hair –

WRONG: Well then?

RIGHT: You win. Here, you sods out there, in the name of the
gods, take my cloak – I'm defecting! [*He throws his cloak
towards the right-hand side of the audience, in the direction
of some of the men he has previously pointed out – to reveal
that he is wearing underneath it an inner garment of distinctly
feminine colour and line. He then runs into the auditorium
and up a gangway on the left-hand side – pausing to dally
flirtatiously with the odd spectator – and eventually vanishes
from view at the rear.*][126]

WRONG [*to Strepsiades*]: Well, now, which do you want? Are   1105
you going to take your son away, or do you want me to teach
him to be an orator?

STREPSIADES: Oh, teach him – don't spare the rod, if necessary
– and be sure to give his teeth a good cutting edge. He should
be able to handle small cases with one side of his mouth while
using the other side for the bigger ones.   1110

WRONG: Don't worry; when you get him back, he'll be a top-
class sophist.

PHEIDIPPIDES [*aside*]: A pale-faced wretch, more like, if you
ask me.

CHORUS [*as* WRONG *leads* PHEIDIPPIDES *into the school and*
STREPSIADES *turns towards his house*]:
  Farewell; [*to Strepsiades*] but we bet it
  You'll come to regret it![127]

[STREPSIADES, *taking no notice, almost dances into his
house in great joy.*]

LEADER [*addressing the competition judges*]:
  We would like to tell you, judges, of the blessings we'll   1115
    accord
  Those who give to both this chorus and this play their just
    reward.

If you want to put the ploughshare to some fallow land
   you've got,
Then we'll see that even in time of drought there's rain
   upon your plot.
If you keep a vineyard, we'll protect it from the double
   bane
1120   Both of soaking with too much and parching with too
   little rain.
But if any mortal treats the Clouds of heaven with
   despite,
We have power to reduce him to a miserable plight.
Both his olives and his grapes and all his other crops will
   fail:
1125   From our powerful slings we'll smite them with those
   slingshots you call hail.
If we see him making bricks, we'll rain, and then we'll give
   him proof
Of our anger when our hailstones smash the tiling of his
   roof.
And if he is getting married (or a friend, or a relation)
We will ruin the festivities with our precipitation.
So all in all, you judges, this we earnestly advise:
1130   You'd be better off in Egypt[128] than not giving us first
   prize!

    [STREPSIADES *comes out of his house. He is counting on*
    his fingers.]

STREPSIADES: Twenty-sixth, twenty-seventh, twenty-eighth;
after that comes the twenty-ninth, and then that day I fear
and dread above all others, the last day of the month, 'Old
1135   and New Day'![129] All my creditors swear that if I don't pay
up, they're going to hand in their court deposits[130] and see me
ruined. And when I ask them for a reasonable little favour –
'Please don't call the loan in now' – 'Give me some more time'
– 'Couldn't we just write it off?' – they all say that's not their
1140   idea of getting paid and call me a villain and say they'll sue.
Well, let them. If Pheidippides has really learned to be an
expert orator, they can't hurt me. I'll soon know if he has.

Let's go to the Thinkery. [*Knocking on the school door*] Boy! 1145
Here, I say! Boy!

SOCRATES [*opening the door*]: Delighted to see you, Strepsiades.

STREPSIADES: Same to you. [*Offering him a present*] I wonder
if you'd accept this?[131] Just as a token of my appreciation. But
my son – has he learnt that Argument that we were listening
to not long ago?

SOCRATES: Yes, he has.   1150

STREPSIADES: Holy Fraud, how wonderful!

SOCRATES: Yes, you'll now be able to defend any and every
lawsuit successfully.

STREPSIADES: Even if the loan was made before witnesses?

SOCRATES: Even if there were a thousand of them.

STREPSIADES [*adopting a tragic pose and tone*]:
Then raise aloft a mighty cry of joy!
O weep, ye moneylenders, for yourselves,   1155
Your capital, and your compound interest!
No longer can ye work your will on me,
Such is the son that's reared within these halls,
The brilliant wielder of a two-edged tongue,   1160
My shield and bulwark, saviour of my house,
Bane of my foes, dispeller of my griefs!
Run, run within, and call him out to me.
[SOCRATES *goes inside.*]
Thy father calls, beloved son; appear.   1165

SOCRATES [*re-emerging with Pheidippides*]:
Here is your offspring.

STREPSIADES [*embracing him*]:
                          O my darling boy!

SOCRATES:
You may depart with him.

STREPSIADES:
                          I whoop with joy!   1170

[SOCRATES *goes back into the school.* STREPSIADES *has a
good look at Pheidippides – whose face, we can see, is
many shades paler than previously – and lets out a cry of
rapture.*]

STREPSIADES: What a gorgeous complexion, son! You've got 'Not guilty' and 'On the contrary' and that famous Attic phrase 'You can't be serious' written all over your face – and
1175 that injured-innocent look that does the trick even if you're caught red-handed! You were my ruin before; now you must be my salvation.

PHEIDIPPIDES: Why, what are you afraid of?

STREPSIADES: Old and New Day.

PHEIDIPPIDES: What, is there a day that's both old and new?

1180 STREPSIADES: Of course there is – and that's when they say they're going to hand in their court deposits.

PHEIDIPPIDES: Well, they're going to lose their money. It's not possible for one day to be two days.

STREPSIADES: How not possible?

PHEIDIPPIDES: Not unless it's also possible for one woman, say, to be old and young at the same time.

1185 STREPSIADES: But that's what the law says: 'summonses to be answerable on Old and New Day'.

PHEIDIPPIDES: Ah, but the meaning of the law has been mis-understood.

STREPSIADES: So what *does* it mean?

PHEIDIPPIDES: Well, our lawgiver Solon was a good demo-crat,[132] right?

STREPSIADES: Yes, but what's that got to do with Old and New Day?

PHEIDIPPIDES: So he fixed the summonses to be for two days,
1190 Old Day and New Day, intending that the deposits should be lodged on New Day, also known as New Moon.[133]

STREPSIADES: Well, in that case, why mention Old Day at all?

PHEIDIPPIDES: To give the defendant a chance to appear a day
1195 early and settle the dispute, so as not to have butterflies in his tummy on the morning of the New Moon.

STREPSIADES: But then why don't the magistrates accept deposits on the New Moon? They only accept them on the day before.

PHEIDIPPIDES: They're acting like the people who taste the
1200 food the day before a festival: early taste, early steal.

STREPSIADES: Nice one! Here [*to the audience*], why are you lot just sitting there like stones, not even laughing? They're a flock of sheep, a heap of earthenware – we intellectuals can exploit them as we please! [*To Pheidippides*] We're in luck, you and me, and I think a song of celebration is called for.   1205

> 'O blest Strepsiades,
>   What brilliance you display,
> And what a son you have!'
>   So everyone will say,
> My friends and neighbours all,   1210
>   In envy at the sight,
> When you go into court
>   And win each case you fight!

Come in now and let's have a party! [*They go into Strepsiades' house.*]

[*Enter* FIRST CREDITOR *– a very fat man – accompanied by his* WITNESS.]

FIRST CREDITOR: Why should anyone want to lend out his money? Better to face the embarrassment of saying no at the   1215
outset rather than have all this trouble afterwards. Here I am, having to bother you with my problems because I need a witness, and also having to make an enemy in my own village. All the same, while I live, I won't put Athens to shame.[134] [*He   1220
is now at Strepsiades' door, and calls out loudly*] I hereby summon Strepsiades –

STREPSIADES [*coming out*]: Who's here?

FIRST CREDITOR: – to attend on Old and New Day.

STREPSIADES [*to the audience*]: I call you to witness that he summoned me for two different days. [*To the creditor*] What is this about?

FIRST CREDITOR: The twelve hundred drachmas you borrowed to buy the ash-coloured horse.   1225

STREPSIADES: Horse! Can you believe it? And you all know that I hate everything to do with horses!

FIRST CREDITOR: Not only did you borrow it, but you swore by all the gods that you would pay.

STREPSIADES: Ah, well, that was before my Pheidippides had learnt his invincible Argument.

1230 FIRST CREDITOR: And now he has, you intend to repudiate the debt?

STREPSIADES: Well, you don't think I sent him to school for nothing, do you?

FIRST CREDITOR: Are you prepared to swear by the gods, in a place of my choosing,[135] that you don't owe me the money?

STREPSIADES: Swear by which gods?

FIRST CREDITOR: Zeus, Hermes and Poseidon.[136]

1235 STREPSIADES: Delighted. I'd give you three obols for the privilege.

FIRST CREDITOR: Well, of all the shameless – !

STREPSIADES [patting him on the stomach]: You know, you'd make quite a good wine-skin once we'd cured your hide.

FIRST CREDITOR: You impudent – !

STREPSIADES: Four gallons it would hold, I think.

FIRST CREDITOR: By Zeus and all the gods, you needn't think
1240 you'll get away with this.

STREPSIADES [laughing uproariously]: 'The gods'! 'Zeus'! How incredibly funny – for those of us in the know!

FIRST CREDITOR: You'll pay for this, make no mistake. And I'm not leaving till you've given me a straight answer. Are you going to pay me back my money or not?

1245 STREPSIADES: Wait a moment and I'll tell you. [He goes into his house.]

FIRST CREDITOR [to his witness]: What do you think he's going to do? Pay, or what?

STREPSIADES [coming out with a kneading-trough]: Where's the man who was demanding money from me? [To First Creditor] Tell me what this is.

FIRST CREDITOR: That? A kneading-trough, of course.

STREPSIADES: And an ignorant person like you dares demand
1250 to be paid? Do you expect me to pay so much as an obol to someone who speaks of a trough instead of a troughena?

FIRST CREDITOR: So you're not going to pay?

STREPSIADES: Not that I know of! Now clear off, will you? Get away from my door! Hurry up!

FIRST CREDITOR: All right, I'm going. But let me tell you, I'm going to lodge that deposit, or may I be damned! [*Exit,* 1255 *accompanied by* WITNESS.]

STREPSIADES [*calling after them*]: Then you'll just be throwing it away after the twelve hundred. And I don't really want that to happen to you just because you were silly enough to use a word like 'trough'.

[*Enter* SECOND CREDITOR, *a much younger man. He is bruised and limping.*]

SECOND CREDITOR [*tragically, singing*]:
Ah me! Ah me!

STREPSIADES: Who's this singing laments? Not one of Carcinus' 1260 gods,[137] is it?

SECOND CREDITOR:
Why wishest thou to know who I may be?
I am a man of sorrows.

STREPSIADES: Then keep them to yourself.

SECOND CREDITOR:
O cruel divinity that smashed my chariot!
Pallas, thou hast destroyed me utterly.[138]   1265

STREPSIADES: Why, what has Tlepolemus ever done you wrong?

SECOND CREDITOR: Stop making fun of me, my man. Tell your son to pay me back the money he had from me. He ought to anyway, and especially when I'm in a state like this.

STREPSIADES: What money is this you're talking about?   1270

SECOND CREDITOR: The money he borrowed.

STREPSIADES: Looks to me you *are* in a bad way!

SECOND CREDITOR: Yes, by the gods, I fell off my chariot.

STREPSIADES: The nonsense you talk suggests you fell off the proverbial donkey![139]

SECOND CREDITOR: Nonsense? I only want my own money back!

STREPSIADES [*in the tones of a doctor breaking bad news*]: I 1275 doubt if you're ever going to recover fully.

SECOND CREDITOR: Why not?

STREPSIADES: I'm fairly sure that you're suffering from some form of concussion of the brain.

SECOND CREDITOR: *I'm* fairly sure that you're going to get a *summons* from me, if you don't pay up.

1280 STREPSIADES: Tell me now: do you think that when Zeus rains, it's new rain every time, or do you think the sun sucks up water from the ground so that he can use it again?

SECOND CREDITOR: I don't know, and I don't care.

STREPSIADES: Then how can you claim the right to have your money back, if you have no knowledge of meteorology?

1285 SECOND CREDITOR: Look, if you're short of cash, you can just pay the interest for now.

STREPSIADES: This 'interest' – what exactly is it?

SECOND CREDITOR: Why, it's just the way that a sum of money keeps getting bigger, month by month, day by day, as time runs on.

1290 STREPSIADES: All right. Now then: do you think the sea has more water in it now than it used to?

SECOND CREDITOR: No, it's the same size; there would be something wrong if it wasn't.

STREPSIADES: So the rivers run into the sea and yet the sea doesn't

1295 get bigger – so how can you claim that as time runs on your money should get bigger? You wretched fool! Go and chase yourself away from this house! Boy – fetch me a goad!

[*A* SLAVE *comes out with a charioteer's goad, and* STREPSIADES *immediately sets to work on the creditor with it.*]

SECOND CREDITOR: Help! Assault!

STREPSIADES: Gee up! What are you waiting for? Get moving, you branded nag!

SECOND CREDITOR: This is criminal outrage![140]

STREPSIADES: Move, won't you? Or else I'll *get* you moving by

1300 poking you right up your thoroughbred arse! [*The* CREDITOR *takes to his heels.*] Retreating, eh? I *thought* I'd get rid of you that way – you and your chariots and wheels and all! [*He goes inside.*]

CHORUS:
Is he not in love with evil,
This old man – in love, I say?

> Having borrowed all this money,   1305
>   He's determined not to pay!
>
> But before this day is ended
>   He'll be rendered broken-hearted,
> And this sophist[141] then will surely
>   Rue the wickedness he started.   1310
>
> For his son's a rhetorician
>   (Which is what his dad desired)
> Armed with Wrong to vanquish every
>   Argument by Right inspired.   1315
>
> Any case, however righteous,
>   He is trained to overcome:
> Soon his father will be praying
>   To the gods to strike him dumb!   1320

[*Screaming is heard from within, and a moment later* STREPSIADES *rushes out, clutching his face and in great agitation;* PHEIDIPPIDES *follows him, looking utterly unconcerned.*]

STREPSIADES: Help, neighbours! Help, kinsmen! Help, men of Cicynna! I'm being beaten up – rescue me! Zeus, my head – my cheeks! [*To Pheidippides*] You abominable villain, do you 1325 dare hit your father?

PHEIDIPPIDES [*coolly*]: Yes, I do.

STREPSIADES [*to the Chorus and the audience*]: Do you hear him? He admits it!

PHEIDIPPIDES: Of course I do.

STREPSIADES: You loathsome young hooligan![142]

PHEIDIPPIDES: More, more! Don't you know I love being called bad names?

STREPSIADES: You gaping arsehole!   1330

PHEIDIPPIDES: Shower me with more of these roses!

STREPSIADES: How *dare* you hit your father?

PHEIDIPPIDES: I'll prove to you that I was perfectly justified in doing so.

STREPSIADES: *Justified!* You utter villain, how could that possibly be?

PHEIDIPPIDES: You argue your case, I'll argue mine, and I guarantee to prove it.

1335 STREPSIADES: *Prove* what you've just said?

PHEIDIPPIDES: Very easily. Now then, which of the two Arguments do you want?

STREPSIADES: Arguments? What Arguments?

PHEIDIPPIDES: You know – do you want Right or Wrong?

STREPSIADES [*bitterly*]: I certainly *have* had you taught to argue
1340 against justice, if you're going to be able to argue convincingly that it's right and proper for a father to be beaten up by his son.

PHEIDIPPIDES: I fancy I will, though; when you've heard me, you won't have a word to utter against me.

STREPSIADES: I'll be very interested to hear what you'll have to say!

CHORUS:
1345   Consider carefully how you can win.
              The facts compel us to believe
              The boy has something up his sleeve:
1350   Observe the shameless frame of mind he's in!

LEADER:
          Now tell us how it came about that this big row took place –
          Why trouble, though, to ask you to? You will in any case!

STREPSIADES: I'll explain, right from the start, how the quarrel
1355 began. You know we were having a big feast. Well, I asked him to take his lyre and sing a song by Simonides, 'The Shearing of Mr Ram'.[143] And straight away he says, 'That's so antiquated, that is – playing the lyre and singing at a drinking party – what do you think we are, women grinding corn?'

PHEIDIPPIDES: Exactly! I wonder I didn't clock you right then
1360 and there. Telling me to *sing*! Who did you think you were entertaining, a treeful of cicadas?

STREPSIADES: That's exactly the way he went on at me – just the way he's talking now. 'And,' he added, 'Simonides was a

rotten poet anyway.' Well, I could barely restrain myself –
but I did. I asked him at least to take a myrtle branch[144] in his
hand and recite me something from Aeschylus. That set him   1365
off again – 'Oh, yes, Aeschylus is a prince among poets – a
prince of hot air and barbarous bombast, who creates words
the size of mountains.' Well, by this time my heart was fairly
thumping, you can imagine. But I bit my lip hard and said,
'All right then, you give us something from one of your   1370
sophisticated modern fellows, whoever they are.' So he
launched straight into some speech by Euripides, about how
a brother – the gods preserve us – how a brother was screwing
his sister – his *full* sister![145] Well, I just couldn't stand it any
longer. I pitched into him, calling him all sorts of foul names,
and then – you know what happens – we were shouting at   1375
each other hammer and tongs. And in the end he jumps up
and starts giving me a pasting, hitting me, throttling me,
pounding me to mincemeat.

PHEIDIPPIDES: And you deserved it. Slagging off Euripides!
He's a genius!

STREPSIADES [*sarcastically*]: Oh, yes, a genius indeed, you –
what can I call you? – oh, forget it, I'll only get hit all over again.

PHEIDIPPIDES: And you'll deserve it again, by Zeus.

STREPSIADES: *Deserve* it? You impudent puppy, who was it   1380
brought you up from a baby, trying to understand from your
infant babbling what it was that you wanted? If you said
'broo', I understood and gave you a drink. If you cried
'mamma', I'd fetch you bread. And the moment you said
'kakka', I'd grab you, take you outside and hold you over the   1385
pit. Not like what happened when you were throttling me
just now. I was screaming and shouting that I needed a crap
– and did *you* take *me* outside, curse you? No, you just kept
choking me until I did a kakka on the spot!   1390

CHORUS:
        Youth's all agog to hear *his* case, I ween.
            For he's committed such a deed
            That, should his coming plea succeed,
        An old man's hide will not be worth a bean!   1395

LEADER [to Pheidippides]:
    It's up to you, disturber of old certainties, to light
    Upon convincing arguments to show that you were right.

PHEIDIPPIDES: It's so delightful to be acquainted with the
1400   wisdom of today, and to be able to despise convention. There
    was a time, you know, when my thoughts were of nothing
    but horses, and in those days I couldn't say three words
    together that made sense. But now my father himself has
    enabled me to put all that behind me. I'm intimate with all
    the newest and subtlest ideas, principles and arguments, and
1405   I'm confident I can demonstrate that it is right and proper to
    chastise one's father.

STREPSIADES: I just wish you'd go back to your horses. I'd
    prefer it even if you kept four of the damn things, rather than
    beat me to a pulp like you've done now.

PHEIDIPPIDES: As I was saying before I was so rudely inter-
    rupted – I will begin by asking you a question or two. When
    I was a child, did you beat me?

1410 STREPSIADES: I did, because I cared for you and wanted to do
    you good.

PHEIDIPPIDES: So beating equals caring. In that case, why is it
    not also right and proper for me to care for you in the same
    way, by beating *you*? On what principle can you claim to
    have the privilege of immunity from physical assault, when I
    did not? I was born free, after all, just as you were. To put it
1415   poetically: 'The son gets thumped; do you think the father
    shouldn't?'[146] You will, no doubt, argue that the custom is
    only for *children* to be beaten; but I would wish to point out
    that old age is proverbially a second childhood. And after all,
    one does expect a higher standard of behaviour from the old
    than the young, so it's only proper that when they do fall
    short they should be severely punished.

1420 STREPSIADES: But you won't find, anywhere, a law that allows
    this to be done to a *father*!

PHEIDIPPIDES: So what? Every law must have been made at
    some time, and made by a human being like you or me, who
    used argument to persuade his contemporaries. Why should
    I be debarred from making another, new law for the future,

saying that sons may also beat their fathers? We won't seek 1425
reparations for all the times we were beaten before this law
came into force; we'll wipe them off the slate. Consider,
again, the animal kingdom – cockerels, for example – where
offspring *fight* their fathers. And what difference is there
between them and us, except that they don't move resolutions
in assemblies?

STREPSIADES: Well, if you're so keen on the life of a cockerel, 1430
why don't you go the whole way and eat manure and sleep
on a perch?

PHEIDIPPIDES: It's not the same thing, silly. Not according to
Socrates it isn't.

STREPSIADES: Well, in that case you'd better not hit me, because
if you do, you'll live to regret it.

PHEIDIPPIDES: Oh, why?

STREPSIADES: Because, just as I have the right to chastise you,
so you will have the right to chastise your son, if you have 1435
one –

PHEIDIPPIDES: And what if I *don't* have one? Then I'll *never*
be able to get my own back for the beatings I got from you, 1436
and *you'll* be laughing all over your dead face![147] And here's 1440
another point too for you to consider.

STREPSIADES: No more, please – they'll be the death of me.

PHEIDIPPIDES: Oh, I don't know. This experience you've had
may prove less bad for you than you think.

STREPSIADES: Why, what good could this behaviour of yours
possibly do me?

PHEIDIPPIDES: Easy. I'll beat up mum too.

STREPSIADES: *What?!* This is really too much!

PHEIDIPPIDES: Suppose I prove to you, with the help of my
trusty Wrongful Argument, that it's right and proper to beat 1445
one's mother?

STREPSIADES: If you do, you're very welcome to throw yourself
off the Acropolis.[148] And you can take Socrates and that 1450
precious Argument with you. [*To the Chorus*] Clouds, this is
your fault. I put my whole fate in your hands, and this is what
you've done to me.

LEADER:
    No, not our fault; you brought it on yourself –
1455   You turned[149] yourself to evil crookery.

STREPSIADES: But why didn't you tell me at the time? I'm an
    old man, and a countryman too; why did you have to lead me
    on?

LEADER:
    We do the same to anyone that we
    Perceive to be in love with wickedness:
1460   We cast him into misery, so he
    May learn that it is right to fear the gods.

STREPSIADES: Ah, holy Clouds, that's harsh – but you're right:
    I shouldn't have tried to cheat my creditors out of their money.
    [To Pheidippides] My dear, dear son – come with me and
1465   let's murder that villain Chaerephon[150] and Socrates for the
    way they swindled both of us.
PHEIDIPPIDES: No, no! I couldn't harm my teachers!
STREPSIADES: Aye, aye! Revere the great Paternal Zeus!
PHEIDIPPIDES: Paternal Zeus indeed! How out of date you
1470   are! Do you mean you think Zeus exists?
STREPSIADES: He does.
PHEIDIPPIDES: No, he doesn't, he doesn't! 'Vortex is king now;
    he's driven Zeus from power.'
STREPSIADES: No, he hasn't. I only believed that because of this
    image here[151] [pointing to a whirlpool-shaped cup standing on
    a pillar in front of the Thinkery]. How stupid could I be, to
    take a piece of earthenware like you for a god!
1475 PHEIDIPPIDES: If you want to yammer to yourself, you can do
    it on your own. [He goes inside.][152]
STREPSIADES: How mad, how insane I was, to let Socrates
    persuade me to discard the gods! [Addressing the image of
    Hermes on a pillar in front of his house] Dear Hermes, don't
1480   be cross with me, don't destroy me. Have pity on me, if a set
    of clever windbags made me take leave of my senses for a
    time. Give me some advice. Should I launch a prosecution

against them,[153] or what do you think? [*He pauses for a reply – and fancies he can see the image moving its head to signify 'no'.*] You're right. I shouldn't bother cooking up lawsuits – I should go right away and set this school for slick talkers on fire. [*Calling into his house*] Xanthias, come here, and bring a ladder and a mattock with you! [*His slave* XANTHIAS *comes out, carrying the items requested.*] Now get up on the roof of that Thinkery and hack it down, if you love your master, until you've brought the whole house down on them! [XANTHIAS *climbs up the ladder and sets to work.*] And someone bring me a lighted torch. I'm going to make this lot pay for what they've done; it'll take more than big talk to save them this time![154]   1485 1490

[*Another* SLAVE *gives him a torch. By now there is a large hole in the roof; many tiles must have fallen inside the building.*]

A STUDENT [*within*]: Help, help!

[XANTHIAS *comes down, passing the mattock to* STREPSI- ADES, *who, with the torch in his other hand, climbs up the ladder.*]

STREPSIADES: Do your job, torch; let's light things up![155] [*He throws the torch into the building, and a fire is soon blazing; meanwhile* STREPSIADES *hacks away at the rafters with the mattock. Several* STUDENTS *rush out of the front door, and see him above them.*]

STUDENT: Hey, you, what are you doing there?   1495

STREPSIADES: Doing? Chopping logic with your rafters, of course.

[CHAEREPHON *appears at an upper window. He has a deathly pale face, with large eyes and the ears of a bat.*]

CHAEREPHON: Help, who's set our house on fire?

STREPSIADES: Remember the last cloak you stole? That's who.

CHAEREPHON: You'll kill us, you'll kill us!

STREPSIADES: That's just what I want to do – if my mattock doesn't fail me, and if I don't fall off and break my neck first.   1500

SOCRATES [*coming out as smoke billows through the door*]: You there on the roof, what are you doing?

STREPSIADES: 'I am walking upon air and attacking the mystery of the sun.'[156]

SOCRATES [*coughing*]: Help, I'm going to suffocate!

1505 CHAEREPHON [*still at his window, seemingly trapped*]: Help, I'm going to be burnt alive! [*He climbs through the window and jumps – straight on to Socrates, who is knocked flat.*]

STREPSIADES [*descending the ladder, while* SOCRATES *and* CHAEREPHON *disengage themselves from each other and scramble to their feet*]: What did you expect, the way you wantonly insulted the gods and scrutinized the back side[157] of the Moon? [*To his slaves, as* SOCRATES, CHAEREPHON *and the* STUDENTS *take to flight*] Chase them, stone them, hit them, for all their crimes! Remember, they wronged the gods!
[STREPSIADES *and the* SLAVES *pursue Socrates and Co., the* SLAVES *hurling some stones after them. When both pursued and pursuers have disappeared, the* LEADER *turns to her colleagues.*]

LEADER:

1510   Lead the way out: we've done, I think I'd say,
          Sufficient choral service for today.

LYSISTRATA

Preface to *Lysistrata*

The Acharnians was an appeal for peace. *Peace*, produced four years later in 421 BC, was a celebration of peace: negotiations with Sparta were nearing completion, and the Peace of Nicias was concluded and sworn only a few days after the performance of the play. *Lysistrata* is the third and last of Aristophanes' 'peace plays' that we possess; it has much in common with the other two, but its spirit is different from either of them. It is a dream about peace, conceived at a time when Athens was going through the most desperate crisis she had known since the Persian War.

Late in 413 news had reached Athens of the total destruction of her expeditionary force in Sicily. At one blow the Athenians found themselves with virtually no navy and, it seemed, with virtually no hope. Spartan land forces had already occupied the strong point of Decelea in Attica; Spartan naval forces might at any moment choose to attack the Peiraeus; many of Athens' subject allies seized the opportunity of changing sides, and Persian provincial governors competed with each other for the honour of bringing back under the Great King's rule the Greeks of Asia Minor who had revolted from his grandfather Xerxes nearly seventy years before, now that the power of Athens, which had dominated and protected them for so long, seemed at last to be finally crumbling.

But, as so often before, swift Athenian action mitigated disaster while Spartan caution squandered the chance of victory. The feared stroke at the Athenian jugular never came, and meanwhile Athens was able to build a new navy, making use of the special reserve fund that had been set aside twenty years before and kept in one of the temples on the Acropolis. In addition a special advisory board of ten *probouloi* was established, with the power to make policy proposals and convene the Council and Assembly; this represented, though only to a limited extent, a break with democratic principle as Athenians understood it, for unlike most magistrates (who were chosen by lot for one year) the *probouloi* were chosen by election and were apparently to hold office indefinitely. They were also a distinctly elderly group: of the two whose names we know, one (the poet Sophocles) was in his mid-eighties, while the other (Hagnon), once a close associate of Pericles, had played little part in public life since Pericles' death in 429. The senile and ineffective *proboulos* in our play may to some extent indicate the public image of this board early in the second (and last) year of its existence.

Lysistrata was produced early in 411, probably at the Lenaea. The new Athenian fleet, based at Samos, had been campaigning in the Aegean for a year, its successes and failures about equally balanced; on the other side there was frequent word of negotiations between Sparta and Persia, though these had not yet borne fruit in an actual alliance. Meanwhile the mercurial Alcibiades, now in exile both from Athens and from Sparta,[1] had come to the court of the Persian satrap Tissaphernes and was intriguing to secure his return to Athens by promising that he could bring Persia into the war on the Athenian side – though only at the price of far-reaching changes in the Athenian constitution. It may have been about the time of the Lenaea that a delegation from Samos, led by Peisander, came to Athens and began to spread this message among those whom they thought politically reliable – the beginning of a process that led, four or five months later, to the temporary overthrow of Athenian democracy. But even if this process had begun at the time when *Lysistrata* was produced, it does not appear that anything was publicly known about it. All that most Athenians could see was that the war was going on as usual and there seemed to be no way out of it – no way, that is, other than the unthinkable option of capitulation.

But comedy specializes in doing the impossible, and in *Lysistrata* fantasy supplies a way out. Even in fantasy, though, it is recognized that Athens cannot end the war on her own: in the play, the women of *all* the warring states have to co-operate in forcing peace upon the men, because they all perceive (as Trygaeus, the hero of *Peace*, had perceived ten years before) that the war is bringing ruin to the whole Greek people and benefiting no one except the Persians – who, it is suggested in both plays, may take advantage of Greek weakness and exhaustion, not only to re-annex the Greek communities of Asia, but even to repeat Xerxes' attempt to bring Greece itself into their empire.

That it was better to be at peace than at war, other things being equal, was a principle theoretically accepted by all Greeks; but other things, all too often, did not seem equal. It was not only that war sometimes appeared to be the only way to protect the honour or even the safety of a community: war also provided unequalled opportunities for the citizen to display courage, for the general to win prestige, for the politician to be able to claim that he had enhanced his city's glory and power. Women, it might be thought, were largely immune from these temptations. They did not fight, they did not compete for the prizes of politics, and whereas the worst that could happen to a man in war was a glorious death,[2] for a woman it could mean decades of misery as a bereaved wife or mother, or even the prospect of not having the chance to *become* a wife and mother in a society in which the unmarried woman had no role and no place.[3] If women perceived this, and if they could unite across the boundaries of the warring states, could they not, would they not, take drastic steps to bring this madness to an end and impose a sensible compromise peace? In this play, this is exactly what they do.

We today find it easy to understand how it might be imagined that a concerted, solid sexual boycott on the part of women could force the men affected to abandon a policy to which these women objected; indeed from time to time one hears of such boycotts actually being threatened in this or that locality, and occasionally the threat is carried out. This would not be the mindset of Aristophanes' essentially male audience. For one thing, the plot requires us to assume that consensual marital sex was the *only* kind of sex available to an Athenian male, or at least the only kind that would give him worthwhile satisfaction; well-known alternatives are simply ignored.[4] For another, it also requires us to assume that women are, or can be persuaded to be, better able than men to endure sexual deprivation – and it was an article of faith with virtually all Greek males (and in comedy in particular, it was normally axiomatic) that the reverse was the case. That Lysistrata's scheme succeeds can thus be explained, in the average spectator's eyes, only by divine support. Aphrodite, the goddess of the sexual process, ensures that the men are quickly brought to the last stage of physical desperation, while the virgin Athena, goddess of the Acropolis where most of the action is set and also a major figure of Spartan cult, through her agent Lysistrata strengthens the women to endure abstention for the time necessary for the scheme to succeed. Nor, indeed, do they rely on the sexual boycott alone: equally important, especially in the first half of the play, is the actual occupation of the Acropolis by the women, which deprives the male Athenian state of access to the money without which it cannot maintain or operate its navy.

Lysistrata (whose name means 'Liquidator of Armies') has a very close connection with Athena; so close that it has been suggested that by the end of the play the two are virtually identified.[5] It has been pointed out that at this time the priestess of Athena Polias (Athena the City- or Acropolis-goddess) – the most important, and the most publicly visible, woman in Athens – bore the very similar name Lysimache ('Liquidator of Battles'), and that Lysistrata is actually made to say (line 554) that if she and her followers are successful they will be known throughout Greece as Lysimaches.[6] It would be a little misleading to claim that the character of Lysistrata represents the priestess Lysimache in the sense, for example, in which the character Paphlagon in *The Knights* represents Cleon; what we can say is that Aristophanes has given her a similar name as part of a process of building a strong association between her, the Acropolis and Athena, with the aim of making the course and outcome of the play seem less like an insubordinate rebellion by women against the lawful authority of the male, and more like the righteous

effectuation of the will of her who was 'our Protectress ...
Athens' own goddess'[7] – but also, as she had shown in the
Trojan and Persian wars,[8] the protectress of Greece as a whole
against enemies to the east.

But in the end, the play remains a dream. Its own script,
indeed, admits as much, when the Chorus offer loans of money
(at first misleadingly spoken of as if they were gifts) with the
promise that, *if ever* peace comes, the loan need not be repaid
(lines 1055–7). In the real world, the Athenian people were
soon, for lack of any apparent alternative, accepting Peisander's
promise of a Persian alliance (not knowing that neither he nor
Alcibiades was in any position to deliver it, if they ever had
been) on the understanding that it would involve 'some
modification of the existing democratic system' – an expression
which deserves a high place in any catalogue of political euphem-
isms. No one could have imagined then what the situation
would be within another year: democracy first abolished and
then restored; Alcibiades in command of the Athenian fleet; and
the Spartans, after two heavy naval defeats, themselves offering
terms of peace – and having them turned down.

NOTES

1. When serving as one of the commanders of the Sicilian expedition
in 415, he had been arrested on charges of sacrilege, escaped, and
defected to Sparta; in 412, however, he had to defect again when
allegations were made (all too plausible in view of his long-standing
reputation) of an affair between him and the wife of the Spartan king
Agis.
2. We hear very little in antiquity about that all too familiar product
of modern war, the disabled survivor; given the primitive state of
medicine and especially of hygiene, it is likely that few of the seriously
wounded would come home alive.
3. The plight of the unmarried forms the climax of Lysistrata's argument in the *agon* (lines 591–7). Similarly, when the orator Lysias
catalogues the crimes of the Thirty (the junta who ruled Athens in
404/3), the culminating atrocity is not that they put over a thousand
citizens to death without any proper trial, but that they 'prevented

many men's daughters from being given in marriage' (Lysias, *Against Eratosthenes* 21).

4. Elsewhere, for example, both in comedy and other texts, it is routinely assumed that a man's female slaves will be sexually available to him; in *Lysistrata* there is almost complete silence about the very existence of female slaves, even to the extent that when Cinesias comes on stage with a baby, he has a *male* slave to look after it.

5. It is striking that in the hymn sung in lines 1279–90, in which the Graces, Artemis, Apollo, Dionysus, Zeus and Hera are invited to join the dance, and credit is given to Aphrodite for bringing the peace, no mention is made of Athena, who in the play as a whole has been far more prominent than any other divinity. Is this because Athena is already present – as Lysistrata – and is, indeed, herself singing the hymn?

6. There had been a similar play on the priestess's name in *Peace* (line 992).

7. *The Clouds*, lines 601–2.

8. We now think of the former as 'mythical' and the latter as 'historical'; but for an Athenian both alike were part of his city's glorious past, and the Persian War had come to share space on public monuments and in official oratory (e.g. at state funerals) with the Trojan War, the Amazons' invasion of Attica, and other episodes of the heroic age.

Characters

LYSISTRATA
CALONICE   } *Athenian women*
MYRRHINE
LAMPITO, *a Spartan woman*
CHORUS OF OLD MEN
CHORUS OF OLD WOMEN *(including their leader*
STRATYLLIS*)*
MAGISTRATE, *one of the ten* probouloi
THREE OLD WOMEN *from the group which has seized*
the Acropolis
FOUR YOUNG WOMEN *from the group which has*
taken Lysistrata's oath
CINESIAS, *husband to Myrrhine*
BABY, *son of Cinesias and Myrrhine*
A SPARTAN HERALD
A SPARTAN PEACE DELEGATE
TWO ATHENIAN PEACE DELEGATES

Silent Characters

ATHENIAN WOMEN, *young and old*
SPARTAN WOMEN
ISMENIA, *a Theban woman*
A CORINTHIAN WOMAN
SCYTHAENA, *servant to Lysistrata*
TWO SLAVES *attending the Magistrate*
FOUR SCYTHIAN POLICEMEN
MANES, *slave to Cinesias*

ATHENIAN AND SPARTAN PEACE DELEGATES
SERVANTS *attending the Spartan delegates*
RECONCILIATION
DOORKEEPER

SCENE: *At first, in front of the houses of Lysistrata and Calonice, somewhere in Athens; later the background building will be reidentified as the west front of the Acropolis. It is early morning.*

[LYSISTRATA *comes out of her house. She looks right and left, with increasing impatience, to see if anyone is coming.*]

LYSISTRATA [*annoyed*]: Just think if it had been a Bacchic celebration they'd been asked to attend – or something in honour of Pan or Aphrodite! You wouldn't have been able to move for all the tambourines.[1] But as it is – not a woman here! [CALONICE's *door opens and she comes out to join* LYSISTRATA.] No, here's my neighbour coming out, at any rate. Good morning, Calonice.   5

CALONICE: Same to you, Lysistrata. What's bothering you, dear? Don't screw up your face like that. Knitted brows really don't suit you.

LYSISTRATA: Sorry, Calonice, but I'm furious. I'm really dis-   10
appointed in womankind. All our husbands think we're such clever villains –

CALONICE: Well, aren't we?

LYSISTRATA: And now look – I've called a meeting to discuss a very major matter, and they're all still fast asleep!   15

CALONICE: Don't worry, darling, they'll come. It's not so easy for a wife to get out of the house, you know. They'll all be hanging round their husbands, waking up the servants, putting the baby to sleep or washing and feeding it –

20 LYSISTRATA: But dammit, there are more important things than
that!

CALONICE: Tell me, Lysistrata dear, what is this thing that
you've called us women together to talk about? Is it a big
thing?

LYSISTRATA: A very big thing.

CALONICE: Big and meaty,[2] you mean?

LYSISTRATA: Very big and very meaty.

CALONICE: Then why on earth aren't they here?

25 LYSISTRATA: That's not what I meant – otherwise they certainly
would have arrived promptly! No, it's an idea that I've been
thinking over and tossing about through many sleepless
nights.

CALONICE: Something pretty flimsy, then, surely, if it's so easy
to toss about?

30 LYSISTRATA: Flimsy? Why, Calonice, we women have the salvation of all Greece in our hands.

CALONICE: In *our* hands? Then Greece hasn't much hope!

LYSISTRATA: The whole future of the country[3] rests with us.
Either the Peloponnesians are all going to be wiped out –

CALONICE: Good idea, by Zeus!

35 LYSISTRATA: – and the Boeotians totally destroyed –

CALONICE: Not all of them, please! Do spare the eels.[4]

LYSISTRATA: – and Athens – well, I won't say it, but you know
what it is that I'm not saying. But if all the women join

40 together – not just us, but the Peloponnesians and Boeotians
as well – then united we can save Greece.

CALONICE: But how can women achieve anything so grand or
noble? What do we ever do but sit at home looking pretty,

45 wearing saffron gowns and make-up and Cimberic shifts and
giant slippers?[5]

LYSISTRATA: But don't you see, that's exactly what I mean to
use to save Greece – those saffron gowns and scents and giant
slippers and rouges and see-through shifts.

CALONICE: How are you going to do that?

LYSISTRATA: I am going to bring it about that no man, for at

50 least a generation, will raise a spear against another –

CALONICE: I'm going to get a gown dyed saffron, by the Holy Twain![6]

LYSISTRATA: – nor take a shield in his hand –

CALONICE: I'll put on a see-through right away!

LYSISTRATA: – or even an icky little sword.

CALONICE: I'm going to buy a pair of giant slippers!

LYSISTRATA: *Now* do you think the women ought to have been here by now?

CALONICE: By Zeus, yes – they ought to have taken wing and flown here! 55

LYSISTRATA: No such luck, old girl; they are Athenian, after all, and can always be relied on to be late.[7] We haven't even had anyone yet from the Paralia, or any of the Salaminians.[8]

CALONICE: Well, I'm sure *they'll* have been *riding over* since the early hours! 60

LYSISTRATA: And the ones I was most expecting and counting on being here first – the Acharnians[9] – they haven't come either.

CALONICE: Well, I'm sure that Theogenes' wife at least will have been putting on all sail to get here.[10] [*Pointing offstage*] But look, here come some of them now. 65

LYSISTRATA [*looking in the opposite direction*]: Yes, and here are some more.

[MYRRHINE *and several other women arrive, some from the left, others from the right.* CALONICE *recoils from one group as if from a loathsome smell.*]

CALONICE: Uggh, where are this lot from?

LYSISTRATA: Stinking Trefoils.[11]

CALONICE: That's why I thought I'd bumped into one!

MYRRHINE [*who has taken a little time to get her breath back*]: We're not late, are we, Lysistrata? [*There is no reply.*] Well? Why aren't you saying anything? 70

LYSISTRATA: Myrrhine, I'm not best pleased with someone who arrives this late when such an important matter is to be discussed.

MYRRHINE: I'm sorry, I had trouble finding my waistband in the dark. If it's that important, don't wait for the rest, tell us about it now.

75 LYSISTRATA: No, let's wait just a moment. The Boeotian and
    Peloponnesian women should be here any time now.
    MYRRHINE: You're right. Ah, here comes Lampito!
       [*Enter* LAMPITO, *accompanied by* ISMENIA *the Theban
       and a* CORINTHIAN WOMAN, *and followed by several
       other* SPARTAN WOMEN. *All their garments are slit at the
       side.*]
    LYSISTRATA: Welcome, Lampito, my beloved Spartan friend!
80   Sweetheart, how absolutely ravishing you look! Such beauti-
       ful colour, such rippling muscles! Why, I bet you could
       throttle a bull.
    LAMPITO: So I cuid, I'm thinking, by the Twa Gods.[12] I'm in
       training – practise heel-to-bum jumps regularly. [*She takes a
       two-footed jump, touching both buttocks with her heels and
       landing on her feet.*]
    CALONICE[13] [*feeling Lampito's breasts*]: A very nice pair you've
       got here, too.
    LAMPITO [*indignantly*]: I'd thank ye not tae feel me over as if
       ye were just aboot tae sacrifice me.[14]
85 LYSISTRATA [*pointing to Ismenia*]: Where does this other girl
       come from?
    LAMPITO: By the Twa Gods, this is the Boeotian representative
       that's come tae ye.
    MYRRHINE [*looking inside her dress*]: Yes, she represents
       Boeotia very well, with those fine broad lowlands!
    CALONICE [*same business*]: And with all the herbage so care-
       fully plucked, too!
90 LYSISTRATA: And this other one?
    LAMPITO: A lass of noble line, by the Twa Gods, a Corinthian.
    CALONICE [*pointing to the Corinthian's well-padded belly and
       buttocks*]: She certainly has noble lines here and here!
    LAMPITO: Now who's the convener of this women's gathering?
    LYSISTRATA: I am.
95 LAMPITO: Then tell us what ye seek of us.
    MYRRHINE: Yes, dear, do tell us just what this important
       business is.
    LYSISTRATA: I will tell you. But before I do, I want to ask you
       just one little question.

MYRRHINE: By all means.

LYSISTRATA: The fathers of your children – don't you miss them when they're away at the war? I know that not one of you has a husband at home.[15]

CALONICE: Mine, my dear, has been away for five months, on the Thracian Coast, keeping an eye on our general[16] there.

MYRRHINE: And mine has been at Pylos for a full *seven* months.[17]

LAMPITO: And as for my mon, if he ever does turrn up at home, straight awa' he's fitted his shield on his arm and flown off agin.

CALONICE: Why, there isn't even anyone now to have an *affair* with – not even the ghost of one. Since the Milesians betrayed us, I haven't even seen one of those six-inch leather jobs which used to help us out when all else failed.

LYSISTRATA: Well then, if I found a way to do it, would you be prepared to join with me in putting a stop to the war?

CALONICE: By the Holy Twain, I would – even if I had to pawn this cloak of mine and drink up[18] the money before the end of the day!

MYRRHINE: And so would I – even if I had to cut myself in two, like a flatfish,[19] and give half of myself for the cause!

LAMPITO: And I too, if I had to climb tae the top of Mount Taÿ-getum,[20] so I cuid see the prospect of peace from the summit.

LYSISTRATA: Then I will tell you my plan: there's no point in keeping it back. Women, if we want to force the men to make peace, we must renounce – [*She hesitates.*]

MYRRHINE: Renounce what? Go on.

LYSISTRATA: Then you'll do it?

MYRRHINE: At the cost of our lives, if need be. [*All indicate enthusiastic agreement.*]

LYSISTRATA: Very well then. We must renounce – sex. [*Strong murmurs of disapproval, gestures of dissent, etc. Several of the company seem on the point of leaving.*] Why are you turning away from me? Where are you going? What does all this pursing of lips and tossing of heads mean? You're all going pale – I can see tears! Will you do it or won't you? Answer me!

CALONICE: I won't do it. Just let the war go on.

130   MYRRHINE: Nor will I. Just let the war go on.

LYSISTRATA: Excuse me, Mrs Flatfish, weren't you offering to cut yourself in half a moment ago?

MYRRHINE: That, or walk through fire, or anything else you
135   want – but renounce sex, never! Lysistrata, darling, there's just nothing like it!

LYSISTRATA [to Calonice]: How about you?

CALONICE: I'd rather walk through fire too!

LYSISTRATA: I didn't realize that we women were such a total lot of nymphos. The tragic poets are right about us after all:
140   shag, calve and dispose of, that's the way we live.[21] My Spartan friend, will *you* join me? Even if it's just the two of us, we might yet succeed.

LAMPITO: Weel, by the Twa Gods, it's a sair thing for a woman tae sleep alone withoot the Big Red One for company – but still I'll say aye, for we must have peace.

145   LYSISTRATA [embracing her]: Oh, Lampito darling, you're the only real woman[22] here!

MYRRHINE: But look, suppose we did renounce – what you said – which may heaven forbid – but if we did, how would that help to end the war?

LYSISTRATA: How? Well, just imagine. We're at home, beauti-
150   fully made up, and we walk around the house wearing sheer lawn shifts and nothing else; the men are all horny and can't wait to leap on us; and we keep our distance and refuse to come to them – then they'll make peace soon enough, you'll see.

155   LAMPITO: Didn't Menelaus drop his sword, I'm thinking, when he got but a wee glimpse of Helen's twa wee apples?[23]

MYRRHINE: But look, what if they just ignore us?

LYSISTRATA: In the words of Pherecrates[24] – you can always fall back on a dead dog.[25]

MYRRHINE: Those imitation things are sheer crap. Anyway,
160   what if they take us and drag us into the bedroom by force?

LYSISTRATA: Cling to the door.

MYRRHINE: And if they beat us, what then?[26]

LYSISTRATA: Just make yourself frigid. There's no pleasure in

it if they have to use force. Make life a misery for them, and
they'll give up trying soon enough. No man is ever going   165
to get satisfaction if the woman doesn't choose that he
should.

MYRRHINE: Well – if you both really think it's a good idea –
then we agree. [*The others indicate assent.*]

LAMPITO: Guid, then we'll see that our men mak peace and
keep it faithfully. But this Athenian riff-raff [*indicating the*   170
audience] – how will ye ever induce *them* tae see sense?

LYSISTRATA: We will, you'll see.

LAMPITO: Not sae lang as their warrships have feet[27] and they
have that bottomless fund o' money in Athena's temple.

LYSISTRATA: Oh, don't think we haven't thought about that!   175
We're going to occupy the Acropolis today. While we take
care of our side of things, all the older women have been
instructed to seize the Acropolis under pretence of going to
make sacrifices.

LAMPITO: A guid notion; it soonds as if it will worrk.   180

LYSISTRATA: Well then, Lampito, why don't we well and truly
confirm the whole thing now by taking an oath?

LAMPITO: Pit the aith to us and we'll sweir.

LYSISTRATA: Well spoken. [*Calling into the house*] Scythaena!
[*A* SLAVE-GIRL *comes outside; she is carrying a large round
wine-bowl. She stares open-eyed about her.*] What are you
staring at? Put that shield face down in front of us. [*The*   185
SLAVE-GIRL *lays the bowl on the ground.*] Now someone
give me the limbs of the sacrificial victim.[28]

MYRRHINE: Lysistrata, what sort of oath is this you're giving
us to take?

LYSISTRATA: Why, the one that Aeschylus talks about somewhere[29] – filling a shield with sheep's blood.

MYRRHINE: But Lysistrata, you can't take a peace oath over a   190
shield!

LYSISTRATA: What do you suggest, then?

MYRRHINE: Suppose we got a white stallion[30] and cut it up?

LYSISTRATA: White stallion indeed!

MYRRHINE: Well, how *are* we going to take the oath, then?

CALONICE: I've got an idea, if you like. Stand a large black cup   195 on the ground, pour in the blood of some Thasos grapes, and swear – to put no water in the cup.

LAMPITO: Och aye, that's the kind of aith I like!

LYSISTRATA [*to Scythaena*]: A cup and a wine-jar from inside, please.

[SCYTHAENA *takes her bowl inside and returns with a cup and jar, both of enormous size. The women crowd around.*]

200   MYRRHINE: My dears, isn't it a whopper?

CALONICE [*picking up the cup*]: Cheers you up even to touch it!

LYSISTRATA: Put the cup down [CALONICE *does so*] and take hold of the sacrificial victim.[31] [*She holds up the jar; all the women lay a hand on it.*] O mighty Goddess of Persuasion, and thou, O Lady of the Loving Cup, accept this sacrifice and look with favour on womankind. [*She pours wine from the jar into the cup.*]

205   MYRRHINE: What lovely dark blood! And how well it flows![32]

LAMPITO: And how sweet it smells forby, by Castor!

CALONICE [*trying to push Myrrhine and Lampito aside*]: Let me take the oath first!

MYRRHINE: Not unless you draw the first lot, you don't!

LYSISTRATA: Lampito and all of you, take hold of the cup. [*All
210   do so.*] One of you repeat the oath after me, and then at the end everyone will confirm that they share in it. I will not allow either lover or husband –

MYRRHINE: I will not allow either lover or husband –

LYSISTRATA: – to approach me in a state of erection. [MYRRHINE *hesitates.*] Go on!

215   MYRRHINE: – to approach me in – a state of – erection – help, Lysistrata, my knees are giving way! [*She nearly faints, but recovers herself.*]

LYSISTRATA: And I will live at home in unsullied chastity –

MYRRHINE: And I will live at home in unsullied chastity –

LYSISTRATA: – wearing my saffron gown and my sexiest make-up –

220   MYRRHINE: – wearing my saffron gown and my sexiest make-up –

LYSISTRATA: – to inflame my husband's ardour.

MYRRHINE: – to inflame my husband's ardour.

LYSISTRATA: But I will never willingly yield myself to him.

MYRRHINE: But I will never willingly yield myself to him.

LYSISTRATA: And should he rape me by force against my will –   225

MYRRHINE: And should he rape me by force against my will –

LYSISTRATA: – I will submit passively and will not thrust back.

MYRRHINE: – I will submit passively and will not thrust back.

LYSISTRATA: I will not raise my slippers towards the ceiling.

MYRRHINE: I will not raise my slippers towards the ceiling.   230

LYSISTRATA: I will not adopt the lioness-on-a-cheesegrater position.[33]

MYRRHINE: I will not adopt the lioness-on-a-cheesegrater position.

LYSISTRATA: If I abide by this oath, may I drink from this cup.

MYRRHINE: If I abide by this oath, may I drink from this cup.

LYSISTRATA: But if I break it, may the cup be filled with water.   235

MYRRHINE: But if I break it, may the cup be filled with water.

LYSISTRATA [to the others]: Do you all join in swearing this oath?

ALL: We do.

LYSISTRATA: Now the sacrifice must be wholly consumed.[34]
[She is about to drink from the cup.]

CALONICE [interposing]: Not all of it, my friend – let's share it, as friends should.

   [Before LYSISTRATA can drink from the cup and pass it round, a shout of triumph is heard backstage.]

LAMPITO: What was that?   240

LYSISTRATA: What I said we were going to do. The Citadel of Athena is now in the women's hands.[35] Well then, Lampito, you'd better go and see to your side of the business at home, but your friends will have to stay here with us as hostages.
[LAMPITO departs; ISMENIA, the CORINTHIAN and the other SPARTAN WOMEN remain.] Now we'll go up on to the Acro-   245
polis, join the others, and make sure the doors are barred.

MYRRHINE: Won't the men be coming soon to try and take the place back?

LYSISTRATA: Let them; they won't bother me. They can threaten

250 what they like – even try to set fire to the place – they won't
make us open the gates except on our own terms.

MYRRHINE: No, by Aphrodite, they won't. We must show that
it's not for nothing that people say 'Damn and blast, but
there's no getting the better of a woman!'

[*All the* WOMEN *retire into the Acropolis, and the doors
are closed. After a short interval there appear, from the
wings, the* CHORUS OF OLD MEN. *They are advancing
slowly and with difficulty, each carrying two olive-wood
logs, a vine-torch and a pot containing live coals.*]

MEN'S LEADER:
Keep moving, Draces, even if your shoulder
255 Aches with the weight of that green olive-wood!
MEN:
Incredible! Impossible!
260   Our women, if you please!
We've kept and fed within our homes
A pestilent disease!

They've seized our own Acropolis,[36]
With bars they've shut the gate!
They hold the image of the Maid,[37]
265   Protectress of our state!

Come on and let us hurry there,
Set down these logs around,
Burn out the whole conspiracy
From Pallas' holy ground!

270 With one accord we vote that all
Have forfeited their life,
And first in the indictment-roll
Stands Lycon's wicked wife![38]

MEN'S LEADER:
What, shall they mock us from the sacred height
Whence we dislodged the great Cleomenes?[39]

MEN:
> He seized our citadel,
>> But didn't go scot-free;   275
> He left with just a cloak, for he'd
>> Giv'n up his arms to me.

> He'd gone in breathing fire,
>> But when he left the place
> He hadn't washed for six whole years
>> And had hair all over his face.   280

> We slept before the gates,
>> A doughty war machine;
> We all of us laid siege to him
>> In ranks of seventeen.

> Now the enemies of the gods
>> And of Euripides[40]
> Have seized the Acropolis and think
>> They can beat us to our knees.

> They never will succeed,
>> For we will take them on,
> And beat them, or our trophy should   285
>> Not stand at Marathon.[41]

[As they struggle to cover the last few yards to their final position in front of the gates]
> I doubt if I have any hope
> Of humping these logs up the slope.
>> I'm feeling all wonky,
>> I haven't a donkey,   290
> But somehow I've still got to cope.
> And I'd better make sure that I've got
> Some fire still alive in my pot –
>> It would really be sad
>> If I thought that I had
> And then found in the end that I'd not.

[*They blow on the coals, which flare up, sending smoke into their faces*]

295   Phew,
          This smoke is so stinging and hot!

          I think a mad dog in disguise
          Has jumped up and bitten my eyes!
               It's a villainous flame
300   Which I'm tempted to name
          'The pig that's been biting the styes'.[42]
          But come, let's go up to give aid
          To our Goddess, the glorious Maid;
               For now is the hour
               To do all in our power –
          Help's useless if help is delayed.
          [*They blow on the coals, as before, with the same result*]
305   Phew,
          This smoke fairly has me dismayed!

MEN'S LEADER: Ah, that's woken the old flame up all right, the
          gods be praised! Now, suppose we put the logs down here,
          put the vine-torch into the pot, set it alight, and then go for
310   the door like a battering-ram? We'll call on them to let the
          bars down, and if they refuse, then we'll set fire to the doors
          and smoke them out. [*All indicate agreement.*] Right, let's put
          this stuff down first. [*They bend to set down the logs, only to
          get the smoke from the pots in their faces again.*] Ugh, this
          smoke! Can any of the generals in Samos come and help?
          [*Eventually he and the others manage to lay down the logs
          and stand upright.*] Well, at least these things aren't crushing
315   my backbone any longer. It's up to you now, pot; get your
          coal aflame, so that I can at least have a lighted torch to use.
          [*Facing left, in what would be the direction of the temple of
          Athena Nike, goddess of Victory*] Our Lady of Victory, be
          with us now, and may we set up a trophy to thee when we
          have defeated the audacious action that these women have
          taken in thy holy Acropolis.
          [*The* MEN *crouch over their pots, trying, without much*

immediate success, to get their torches lit. Meanwhile the
CHORUS OF OLD WOMEN, *led by* STRATYLLIS, *are heard*
approaching from the opposite direction.]

STRATYLLIS [*off*]:
  I think I see a smoky shimmer rising.
  They've lit a fire, my friends; we've got to hurry!   320
WOMEN [*off, approaching*]:
      Come swiftly, fly, before
        Our comrades burn to ash
      In wind-fanned flames stirred up
        By old men foul and rash!   325

      But have we come too late?
        It's early in the day,
      But at the fountain-house
        We suffered great delay.

      The crowd, the jostling crush,
        As slaves with bold tattoos[43]   330
      Knock pitchers right and left
        To reach the front of queues –

    But we filled ours, and come to the defence
    Of our beleaguered fellow-citizens!

[*The* WOMEN *now come into view, carrying pitchers of*
water on their heads.]
      We hear some old half-wits   335
        Are coming (blast their eyes!)
      With logs upon their backs
        Of quite enormous size,

      And mouth the direst threats –
        To turn our friends to coal.   340
[*Raising arms in prayer towards the Acropolis*]
      O Maid, let this not be –
        They must achieve their goal,

Save Athens and all Greece
From lunacy and war,
For that, O Maid, is what
They've seized your temple for.

345

Child of the Lake,[44] if fire should gird them round,
Join our brigade until the flames are drowned!

[STRATYLLIS, *leading the women, almost collides with the*
MEN'S LEADER, *who has at last got his torch lit and is*
preparing to lead his colleagues in an attack on the doors.]

350 STRATYLLIS [*to the women*]: Hold it! What have we got here?
A gang of male scum, that's what! No man who had any
decency, or any respect for the gods, would behave like this!

MEN'S LEADER: Well, did you ever – ! A swarm of women
reinforcements *outside* the walls, as well!

STRATYLLIS: What are you so frightened for? Are there *that*
355 many of us? Mind you, there's thousands more where we've
come from!

MEN'S LEADER [*to a comrade next to him*]: Phaedrias, are we
going to let them go on jabbering like this? Shouldn't we be
breaking our logs on their backs now?

STRATYLLIS [*to her followers*]: Let's put down our pitchers
too. We don't want to be encumbered if it should come to a
fight.

360 MEN'S LEADER [*raising his fist*]: Someone ought to give them a
Bupalus[45] or two on the jaw – that might shut them up for a
bit!

STRATYLLIS [*presenting her cheek to be struck*]: All right; there
you are; hit me; I won't shy away. Only, if you do, no *other*
bitch will ever grab your bollocks again![46]

MEN'S LEADER: If you don't keep quiet, you old crone, I'll flay
you out of your skin!

365 STRATYLLIS: If you so much as touch Stratyllis with the tip of
your finger –

MEN'S LEADER: If I bash you up with both fists, what's your
terrifying threat?

STRATYLLIS: I'll tear out your lungs and guts with my teeth!

MEN'S LEADER [*backing off; to his comrades*]: Euripides was
right! 'There is no beast so shameless as a woman!'[47]

STRATYLLIS: Rhodippe! Everybody! Take up – *jars*! [*All pick*   370
up their pitchers again.]

MEN'S LEADER: What have you brought water here for, you
goddamned scum?

STRATYLLIS: Well, how about *you*, you old corpse? What's that
torch for? Your funeral pyre?

MEN'S LEADER: No – for your friends in there, for *their* funeral
pyre.

STRATYLLIS: And *we've* got the water here to put your pyre
out!

MEN'S LEADER: Put our pyre out?   375

STRATYLLIS: Just you wait and see!

MEN'S LEADER: I'm just wondering whether to give *you* a light
roasting right away.

STRATYLLIS: If you've got some soap, I'll be happy to give you
a bath!

MEN'S LEADER: A *bath*, you rotting relic?

STRATYLLIS: A wedding bath,[48] if you like.

MEN'S LEADER: Of all the barefaced –

STRATYLLIS: I'm not a slave, you know.

MEN'S LEADER: I'll shut your big mouth!   380

STRATYLLIS: Now then, now then, you're not sitting on a jury
now.[49]

MEN'S LEADER [*to Phaedrias, as both brandish their torches*]:
Go on, set her hair on fire!

STRATYLLIS: Water, do your duty! [*All the* WOMEN *fling water*
over the men.]

MEN:
        Help, I'm soaking!

WOMEN [*with mock concern*]:
                            Was it hot? [*They throw more*
        water.]

MEN:
        No, it certainly was not!
        Stop it, will you? Let me go!

WOMEN:
>We're watering you to make you grow.

MEN:

385
>Make us grow? With all this shivering
>We're already dry and withering!

WOMEN [*pointing to the men's pots*]:
>Well, you've got a handy fire –
>Warm up to your heart's desire!

[*At this point there unexpectedly enters an elderly* MAGIS-
TRATE *of severe appearance, wearing a full-length outer
garment, attended by two* SLAVES *carrying crowbars and
four* SCYTHIAN POLICEMEN *equipped with bows, quivers
and whips. The* WOMEN *put down their empty pitchers
and await developments. The* MAGISTRATE *at first takes
no notice either of them or of the men.*]

MAGISTRATE: Apparently it's the same old story – the unbridled
licentiousness of the female sex displaying itself. All their
banging of drums and shouting in honour of that Sabazius
390   god, and singing to Adonis on the roofs of houses.[50] I remember once in the Assembly – Demostratus, curse him, was
saying we ought to let the Sicilian expedition sail, and this
woman, dancing on the roof, she cried, 'O woe for Adonis!'[51]
Then Demostratus went on to say we should enlist some
395   heavy infantry from Zacynthus, and the woman on the roof
– she'd had a bit to drink, I fancy – she goes, 'Mourn for
Adonis!' But that dirty villain from the Ragers clan[52] just
blustered on regardless. That's the sort of impudent behaviour
you get from women.

MEN'S LEADER [*approaching Magistrate*]: Wait till you hear
400   what *this* lot have done. We have been brutally assaulted, and
what is more, we have been given an unsolicited cold bath
out of those pitchers, so that all our clothes are wringing wet
as if we were incontinent!

MAGISTRATE: By Poseidon of the Briny, can you be surprised?
405   Look at the way we pander to women's vices – we positively
teach them to be wicked. That's why we get this sort of
conspiracy. When we go to the shops, for example, and say

to the goldsmith: 'Goldsmith, that necklace you mended for my wife – she was dancing last night and the pin[53] slipped out of the hole. Now I've got to go across to Salamis; so if you've got time, could you go over to my place tonight and fit a pin in her hole, please?' Or perhaps we go into a shoemaker's, a great strapping young fellow with a great strapping organ, and we say, 'Shoemaker, the strap on my wife's sandal is hurting her little pinkie[54] – it's rather tender, you know. Could you go over around lunchtime perhaps and loosen it up, make the opening a little wider?' That's what' led to things like this. Here am I, a member of the Advisory Board,[55] having found a source of supply for timber to make oars,[56] and now requiring the money to pay for it, and I come to the Acropolis and find these women have shut the door in my face! No good standing around, though. [*To the two slaves*] Let's have the crowbars, and we'll soon put a stop to this nonsense. [*The* SLAVES *are slow to respond.*] What are you gawping like that for, you fool? And you too? Daydreaming about wine-shops, eh? Let's get these bars under the gates and lever them up – you on that side, and I'll take a hand on this side.

[*Before the crowbars can be moved into position, the doors open and* LYSISTRATA *comes out.*]

LYSISTRATA: No need to use crowbars; I'm coming out of my own free will. What's the use of crowbars? It's not crowbars that we need, it's intelligence and common sense.

MAGISTRATE: You disgusting creature! Constable! [*One of the* POLICEMEN *steps forward.*] Take her and tie her hands behind her back.

LYSISTRATA: By Artemis, if he so much as touches me, I'll teach him a lesson, servant of the state though he is!

[*The* POLICEMAN *hesitates.*]

MAGISTRATE: Frightened, eh? Constable! [*A* SECOND POLICE-MAN *steps forward.*] Hold her tight and tie her up, both of you, and be quick about it.

[*Before they can do so, a ferocious-looking* OLD WOMAN *comes out of the Acropolis and belligerently confronts them.*]

FIRST OLD WOMAN: If you so much as lay a finger on her, by

440   Pandrosus,[57] I'll hit you so hard you'll shit all over the place!

MAGISTRATE: What language![58] Constable! [*A* THIRD POLICE-
MAN *comes forward.*] Tie this one up first, since she won't
hold her tongue.

[*Before he can do so, a* SECOND OLD WOMAN *comes out
of the Acropolis.*]

SECOND OLD WOMAN: By the Bringer of Light,[59] if you touch
her, you'll soon be nursing a black eye!

445   MAGISTRATE: What's all this? Constable! [*The* FOURTH
POLICEMAN *comes forward.*] Lay hold on her. I'm going to
put a stop to these sallies.[60]

STRATYLLIS [*intervening to confront Fourth Policeman*]: By the
Bull Goddess,[61] if you go near her, I'll tear out your hair till
you scream and scream!

450   MAGISTRATE: Heaven help me, I've no more archers! But we
mustn't let ourselves be worsted by women. Fall into line,
constables, and let's charge them.

[*The* POLICEMEN, *together with the* MAGISTRATE, *regroup
themselves in line, facing the women.*]

LYSISTRATA: If you do, by the Holy Twain, you'll find we've
got four whole companies of fully armed fighting women
inside there!

455   MAGISTRATE [*calling her bluff, as he thinks*]: Constables, twist
their arms behind them.

LYSISTRATA [*calling into the Acropolis, as the* POLICEMEN
advance on her and her comrades]: Come out, the reserve, at
the double! Come on, daughters of the porridge and vegetable
market! Come on, innkeepers, bakers and garlic-vendors! [*A
squad of tough* OLD WOMEN, *fully armed, come out of the
Acropolis. They divide into four groups, each of which sets
upon one of the policemen.*] Drag them down! Hit them! Beat

460   them up! Shout rude words in their faces! [*The* POLICEMEN
*are quickly brought down, punched and kicked, but manage
to scramble to their feet and take flight.*] Stop – withdraw –
no stripping the corpses![62]

[*The armed* WOMEN *retire into the Acropolis.*]

MAGISTRATE [*his hand to his head*]: My bowmen have been
utterly defeated!

LYSISTRATA: Well, what did you expect? Did you think you
were fighting slaves – or that women couldn't have any 465
stomach for a fight?

MAGISTRATE: They certainly do – any time a tavern-keeper tries
to cheat them!

MEN'S LEADER:
Our worthy magistrate, why waste your words
On these sub-human creatures? Don't forget,
They gave us all a bath when fully clothed, 470
And that without the benefit of soap!

STRATYLLIS:
If you resort to wanton violence,
You can't complain if you get hit right back!
We only want to stay demure at home
Doing no harm, disturbing not a twig –
But he who would provoke me should remember 475
That those who rifle wasps' nests will be stung!

MEN:
    Monsters, enough! Our patience now is gone.
  [*To the Magistrate*]
      Command them now to tell
Just *why* they're barricaded here upon 480
    Our hallowed citadel.

MEN'S LEADER:
Now question her, and don't give way, and test her every
    claim;
Meek submission on such issues would be cause for lasting 485
    shame.

MAGISTRATE [*to Lysistrata*]: Well, the first thing I want to
know is – what in Zeus' name do you mean by shutting and
barring the gates of our own Acropolis against us?

LYSISTRATA: We want to keep the money safe and stop you
from waging war.

MAGISTRATE: The war has nothing to do with money –

LYSISTRATA: Hasn't it? Why did Peisander, and all those 490
 other office-seekers, always keep stirring up trouble?[63] To get

more opportunities for stealing public funds, of course! Well, as far as that's concerned they can do what they like, *but* they're never going to get their hands on the money in there.

MAGISTRATE: Why, what are you going to do?

LYSISTRATA: Do? Why, we'll take charge of it.

MAGISTRATE: *You* in charge of state money?

495 LYSISTRATA: Well, what's so strange about that? We've always been in charge of all your housekeeping finances.

MAGISTRATE: But that's not the same thing.

LYSISTRATA: Why not?

MAGISTRATE: Because the money here is needed for the war!

LYSISTRATA: Ah, but you shouldn't be *at* war.

MAGISTRATE: How else can we keep the City safe?

LYSISTRATA: *We'll* see it's kept safe.

MAGISTRATE: *You!!!*

LYSISTRATA: Us.

MAGISTRATE: This is intolerable!

LYSISTRATA: We're going to save you, whether you like it or not.

MAGISTRATE: What an outrageous thing to say!

500 LYSISTRATA: Annoyed, are you? It's still got to be done!

MAGISTRATE: But, Demeter! It's against Nature!

LYSISTRATA [*very sweetly*]: We *must* see that you're safe, my dear sir.

MAGISTRATE: Even if I don't want you to?

LYSISTRATA: All the more if you don't!

MAGISTRATE: Anyway, how do *you* come to have taken an interest in matters of war and peace?

LYSISTRATA: We'll tell you.

MAGISTRATE [*on the brink of a violent outburst*]: You'd better or else!

LYSISTRATA: Listen, then – and try and keep those hands of yours under control.

505 MAGISTRATE: I can't – my anger is getting the better of me –

FIRST OLD WOMAN [*interrupting*]: If you don't, you'll be the one that suffers most!

MAGISTRATE: May those words fall on *your* head, you old croaker! [*To Lysistrata*] Go on.

LYSISTRATA: I will. Always till now we have controlled our feelings and uncomplainingly endured whatever you men did – and in any case you wouldn't let us say a word. But don't think we approved! We knew everything you were up to. 510 Many a time we'd hear at home about some major political blunder of yours, and then when you came home we'd be inwardly in great distress but we'd have to put on a smile and ask you: 'In the Assembly today, what did you decide to inscribe on the stone underneath the Peace Treaty?'[64] And what did my husband always say? 'Shut up and mind your 515 own business!' And I did.

STRATYLLIS: *I* wouldn't have done!

MAGISTRATE [*ignoring her; to Lysistrata*]: You'd have been for it if you hadn't!

LYSISTRATA: Exactly – so I kept quiet. But sure enough, next thing we knew you'd take an even sillier decision, and then we might go so far as to ask, 'Husband, why are you men persisting with this stupid policy?' Whereupon he'd glare at me and say 'Back to your spinning, woman, or you'll have a headache for 520 a month. "Let war be the care of the menfolk!"'[65]

MAGISTRATE: Quite right too, by Zeus.

LYSISTRATA: Right? That we should not be allowed to make the least little suggestion to you, no matter how much you mismanage your affairs? But *now* every time two men meet in the street, what do they say? 'Isn't there a *man* in the country?' And the answer comes, 'Not one'. That's why we 525 women got together and decided to unite and save Greece. What was the point of waiting any longer? So let's make a deal. You listen to us – and it'll be good advice we give – listen to us and keep quiet, like you made us do, and we'll set you to rights.

MAGISTRATE: *You* set *us* to rights? Insufferable! I'm not standing for this –

LYSISTRATA: Silence!

MAGISTRATE: You, damn you, a woman with a veil on her 530 head, order *me* to be silent? Gods, let me die!

LYSISTRATA: Well, if that's what's bothering you –

[*During the ensuing song* LYSISTRATA *removes her veil*

and puts it on the Magistrate's head, and the FIRST OLD
WOMAN *gives him her work-basket.*]

LYSISTRATA:
Just cover your head with this veiling of mine –
FIRST OLD WOMAN:
535   Take this basket –
LYSISTRATA:
                                    – And not one word more;
Hitch your robe up, chew beans,[66] and card wool all
        the day,
And *women* will deal with the war!

STRATYLLIS [*to the women's chorus*]:
Move forward from the pitchers – lend a hand
540   Of succour to our comrades' gallant stand!
WOMEN:
I'll dance for ever, never will I tire,
        To aid our champions here;
545   For they have courage, wisdom, charm and fire,
        And hold our City dear.

STRATYLLIS [*to Lysistrata*]:
Now, bravest of all mothers and all nettly grannies too,
550   To battle! Do not weaken, for the wind is fair for you.
LYSISTRATA: So long as Aphrodite of Cyprus[67] and her sweet
    son Eros breathe hot desire over our bosoms and our thighs,
    and so long as they cause our menfolk to suffer from long,
    hard, truncheon-shaped tumescences – then I believe that
    before long we will be known throughout Greece as the
    Liquidators of War.[68]
555 MAGISTRATE: Why, what will you do?
LYSISTRATA: Well, for one thing, we'll stop people going shop-
    ping in the Market Square in full armour, like lunatics.
FIRST OLD WOMAN: Well said, by Aphrodite!
LYSISTRATA: You see them every day – going round the veg-
    etable and pottery stalls armed to the teeth. You'd think they
    were Corybants![69]

MAGISTRATE: Of course; that's what a brave man *should* do.[70]

LYSISTRATA: But a man carrying a shield with a ferocious Gorgon on it – going and buying minnows at the fishmonger's! Isn't it ridiculous?   560

FIRST OLD WOMAN: Like that long-haired cavalry captain I saw, coming into the Square on horseback, buying porridge from an old stallholder and stowing it in his helmet! And there was a Thracian too – brandishing his leather shield and his javelin like King Tereus.[71] The woman on the fig stall fainted with fright, and he swallowed all her ripe figs!

MAGISTRATE: But the international situation at the moment is   565
in hopeless confusion. How do you propose to unravel it?

LYSISTRATA: It's very easy.

MAGISTRATE: Would you explain?

[LYSISTRATA *takes the work-basket which the* MAGISTRATE *has been holding, and uses its contents to illustrate her exposition.*]

LYSISTRATA: Well, consider how we deal with a tangled skein of wool. We take it like this, and with the help of our spindles we pull it gently, now in this direction, now in that, and it all unravels. That's how we'll unravel this war, if you'll let us, unpicking it by sending diplomatic missions, now in this   570
direction, now in that.

MAGISTRATE: How stupid can you get, thinking you can solve serious problems with wool and skeins and spindles?

LYSISTRATA: Actually, if *you* had any sense, you'd run the whole City entirely on the model of the way we deal with wool.

MAGISTRATE: How do you make that out?

LYSISTRATA: Imagine the citizen body is a raw fleece. You start by putting it in a bath and washing out the dung; then lay it   575
on a bed, beat out the villains with a stick and pick out the burrs. Then you have to deal with the cliques, who knot themselves together to get chosen for public office; you must card those out and pick off their heads. Then you card all the wool into the work-basket of Civic Goodwill – including   580
everyone, immigrants, friendly foreigners – yes, and even those who are in debt to the Treasury! Not only that. There are many other states which are colonies of Athens.[72] At the

585 moment these are lying around all over the place, like little flocks of wool. You should pick them up, bring them here, and put them all together in one great ball of wool – and from that you can weave the People a nice warm cloak to wear.

MAGISTRATE: Burrs – balls of wall – all this nonsense! What right have you women to talk like this? What have you ever done for the war effort?

LYSISTRATA: Done, curse you? We've contributed to it twice
590 over and more. For one thing, we've given you sons, and then had to send them off to fight.

MAGISTRATE: Enough, don't open old wounds.

LYSISTRATA: For another, we're in the prime of our lives, and how can we enjoy it, with our husbands always away on campaign and us left at home like widows? And quite apart from us married women, what about the unmarried ones who are slowly turning into old maids?

MAGISTRATE: Don't men grow old too?

595 LYSISTRATA: But it's not the same thing, is it? A man comes home – he may be old and grey – but he can get himself a young wife in no time. But a woman's not in bloom for long, and if she isn't taken quickly she won't be taken at all, and before long she's left sitting at home hoping to see some omen foretelling a happier future.

MAGISTRATE: But any man who can still get himself to stand erect –[73]

[*During the following song the* MAGISTRATE *is decked out as a corpse ready to be taken to the grave, the* WOMEN *putting on him various adornments which they themselves have been wearing.*]

LYSISTRATA:
    You should have been dead long ago!
600   There's a grave-plot all ready, you know.
        Buy a coffin – I'll bake
        You a nice honey-cake[74] –
    And here is a garland or so.

FIRST OLD WOMAN:
    Here's some ribbons – they'll make you look swell –

SECOND OLD WOMAN:
>   And here's a tiara as well –
LYSISTRATA:
>   So why do you wait?
>   You'll make Charon[75] late!   605
>   Last call for the next boat to Hell!

MAGISTRATE [*fuming*]: This is outrageous! I shall go at once
and show my colleagues just what these women have done to   610
me. [*Exit, with his* SLAVES.]
LYSISTRATA [*calling after him*]: What's your complaint? You
haven't been properly laid out? Don't worry; we'll be with
you early the day after tomorrow to make the post-funeral
offerings![76]

> [*She and the two* OLD WOMEN *go back into the Acropolis.
> By now the logs, fire-pots, pitchers, etc., have been removed
> from the performing area, and the two* CHORUSES *face
> each other across it.*]

MEN'S LEADER:
>   No time to laze; our freedom's now at risk;
>   Take off your cloaks, and let the dance be brisk!   615
>   [*The* MEN *remove their outer garments.*]
MEN:
>   There's more in this than meets the eye,
>   Or so it seems to me.
>   I smell the odour very strong
>   Of Hippias' tyranny![77]
>   These Spartan rogues are at their tricks   620
>   (Their agent's Cleisthenes[78]) –
>   It's them that's stirring up these dames
>   To steal our jury fees![79]   625

MEN'S LEADER:
>   Disgraceful! – women venturing to prate
>   Of war and arms and high affairs of state!
>   A pact with Spartans they would have us make –
>   And he who trusts a Spartan, trusts a snake![80]

630   This is an anti-democratic plot –
       And shall we yield to tyrants? No, we'll not!
       I'll be alert for anything they try;
       I'll do my shopping in full panoply.
       As once our Liberators did, so now
       'I'll bear my sword within a myrtle bough',
       And stand beside them, thus[81] –
           [*Striking an attitude, right leg thrust forward, right arm
           raised as if swinging back a sword*]
                                        – and, what is more,
635   Give this old bag a sock upon the jaw!
       [*He brandishes his fist at Stratyllis.*]

STRATYLLIS:
       If you do such a thing, we tell you plain,
       Your mum won't recognize your face again!
       Let's start by taking off our mantles too,
           [*The* WOMEN *do so*]
       And, citizens, address ourselves to you.
WOMEN [*addressing the audience*]:
           I shall give good advice to the City:
640   For my nurture, I owe her no less.
           I became, at the age of just seven,
               An Acropolis child priestess;[82]
           Then, after I'd served as a Grinder,[83]
               To Brauron, aged ten, I went down
645   As a Bear in the rites of the Foundress,
               And discarded my saffron-dyed gown;[84]
           And finally I was selected
               The ritual basket to bear,[85]
           With a string of dried figs for a necklace[86]
               And a face most surpassingly fair.

STRATYLLIS:
       See why I think I owe you good advice?
       And please don't look on me with prejudice:
       My gender has no bearing on the question
650   Whether I'm offering you a good suggestion.

I'm a full member of your civic club:
I give you *men*, that's how I pay my sub.
And what do *you* lot pay? Where's all the gold
Your fathers took from Persian foes of old?
You've squandered it, and live instead on tax[87] –
In paying which you're something worse than lax.
In fact, all thanks to you, our situation   655
Is that we're on the brink of liquidation!
What can you answer? Vex me any more,
And this raw-leather boot will sock *your* jaw!
    [*She raises her leg as if to kick the men's leader.*]

MEN:

    This sheer outrageous impudence
        Grows yet more aggravated!   660
    Why don't we act in self-defence?
        Or are we all castrated?

MEN'S LEADER:

Let's not be wrapped in fig-leaves[88] – let's be men
Who *smell* like men! Come on now, strip again!
    [*The* MEN *remove their tunics.*][89]

MEN:

    Come on, you Whitefeet, who of yore
    Against the tyrants went to war,[90]   665
        In days when we were men!
    It's time to shake off age, arouse
    The dormant strength our limbs still house,   670
        And be like youths again.

MEN'S LEADER:

If once we let these women get the semblance of a start,
Before we know, they'll be adept at every manly art.
They'll turn their hands to building ships, and then they'll
    make a bid
To fight our fleet and ram us, just like Artemisia did.[91]   675
And if to form a cavalry contingent they decide,

They'd soon be teaching *our* equestrian gentry how to ride!
For riding (of a certain kind) suits women to a T:
At the gallop they stay mounted and don't slip off easily.[92]
If you look at Micon's painting,[93] you will see the sort of
   scene –
The Amazons on horseback, fighting Athens' men, I mean.

680 I think that we should take them by the scruff o' the neck, I
   do,
And clap them in the stocks – and I will start by seizing *you*!
   [*He makes as if to seize Stratyllis, but she easily evades
   him.*]

WOMEN:
     If you ignite my wrath, I vow,
       By both the Holy Twain,
     I'll turn into a savage sow,
685   Tear out your hair,[94] and then hear how
       You scream and scream with pain!

STRATYLLIS:
     Let's smell like *women*, armed to teeth with rage!
     Let's take *our* strip-act to the second stage!
     [*The* WOMEN *remove their remaining garments.*][95]
WOMEN:
     The man who lays a hand on me
     Will never more eat celery[96]
690   Or beans – he won't be able.
     One word from you, and I will strike;
     I'll smash your eggs in rage, just like
695   The beetle in the fable.[97]

STRATYLLIS:
While my Theban friend Ismenia lives, and Spartan
   Lampito,
I'm not bothered in the slightest whether you complain or no.
You cannot stop us, though you pass your motions six times
   o'er:
You're loathed by all and sundry, and by the folk next door.

I had the girls round yesterday to share a sacred meal   700
For Hecate; our neighbour, who's a fine Boeotian eel –
I'm very fond of her – had been asked round,[98] but we were
    told
That, thanks to your decrees, we couldn't have her, hot or
    cold!
Will you ever give this passing of decrees up? Will you
    heck –
Unless we grab your leg and haul you off to break your   705
    neck!

    [*She makes as if to seize the Men's Leader by the leg; with
    some difficulty, he evades her grasp. At this the* MEN,
    *accepting defeat for the time being, retire down stage away
    from the Acropolis entrance, while the* WOMEN *move closer
    to the gates. Presently* LYSISTRATA *comes out of the gates,
    in some agitation, and paces anxiously about, until* STRA-
    TYLLIS *addresses her in tragic tones.*]

STRATYLLIS:
    O sovereign of this action and this plot,
    Why from thy fortress com'st thou grim-look'd out?
LYSISTRATA:
    'Tis women's fickle, cowardly thoughts and deeds
    That make me pace despondent to and fro.
WOMEN [*singing*]:
    What sayest thou, what sayest thou?   710
LYSISTRATA [*singing*]:
    'Tis true, ah, tis true!
STRATYLLIS:
    But what's amiss? Grudge not to tell thy friends.
LYSISTRATA:
    Silence boots not, and yet 'twere shame to speak.
STRATYLLIS:
    Hide not the ill that we are suffering from.
LYSISTRATA:
    Few words it takes to say: we need a fuck.   715
WOMEN [*singing*]:
    Ah, Zeus!

LYSISTRATA:
Why cry the name of Zeus? –
[*In her ordinary voice*] Anyway, that's the way it is. I just can't keep them to their vow of abstinence any longer;
720 they're deserting right and left. One I caught opening up a hole ... in the wall near Pan's Grotto; another was letting herself down on a pulley-cable;[99] another one yesterday[100] I pulled down by the hair when she was about to fly down to
725 Orsilochus' place on sparrow-back![101] And they invent every kind of excuse just to be allowed to go home. Here's one now. [*To First Woman, who has come out of the Acropolis swiftly and stealthily*] Hey, you, where do you think you're going?

FIRST WOMAN: I want to go home. I've got some fleeces there –
730 imported from Miletus – and the moths will be eating them up.

LYSISTRATA: No nonsense about moths. Come back here.

FIRST WOMAN: But I swear by the Holy Twain, I'll come right back. I'll only spread them on the bed.

LYSISTRATA: You're not spreading anything on any bed, and you're not going anywhere.

FIRST WOMAN: And I'm to leave my fleeces to be ruined?

LYSISTRATA: If necessary, yes.

[*A* SECOND WOMAN *runs out of the Acropolis.*]

735 SECOND WOMAN: Help! My flax, my superfine flax! I left it at home, and I'd forgotten to peel the bark!

LYSISTRATA: Here's another – this time it's unpeeled flax. [*To Second Woman, who has now almost reached the exit-passage*] Come back here.

SECOND WOMAN: But I will, by the Bringer of Light, as soon as I've stripped it bare!

740 LYSISTRATA: I'm not having any stripping bare – otherwise they'll all want to do the same.

[*A* THIRD WOMAN *runs out of the Acropolis, clutching her bulging belly.*]

THIRD WOMAN: Not yet, holy Eileithyia,[102] not yet! Wait till I've got off sacred ground!

LYSISTRATA: What's all this nonsense?

THIRD WOMAN: The baby's coming any minute!

LYSISTRATA: But you weren't even pregnant yesterday!   745

THIRD WOMAN: Well, I am today! Lysistrata, let me go home right away. The midwife's waiting.

LYSISTRATA: What's this yarn you're spinning? [*Pokes her stomach*] Rather hard, isn't it? What have you got there?

THIRD WOMAN: Why, the baby must be a boy![103]

LYSISTRATA [*tapping with her knuckles*]: Nonsense! This is something metallic – and hollow – let's have a look at it. [*She   750 lifts up Third Woman's dress to reveal a large bronze helmet.*] You ridiculous fool – pretending to be pregnant with Athena's sacred helmet![104]

THIRD WOMAN: But I *am* pregnant, I swear.

LYSISTRATA: So what's the helmet for?

THIRD WOMAN: Well, I thought – if I found the baby was coming before I got out of the Acropolis – I could nest in the helmet, like a pigeon, and give birth there.   755

LYSISTRATA: No good trying to wriggle out of it. You're caught. You can stay here until your helmet has been carried round the hearth.[105]

THIRD WOMAN: But I can't sleep in there any longer, since I saw the Guardian Serpent![106]

SECOND WOMAN: I can't either! Those owls with their infernal   760 honking[107] never let me get to sleep!

LYSISTRATA [*firmly*]: Tall tales will get you nowhere, ladies. I know you miss your husbands; but don't you realize they miss you as well? Think of the sort of miserable nights *they'll*   765 be spending. Be strong, my friends; you won't have to endure much longer. There is an oracle [*unrolls a scroll*] that we will triumph if only we don't fall out among ourselves. I have it here.

    [*The* WOMEN *all gather round her.*]

THIRD WOMAN: What does it say?

LYSISTRATA: Listen. [*Reads*]

'When that the swallows escape from the hoopoes[108] and   770
    gather together,
Keeping away from the cock-birds,[109] then trouble and
    sorrow will perish,

Zeus will make high into low –'

THIRD WOMAN: Will *we* lie on top from now on, then?

LYSISTRATA:

775 'But if the swallows rebel and fly from the sacred enclosure,
Then 'twill be patent to all that there's no bird that's so
nymphomaniac.'

THIRD WOMAN: Zeus and all the gods, that's pretty blunt!

LYSISTRATA: Then let us not give up the fight, hard though it is

780 to endure. It would be disgraceful, dear comrades, would it
not, to betray the oracle now.

[*All go into the Acropolis, leaving the two* CHORUSES *on
stage – still unclad. They confront each other.*]

MEN:

I heard in boyhood many a tale;
    I'd like to tell you one,
About a stripling long ago –
785   His name, Melanion.

From women and from wedlock's bond
    This young Melanion fled,
Preferring life in desert wastes
    And barren hills instead.

790 He hunted hares with nets, although
    He only had one hound;
He hated women so, he ne'er
    Came back to his native ground.

Yes, he was truly wise, this lad,
    Loathed females through and through,
795 And following his example we
    Detest the creatures too![110]

MEN'S LEADER [*to Stratyllis*]:
    Old thing, I want to kiss you.

STRATYLLIS [*shying away*]:
    Not till you give up onions!

MEN'S LEADER:

> Old thing, I want to *kick* you!
> [*He kicks a leg in the air.*]

STRATYLLIS [*pointing and laughing*]:

> Look at that hairy bottom! 800

MEN:

> A hairy crotch is evidence
>   Of courage, don't you know!
> Myronides was shaggy-arsed,
>   And so was Phormio.[111]

WOMEN:

> You told a little tale, and now 805
>   I'd like to do the same:
> The story of a wandering man,
>   And Timon[112] was his name.

> His face was hedged on every side
>   With prickly brier and thorn;[113] 810
> Some said he was no mortal's son
>   But of a Fury[114] born.

> This Timon went away and lived
>   So far from human ken
> Because he loathed most bitterly
>   The wickedness of *men*. 815

> Yes, hating their depravity,
>   Their company he abhorred;
> He cursed them long and loud and deep –
>   But *women* he adored. 820

STRATYLLIS [*threateningly, to Men's Leader*]:

> Like me to punch your jaw there?

MEN'S LEADER [*ironically*]:

> No, no! I cringe with terror!

STRATYLLIS:
>Would you prefer I *kicked* you?
MEN'S LEADER:
>What, and display your man-bag?

STRATYLLIS:
825
>>At least, despite our age, it's not
>>>With hairy mantling fringed:
>>We regularly use the lamp
>>>To get it closely singed.[115]

[*Both* CHORUSES *now withdraw to the edges of the orchestra. The* WOMEN *take with them both their own discarded clothing – which they will unobtrusively re-don during the ensuing scene – and also that of the men.* LYSISTRATA *appears on the ramparts, and looks off to right and left. Suddenly she sees something in the distance that makes her cry out in delight.*]

830 LYSISTRATA: Hey! Women, women, come here quickly!
[*Several women join her, among them* CALONICE *and* MYRRHINE.]

CALONICE: What's the matter? What are you shouting about?

LYSISTRATA [*pointing off*]: A man! There's a man coming – and by the look of him he's been driven half mad by the mystic power of Aphrodite! O Lady of Cyprus, Paphos and Cythera, stay with us on the long hard road!

835 CALONICE: Where is he, whoever he is?

LYSISTRATA: There, down by the shrine of Chloe.[116]

CALONICE: Yes, I can see him. But who on earth is he?

LYSISTRATA: Have a look, all of you. Does anyone know him?

MYRRHINE: Yes, by Zeus! It's Cinesias, my husband!

LYSISTRATA: Well then, it's over to you now. Keep him on
840
tenterhooks – slow-roast him – tantalize him – lead him on – say no, say yes. You can do anything – except what you swore over the cup not to do.

MYRRHINE: Don't worry, I'll do as you say.

LYSISTRATA: I'll stay here and start turning the spit. Off you all go.

[*All go within except* LYSISTRATA. *Enter, left,* CINESIAS, *his enormous phallus fully erect. He is followed by a male slave,* MANES, *who carries a* BABY.]

CINESIAS [*to himself*]: Gods help me! These terrible cramps   845
  and spasms – it's just as though I was on the rack!

LYSISTRATA: Who *stands* there?

CINESIAS: Me.

LYSISTRATA: A man?

CINESIAS: I certainly am!

LYSISTRATA: Well, off with you.

CINESIAS: And who do you think you are, sending me away?

LYSISTRATA: I'm on daytime sentry duty.

CINESIAS: Then, for the gods' sake, ask Myrrhine to come out   850
  to me.

LYSISTRATA: You want me to get you Myrrhine? Who might
  you be?

CINESIAS: Her husband – Cinesias from Paeonidae.[117]

LYSISTRATA [*effusively*]: How lovely you're here, darling!
  Yours is a name we know very well, because it's for ever in   855
  your wife's mouth. She can't eat an egg or an apple but she
  says, 'To the health of Cinesias'.

CINESIAS [*breathing more rapidly*]: You gods!

LYSISTRATA: It's true, I swear by Aphrodite. And if we happen
  to get talking about men, she always says, 'The rest are   860
  nothing to my Cinesias!'

CINESIAS: Come on, then, and bring her to me!

LYSISTRATA: Well, aren't you going to give me anything?

CINESIAS [*with a suggestive gesture*]: Sure I'll give you something, if you like. [*When* LYSISTRATA *makes no response*]
  Well, I've got this; so what I've got, I'll give to you. [*He
  throws her up a purse.*]

LYSISTRATA: Right, I'll go and get her. [*She disappears.*]

CINESIAS [*calling after her*]: Quickly, please! – I've no joy in   865
  life any longer, since she's left home. It pains me to enter the
  place, it all seems so empty, and I've no appetite to eat
  anything – because I'm permanently rigid!

  [MYRRHINE *appears on the ramparts, speaking back to
  Lysistrata within.*]

870 MYRRHINE: I love him, I love him! But he doesn't *want* to be
       loved – not by me. Don't ask me to go out to him.
     CINESIAS [*calling up to her*]: Myrrie baby,[118] why on earth not?
       Come down here.
     MYRRHINE: No, I will not.
     CINESIAS: Aren't you going to come down when I call you,
       Myrrhine?
875 MYRRHINE: You don't want me really.
     CINESIAS: Not want you? I'm *dying* for love of you!
     MYRRHINE: I'm going. [*She turns to go back inside.*]
     CINESIAS: No – don't – listen to your child! [*He takes the baby
       from Manes.*] Go on, go on, say mamma!
     BABY: Mamma, mamma, mamma!
880 CINESIAS: What's wrong with you? Surely you can't harden
       your heart against your baby! It's five days now since he had
       a bath or a suck.
     MYRRHINE: I pity him all right. His father clearly doesn't care
       much about him.
     CINESIAS: For heaven's sake, won't you come down to your
       own child?
     MYRRHINE: The power of the maternal instinct! I have to come
       down, I have no choice. [*She leaves the ramparts.* CINESIAS
       returns the baby to Manes.]
     CINESIAS: Absence certainly does make the heart grow
885   fonder![119] She looks a lot younger to me, and she has such a
       soft fetching look in her eye! And all this spurning and
       coquetting – why, it just inflames my desire even more!
          [MYRRHINE *comes out through the door. Ignoring* CINES-
       IAS, *she goes straight to the baby and takes it in her arms.*]
     MYRRHINE: My sweet little babykins! You've got such a
890   naughty daddy, haven't you? Let mummy kiss you, sweetie.
       [*She kisses and cuddles the baby.*]
     CINESIAS: Look, poor thing, why do you behave like this,
       listening to these other women? You're giving me such pain,
       and you're giving yourself pain too. [*He attempts to caress her.*]
     MYRRHINE [*brushing him off*]: Keep your hands off me!
     CINESIAS: And our things at home – the goods we own
895   together[120] – they're going to ruin!

MYRRHINE: I don't care!

CINESIAS: What, you don't care if the hens are pulling all your wool to pieces?

MYRRHINE: No, I don't.

CINESIAS: And the secret rites of Aphrodite? How long is it since you celebrated them? [*Putting his arm around her*] Come along home.

MYRRHINE [*wriggling free*]: No, I won't. Not until you men reach a settlement and stop the war. 900

CINESIAS: Then, if you want, we'll do that.

MYRRHINE: *Then*, if you want, I'll go home. Till then, I've sworn not to.

CINESIAS: But won't you at least lie down with me? It's been such a long time!

MYRRHINE: No. Mind you, I'm not saying I don't love you . . . 905

CINESIAS: You do, Myrrie love? Why won't you, then?

MYRRHINE: What, you idiot, in front of the baby?[121]

CINESIAS: No – er – Manes, take it home. [*The baby is returned to Manes, who departs homeward with it.*] All right, that's it out of the way. Let's lie down. 910

MYRRHINE: Don't be silly, there's nowhere we can do it here.[122]

CINESIAS: What's wrong with Pan's Grotto?

MYRRHINE: And how am I supposed to purify myself before going back into the Acropolis?

CINESIAS: That's easy; you can bathe in the Clepsydra Spring.[123]

MYRRHINE: You're not asking me to break my oath!

CINESIAS: On my own head be it. Forget about that oath. 915

MYRRHINE: All right, I'll go and fetch a bed.

CINESIAS: Why not on the ground?

MYRRHINE: By Apollo, cheap little fart though you are,[124] I don't think as little of you as that! [*She goes off into the right-hand wing of the* skene, *which represents Pan's Grotto.*]

CINESIAS: Well, at least she loves me, that's pretty clear!

MYRRHINE [*returning with a portable bed, which she puts down before the grotto entrance*]: Here you are. You just lie down, while I take off my – Blast it! We need a – a – a mattress. 920

CINESIAS: Mattress? *I* certainly don't!

MYRRHINE: Oh, yes, by Artemis! You don't mean you want us
to do it on the cords!

CINESIAS: At least give us a kiss first.

MYRRHINE [*doing so*]: There. [*She goes into the grotto.*]

CINESIAS: Mmmm! Come back quickly!

925   MYRRHINE [*returning with a mattress, which she lays on the
bed*]: There. Now just lie down, and I'll undress. [*She unpins
herself at the shoulders, and then breaks off.*] But look – um
– a pillow – you haven't got a pillow!

CINESIAS: I don't want one.

MYRRHINE: But I do! [*She goes into the grotto.*]

CINESIAS: This is a Heracles' supper[125] and no mistake!

MYRRHINE [*returning with a pillow*]: Go on, up you get. [CIN-
ESIAS *rises; she puts the pillow in place; he lies down again.
Speaking half to herself*] Is that everything?

930   CINESIAS: Yes, it is. Come to me now, precious.

MYRRHINE [*her back to him*]: I'm just undoing my breastband.
Remember, don't let me down over what you said about
making peace.

CINESIAS: May Zeus strike me dead if I do!

MYRRHINE: But look now, you haven't got a blanket!

CINESIAS: By Zeus, I don't *need* one! All I need is a *fuck*!!

935   MYRRHINE: Don't worry, that'll come. I'll be back very quickly.
[*She goes into the grotto.*]

CINESIAS: This woman and her bedclothes will be the end of
me!

MYRRHINE [*returning with a blanket*]: Raise yourself up.

CINESIAS [*standing up while* MYRRHINE *spreads the blanket
on the bed*]: Can't you see that happened long ago [*gesturing
at his phallus*]?

MYRRHINE: Do you want me to put scent on you?

CINESIAS: No, dammit, I don't!

MYRRHINE: Too bad then, because I'm going to anyway! [*She
goes into the grotto.*]

940   CINESIAS: Zeus, make her spill the stuff!

MYRRHINE [*returning with a scent bottle*]: Hold out your hand
and you can rub it on.

CINESIAS [*sniffing the scent in his hand*]: I don't care for it. It's not at all sexy, and it reeks of prevarication!

MYRRHINE [*pretending to sniff it in her turn*]: Why, silly me, I brought the wrong one!

CINESIAS: Well, never mind, my dear, let it be.   945

MYRRHINE: Don't talk such nonsense. [*She goes inside with the bottle.*]

CINESIAS: A curse on the man who invented perfume!

MYRRHINE [*returning with another scent bottle, slender and cylindrical in shape*]: Here, take this bottle.

CINESIAS [*pointing to his phallus*]: I've got too much bottle already! Now just lie down, damn you, and don't bring me anything more for any reason.

MYRRHINE: I will, I swear. I'm taking my shoes off now. But   950
darling, don't forget to vote for making peace!

CINESIAS: I'll think it over. [*He stretches out his arm to draw Myrrhine towards him. It clasps empty air, and, turning his head, he sees her vanishing into the Acropolis. He leaps to his feet.*] She's gone! She's done me and diddled me! Just when I was all ripe and peeled for her, she ran away! [*Sings:*]

> O what, tell me what, is there left for me to do?
> And, robbed of her beauty, who's there for me to   955
>   screw?
> Philostratus,[126] I need you, do come and help me
>   quick:
> Could I please hire a nurse for my poor young orphan
>   prick?

MEN:

> It's clear, my poor lad, that you're in a wretched
>   way.
> And I pity you – O alack and well-a-day!   960
> What heart, what soul, what bollocks[127] could long
>   endure this plight,
> Having no one to shag in the middle of the night?   965

CINESIAS:
　　　O Zeus! Help me, Zeus! These cramps, they torture me!
MEN:
　　　It's that female's fault – a loathsome pest is she.
WOMEN:
970　　No, she's an utter darling, a total sweetie-pie!
MEN:
　　　Some darling! A villain of foul and filthy dye!

CINESIAS:
　　　A villain, a villain, that's what she is! O Zeus,
　　　I've got a small miracle I'd like you to produce:
　　　To have a whirlwind catch her, just like a heap of hay,
975　　And waft her aloft, take her up, up and away –

　　　And then let it drop, after tossing her around,
　　　So down from the sky she will fall back to the ground,
　　　And make a spot-on landing, with legs spread out all
　　　　　wide,
　　　Just where this cock-horse is set up for her to ride!

　　　[*Enter a* SPARTAN HERALD. *He has a curious bulge under
　　　the lower part of his cloak.*]
980 HERALD: Where is the Athenian Senate,[128] or Executive, or
　　　whatever ye ca' them? I hae some news for them.
　　　CINESIAS:[129] And what might you be? A man, or a walking
　　　phallus?
　　　HERALD: I'm a herald, my lad, by the Twa Gods, and I've come
　　　frae Sparrta tae talk aboot a settlement.
985 CINESIAS [*pointing to the bulge*]: Which is why you've got a
　　　spear hidden in your clothes, I suppose?
　　　HERALD [*turning his back on him*]: No, I hanna.
　　　CINESIAS: What are you turning away for, then? Why are you
　　　holding your cloak away from your body like that? Did you
　　　get a swollen groin on the way here?
　　　HERALD [*indignantly turning back to face him*]: The man's
　　　mad, by Castor! [*He angrily raises a hand within his cloak –
　　　and in so doing accidentally reveals his erect phallus.*]

CINESIAS: Well, well, you rogue! Another *club member*!

HERALD: No, no, by Zeus – dinna blather.   990

CINESIAS: Well, what's this sticking out here, then?

HERALD: A Sparrtan walking-stick.[130]

CINESIAS: Oh yes, if *this* [*indicating his own phallus*] is one too. You needn't think I'm a fool; you can tell me the truth. What is the present situation in Sparta?

HERALD: It's a total cock-up through all Laconia.[131] All our   995
allies ha' risen, and they're standing absolutely firrm. And we've no got Pellene![132]

CINESIAS: What's the cause of this affliction? Do you think Pan was responsible?[133]

HERALD: Och, noo. It was Lampito, I'm thinking, that began it, and then a' the ither women – almost as though at a given   1000
signal – they a' barred the men from their barrels.

CINESIAS: So how are you getting on?

HERALD: Verra badly, verra badly. We a' walk roond the toon stooped over, as if we were carrying lamps.[134] D'ye ken, the women won't even let us sae much as touch their wee berries,[135] till we a' consent tae mak a general peace for the whole   1005
o' Greece.

CINESIAS: Ah, now I see the plot! They're all in it – all the women everywhere. Tell your people at once to send delegates here with full powers, to negotiate for peace. And I'll present   1010
this di . . . document to the Council and tell them to choose delegates to represent Athens.

HERALD: That's a' fine by me. I'll fly.

[*The two depart in opposite directions. The two* CHORUSES *return to the centre of the orchestra; the* WOMEN *are carrying the men's clothes.*]

MEN'S LEADER:
There is no beast more stubborn than a woman,
And neither fire nor leopard is more ruthless.   1015

STRATYLLIS:
If you know that, why do you fight us still?
We would be faithful friends, if you would let us.

MEN'S LEADER:
Women I loathe, both now and evermore.

STRATYLLIS:
Well, when you like. But really, standing naked,
1020   You do look stupid! I'm not going to leave you
In such a state. Come on, put on your tunic.
        [*She dresses him in the tunic; and the other* WOMEN *follow her example.*]

MEN'S LEADER:
That wasn't a bad turn you did me then;
When I in anger doffed it – *that* was bad.

STRATYLLIS:
You look more like a man now[136] – not so comic.
        [*Examining him closely*]
1025   And if you weren't quit such a *nasty* man,
I'd long ago have taken out that creature
That's in your eye.

MEN'S LEADER:
                              Oh, *that* is what it was
Was murdering me! Look, take this ring of mine
And scoop it out,[137] and show it me. I tell you,
I've had it biting me for quite a time.

STRATYLLIS:
1030   All right – though really, you've got *such* a temper!
        [*She explores his eye carefully with the ring.*]
Great Zeus, that *is* some gnat!
        [*She extracts the insect and shows it to him.*]
                              Just look at it!
It must be from the Marsh of Marathon!

MEN'S LEADER:
I'm very grateful. It was digging wells,
It was, and now my eyes are streaming tears.

STRATYLLIS:
1035   I'll wipe them, then –
        [*As she does so*]
                              – you *are* a naughty man, though –
And kiss you.

MEN'S LEADER:
            No, you don't.
ALL THE WOMEN: Oh, yes, we do!
    [*And each of them kisses one of the men.*]
MEN'S LEADER:
    Damn your cajolery! Still, the saying's true –
        We can't live *with* you, we can't live *without* you!
    Let us make peace, that's what we ought to do;   1040
        If you don't hurt us, we will never flout you.
    Let our division now be dead and done:
    Let us unite and sing our songs as one.

    [*The two* CHORUSES *unite into a single chorus of twenty-four members.*]

CHORUS:
        No citizen need fear that we
            Will dent his reputation;   1045
        We rather think you've had enough
            Of toil and tribulation.

        So mockery is out for now,
            Its opposite is in!
        We've lots of goodies waiting here
            For all of you to win.

        If you should need a spot of cash –   1050
            Two hundred drachmas,[138] say –
        Just let us know and call on us
            And take a purse away!

        What's more, we guarantee that if
            The war should ever end,   1055
        You won't be liable to repay
            The money that we lend![139]

We're entertaining some friends from Carystus tonight;

1060   They're fine upstanding men, and the menu's just right!

There's a special soup, and I've chosen for sacrifice

A young porker whose flesh will be good and tender
            and nice.[140]

So come to my house today; don't hesitate –

1065   Have a bath and come over, you and your kids – don't
            be late.

Walk in – no questions – as if you were in your own
            place.

1070   (Oh, I should have said, *the door will be shut in your
            face*.)

[*Enter a party of* SPARTAN DELEGATES, *with the now
familiar bulge in their clothes. They are attended by*
SLAVES, *who remain in the background*.]

LEADER:

Here's the long-bearded Spartan delegation. Why, you'd
            swear

That each of them was carrying a pig-cage[141] under there!

1075   [*To the Spartans*] Welcome, gentlemen of Laconia. How are
            you doing?

FIRST SPARTAN: I've no need tae answer that in words; ye can
            see for yersel's how we're doing. [*The* SPARTAN DELEGATES
            drop their cloaks, revealing their erect phalli.]

LEADER: Whew! You're certainly in a state of severe tension –
            the crisis is getting more inflamed than ever!

1080   SPARTAN: It's beyond worrds. There's nothing tae be said: anely
            let someone mak peace for us, nae matter who, nae matter
            how.

            [*A party of* ATHENIAN DELEGATES *is seen approaching
            from the other direction*.]

LEADER: Ah, here are our true-born Athenian representatives,
            leaning forward like wrestlers[142] and holding their cloaks

1085   clear of their stomachs – or are they just suffering from excess
            abdominal fluid?[143]

FIRST ATHENIAN: Will somebody tell us where Lysistrata is? Because we men are – well, you can see how we are. [*The* ATHENIANS *drop their cloaks, and are seen to be in the same condition as the Spartans.*]

LEADER [*aside to the Chorus*]: Both got the same affliction, haven't they? [*To the Athenian Delegates*] What does it give you? Cramp attacks in the small hours?

FIRST ATHENIAN: If only that were all! It's killing us. If we don't   1090 make peace right away, we'll all end up shagging Cleisthenes!

LEADER: Hadn't you better put those cloaks on again? You wouldn't want your sacred emblems mutilated,[144] would you?

FIRST ATHENIAN: You're right, you know. [*The* ATHENIANS   1095 *pick up their cloaks and put them back on.*]

SPARTAN: Aye, indeed, by the Twa Gods. Here, let's pit them on agin. [*He and the other* SPARTANS *do so.*]

FIRST ATHENIAN [*taking notice of the Spartans for the first time*]: Welcome, Laconians! This is a pretty pass we've all come to!

SPARTAN: Not sae bad as it wuid be, my dear fellow, if those men[145] had seen us in this state.

FIRST ATHENIAN: Well, now, let's have some straight talking.   1100 What are you here for?

SPARTAN: We're a delegation come tae mak peace.

FIRST ATHENIAN: That's good to hear. So are we. Why don't we ask Lysistrata to join us? She's the only person who can bring about a true reconciliation.

SPARTAN: Aye, by the Twa Gods, call her, and call Lysistrat*us*   1105 too if ye choose![146]

[*The portal of the Acropolis opens wide, and* LYSISTRATA *appears.*]

FIRST ATHENIAN: No need to call her, it seems; here she is!

CHORUS:

Hail, bravest of all women! To your charms all Greeks surrender!

Now be awesome, gentle, noble, common, proud, experienced, tender:

1110   The two great warring states now share the joint
            determination
        To submit all points of quarrel to your binding
            arbitration.

LYSISTRATA: It's not hard, if you catch them when they're eager
    for it and aren't trying to exploit each other. We'll soon see.
    Reconciliation! [*A beautiful, naked young woman*, RECON-
1115   CILIATION, *comes out of the Acropolis*.] Bring the Spartans
    to me first of all. Don't be rough or brusque; handle them
    very gently, not in the brutal way our menfolk used to do,[147]
    but in the friendly, intimate way that a woman does. If he
    won't give you his hand, take him by the tool. [*The chief*
    SPARTAN DELEGATE, *who had been hesitating whether to
    offer his hand to Reconciliation, now does so, and she leads
    him and his colleagues to stand on one side of Lysistrata*.]
1120   Now bring the Athenians here too. You can take hold of any
    part they offer you. [RECONCILIATION *brings the* ATHENIAN
    DELEGATES *to stand at Lysistrata's other side*.] Now you
    Spartans stand right next to me on this side, and you
    Athenians on that side, and listen to what I have to say.

        I am a woman, but I'm not a fool:
1125   I have my share of native wit, and also
        I've often heard my father's conversations
        With other older men.[148] Now, listen, both:
        My words to you are harsh – but you deserve them.
        You worship the same gods at the same shrines,
1130   Use the same lustral water,[149] just as if
        You were a single family – at Olympia,
        Delphi, Thermopylae – how many more
        Could I make mention of, if it were needed?
        And yet, though threatened by barbarian foes,[150]
        You ruin Greece's towns and slay her men.
1135   Here ends the first part of my argument.

FIRST ATHENIAN [*whose eyes have been fixed on Reconcili-
    ation*]: How much longer? I'm dying of erectile hyper-
    function!

LYSISTRATA:
        Now, turning to you Spartans: d'you remember

How Pericleidas came to Athens once,
And sat a suppliant at their holy altars,   1140
With blood-red martial cloak and death-white face,
Imploring them to send a force to help you?
For then two perils threatened you at once:
Messenia, and Poseidon with his earthquake.
So Cimon took four thousand infantry
And saved all Lacedaemon.[151] That is how   1145
Athens has treated you – and do you ravage
The lands of those who are your benefactors?

FIRST ATHENIAN: Yes, Lysistrata, they're in the wrong.

SPARTAN [*absently, his eyes on Reconciliation*]: We're in the
wrong. But that's an incredible bum she has!

LYSISTRATA:
Don't think, Athenians, you are guiltless either.
Remember once you wore the smocks of slaves,   1150
Until the Spartans came in arms, and slew
Many Thessalian men, and many allies
And friends of Hippias.[152] Upon that day
They alone helped you drive him out; they freed you,   1155
Enabled you to throw that smock aside
And gave you back a thick warm cloak to wear.

SPARTAN: I hanna seen a nobler woman [*meaning Lysistrata*].

FIRST ATHENIAN: Nor I a prettier pussy [*meaning Reconciliation's*].

LYSISTRATA:
Thus each of you is in the other's debt:
Why don't you stop this war, this wickedness?   1160
Yes, why don't you make peace? What's in the way?
[*During the ensuing dialogue both negotiators map out
their respective demands upon Reconciliation's person.*]

SPARTAN: We're willing, if ye'll give us back this roond hill
[*Reconciliation's bottom*].

LYSISTRATA: What round hill?

SPARTAN: Pylos. We've set oor herrts on it and been probing
aroond it for years.

FIRST ATHENIAN: By Poseidon, you shan't have it!   1165

LYSISTRATA: No, give it them.

FIRST ATHENIAN: Then who will we be able to arouse . . . to revolt?[153]

LYSISTRATA: Well, you ask for something else in exchange.

FIRST ATHENIAN: Very well . . . give us these Prickly Bushes
1170 here, and the Malian Gulf behind them, and the Long Legs –
I mean the Long Walls of Megara.

SPARTAN: Ye're no going to get *everything*,[154] my guid man, by
the Twa Gods!

LYSISTRATA: Let it be – don't quarrel over a pair of legs – I
mean walls.

FIRST ATHENIAN: I'm ready to strip off now and get down to
some husbandry.

SPARTAN: And I'm wanting to get stuck into the muck.[155]

1175 LYSISTRATA: Time enough to do that when you've made peace.
Please decide whether you want to do so, and also discuss it
with your allies.

FIRST ATHENIAN: Allies, ma'am? Look at the state we're in! We
1180 know what the allies will want: the same as we do – *a fuck!!*

SPARTAN: *Oor* allies cerrtainly will.

FIRST ATHENIAN: And so will the Carystians, I'm sure!

LYSISTRATA: Fine then. Now will you please maintain purity,
so that we women can entertain you on the Acropolis with
1185 the food and drink we brought in our picnic boxes. And over
that you can clasp hands and swear to the treaty. And then,
let everyone go home, taking his wife with him!

FIRST ATHENIAN: Let's go, right away.

SPARTAN [*to Lysistrata*]: Lead us where ye will.

FIRST ATHENIAN: Yes, and quickly.

[LYSISTRATA, *accompanied by* RECONCILIATION, *leads
both delegations into the Acropolis. The Spartans'* SLAVES
remain outside; some sit down on the steps.]

CHORUS:
1190   Embroidered horsecloths – magnificent robes –
                Gold jewellery – whatever you need,
           If your daughter's been given a basket to bear,[156]
                Or your son a processional steed:

What I have of these things, for the taking it's yours;   1195
   The seals on the chests are quite weak;
You can break them, and then from the contents within
   Take freely whatever you seek.

You should look very closely to see what there is,   1200
   Explore every cranny with care;
For unless you have got sharper eyesight than me,
   You'll find there ain't anything there!

If anyone who's short of bread
Has slaves and kids that must be fed,   1205
I've lots of wheat, a first-rate sort –
For one giant loaf, use just one quart.

Let anyone who feels a lack
Of food, come round with bag or sack: 1210
I've told my Manes he must be
Prepared to give you wheat for free.

One thing I should have said before –
You'd better not come near the door.
I hereby give you notice to
Beware the dog – she'll go for you!   1215

FIRST ATHENIAN [*within; sounding rather drunk*]: Open the
door here! [*The door begins to open; immediately the speaker
barges past the Doorkeeper, knocking him over.*] Why didn't
you get out of the way? [*He is joined by some of the other*
ATHENIAN DELEGATES; *all are wearing garlands, carrying
torches, and evidently drunk. He sees the Spartans' Slaves,
but does not realize who they are.*] What are you sitting there
for? Do you want me to burn you up with my torch? [*The*
SLAVES *retreat from the door.*] A low-grade comic cliché,
that, though. I won't do it. [*Some protests from the audience.*]
Oh – very well – it gives me pain, but to please you, I'll go   1220
through with it.

SECOND ATHENIAN: And we'll be with you and share your

pain. [*They brandish their torches at the Slaves, who are still hovering near the door.*] Off with you – or shall we pull out that hair of yours and see how you shriek?

FIRST ATHENIAN: Yes, off with you – the Spartans will soon be coming out after the banquet, and they won't want you getting in their way!

[*The* SLAVES *are driven away.*][157]

1225 SECOND ATHENIAN: Never known a party like it. The Spartans were really fun to be with, weren't they? And we kept our wits pretty well, considering how sozzled we were.

FIRST ATHENIAN: Not surprising, really. We couldn't be as stupid as we are when we're sober. If the Athenians took my
1230 advice they'd always get drunk when going on diplomatic missions. As it is, you see, we go to Sparta sober,[158] and so we're always looking for ways to make things more complicated. Result is, we don't hear what they do say, and we hunt
1235 for implications in what they don't say – and we bring back quite incompatible reports of what went on. *This* time, on the other hand, everything seems splendid. If one of them starts singing 'Telamon' when he should be singing 'Cleitagora',[159] all we do is applaud and swear blind that – [*The* SLAVES *are seen returning.*] Here comes this lot back again. Bugger off, will you, you scum!

[*The* SLAVES *are again driven off.*]

1240 SECOND ATHENIAN: Just as well. They're coming out now.

[*The* SPARTAN DELEGATES *come out of the Acropolis. Their leader carries a pair of bagpipes.*[160]]

SPARTAN [*to the stage piper*]: Here, my dear fellow, tak the pipes, and I'll dance a two-step and sing a bonny song in honour o' the Athenians and of oursel's forby.

1245 FIRST ATHENIAN: Yes, do, do. I do like watching a Spartan dance.

[*The* PIPER *takes the pipes and strikes up. The* SPARTAN *dances a solo as he sings.*]

SPARTAN:

Send me thy child,[161] the Muse of fame,
1250   Who knows the pride of Sparta's name
           And Athens' feats at sea,
           O holy Memory:

How once they focht in days of yore
Close by the Artemisium shore –
   Fu' godlike were their deeds,
   And well they whipped the Medes.

Leonidas led *us* from home:
Like boars, oor cheeks ran white wi' foam,   1255
   Like boars, oor teeth we whet,
   And doon oor legs ran sweat.

The Persian men they filled the land   1260
In numbers mair than grains o' sand,
   Whom we opposed that day
   At famed Thermopylae.

O Artemis the Virgin Queen,
Thou huntress o' the forests green,
   Come hither, Maiden fair,
   And in oor treaty share;

O mak oor pact endure for aye   1265
In friendship, bliss and wealth; and may
   All cunning foxes[162] cease
   To jeopardize oor peace!   1270

[*The portals open again, and* LYSISTRATA *appears, wearing the aegis of Athena,*[163] *and flanked by all the* ATHENIAN *and* SPARTAN WOMEN.]

LYSISTRATA: Well gentlemen, so it's all happily settled. Spartans, here are your wives back. And [*to the Athenians*] here are yours. Now form up everyone, man beside wife and wife   1275 beside man, and let us have a dance of thanksgiving –
And let us for the future all endeavour
Not to repeat our errors, never ever!

[*During the ensuing song by* LYSISTRATA, *the* WIVES *rejoin their* HUSBANDS, *and the couples move into formation for the dance that will follow; they occupy the centre of the*

orchestra, while the CHORUS *– also paired off in couples –*
are grouped at the edges.]

Come, let us on the Graces call,
1280   Apollo next who healeth all,
On Artemis and Hera too,
On Bacchus 'mid his maenad crew,[164]
1285   And most on Zeus above:

Let all the gods come witness now
The making of our solemn vow
To keep and never to evade
1290   The peace that Aphrodite made,
The goddess who is Love!

CHORUS [*dancing*]:
Hurrah! Apollo, hail!
Let's kick it high and free
And pray for victory![165]
Evoi, evoi! Evai, evai![166]

LYSISTRATA:
1295   Over to you, our Spartan brother:
We've had one new song, so give us another!
SPARTAN [*singing as the couples dance*]:
Muse o' Laconia, come from the mountains,
Sing the song that a Spartan ought,
Sing o' the noble Castor and Pollux
Who by Eurotas[167] take their sport.

1300   Sing of Athena's brazen temple,
Sing of Apollo's noble seat.[168]
Step it and prance, ye lively dancers,
1305   Let us praise Sparta wi' lips and feet!

Sparta delights in sacred dance,
The beating o' feet upon the groond,
When by Eurotas the girls like fillies
1310   Raise the dust as they prance aroond,

Shaking their tresses like Bacchic maenads
    Who sport and brandish their holy rods.[169]
And who but Helen, the pure[170] and comely,
    Leads their Chorus in dance to the gods?   1315

Clap your palms, and leap like a deer, and
    Raise up your hands to bind your hair!
And sing in praise of the warrior goddess   1320
    Of Sparta's Bronze Hoose, Athena the fair!

[*All depart, dancing, the* CHORUS *singing a hymn*[171] *to Athena.*]

Notes

THE ACHARNIANS

1. *when Cleon coughed up his thirty grand*: Evidently Cleon had been compelled by 'the Knights' (the rich young men who formed the Athenian cavalry corps) to relinquish some money which he was alleged to have acquired dishonestly; it is entirely obscure how this was done, what precisely the allegation was, and how Cleon was able to avoid heavy punishment (it has even been suggested that the whole incident took place not in real life but in an earlier comedy). Here and elsewhere I quote all large sums of money in drachmas; the Greek text often uses larger units (the mina of 100 drachmas, or the talent of 60 minas = 6000 drachmas). It is meaningless to attempt to give equivalents in modern currencies, but a drachma was a common daily wage for a hired workman or soldier.

2. *Theognis*: A tragic poet whose 'frigidity' had earned him the nickname 'Snow'.

3. *Chaeris*: The second worst lyre-player of his day, according to the comic poet Pherecrates. There was a piper of the same name, to whom comedy gave an equally low musical rating (see line 866); he may or may not have been the same person as the lyre-player.

4. *Orthian tune*: A martial tune composed by the famous seventh-century poet/musician Terpander of Lesbos.

5. *red rope*: When an Assembly was due to begin, all exits from the Market Square (Agora) not leading to the Pnyx were blocked, and the Scythian policemen marched from end to end of the square holding between them a rope freshly painted red, so that any who did not quickly leave for the Pnyx were branded for the day (and liable to a fine).

6. *the Executive*: Each of the ten 'tribes' supplied fifty members to the Council (Boule), and each tribal delegation formed a committee which managed the business of Council and Assembly for one tenth of the

year. The members of this committee were called the *prytaneis*, here rendered as 'the Executive'.

7. *sale-free zone*: On the hard-to-render pun here on *priō*, 'buy!', and *priōn*, 'saw(yer)', see Introduction, p. xxxviii.

8. *addressing the 'public'*: In this scene the audience were probably deemed to represent the mass of the Assembly.

9. *consecrated enclosure*: Before the Assembly was formally opened, a sucking-pig was carried round the Pnyx, sacrificed, and its blood sprinkled over the meeting area as a rite of purification.

10. *Who wishes to speak?*: The standard formula for opening an Assembly debate.

11. *My ancestor . . . immortal*: This is a wild distortion of mythical genealogies associated with the Eleusinian Mysteries, with some quite ordinary Athenian names (Phaenarete, Lycinus) mixed in. In real myth, a character with a pedigree like this (only one sixteenth divine) would certainly have been mortal.

12. *peacocks*: Alluding to a gift of peacocks made some time before by the Persian king to an Athenian ambassador, probably Pyrilampes (whose son Demos later let visitors view them for a fee).

13. *Ecbatana*: Not the name of a divinity, but a city – the capital of the Medes, modern Hamadan in western Iran.

14. *in the year when Euthymenes was archon*: This was the year that began in summer 437 BC; so the ambassadors have been away for eleven years, and each of them has 'earned' himself some 8000 drachmas (quite apart from the entertainment and presents they received from the king).

15. *Cranaus*: A mythical king of Athens.

16. *shitting on the Golden Hills*: Persia was believed to contain mountains of solid gold – but these 'golden hills' could also be dunghills!

17. *And how long . . . moon?*: This is a literal rendering of the Greek; the English word-play is pure serendipity.

18. *oven-baked oxen*: The Persians did indeed roast oxen whole in a furnace (*kaminos*) on special occasions (such as birthdays); instead of *kaminos* the ambassador absurdly says *kribanos*, 'oven for baking bread'.

19. *hoodwin*: Greek *phenax*, not the name of any actual bird, but invented for the sake of the pun on *phenakizein*, 'hoodwink, cheat', in the next line. Cleonymus was a politician celebrated at this time mainly for his weight, later (from *The Clouds* onwards) for having allegedly thrown away his shield in battle.

20. *Great King's Eye*: The actual title of certain high Persian officials.

The second part of the Eye's name suggests well-known Persian names such as Artabanus; the meaning of the first part is obvious.

21. *oar-sleeve . . . eye*: Warships often had large eyes painted on their port and starboard bows; but Pseudartabas' partly swathed eye also reminds Dikaiopolis of a warship's oar-holes, which were fitted with leather covers (forming a sleeve round the oar) to keep out the sea, and his movements are very gingerly (since the actor cannot see where he is going) like those of a large ship in narrow waters.

22. *Yawonian*: I.e. 'Ionian', the usual term for Greeks in the languages of south-west Asia.

23. *wide carts*: In the Greek the Ambassador interprets the first half of *chauno-prōkte*, 'gaping-arsed', as a mispronunciation of *achanē* (a large unit of volume, nearly 2.5 cubic metres); the second half he ignores.

24. *indicates . . . 'no'*: The ancient Greek gesture for this purpose was to raise the chin (i.e. a reversed nod).

25. *Cleisthenes*: A continual target of the comic poets for his effeminacy; his smooth chin made him all too conspicuous in a society where beards were universal. Aristophanes makes him a character in *The Poet and the Women*.

26. *famous wrestler*: Literally, 'son of Sibyrtius' (the proprietor of a well-known wrestling school); the designation is sarcastic.

27. *'O thou . . . arse!'*: Adapted, drastically, from an unknown play of Euripides.

28. *Strato*: Nothing is known of him, except that he too was beardless; he is again mentioned alongside Cleisthenes in *The Knights*.

29. *City Mansion*: The *Prytaneion*, the building containing the sacred hearth of the city, where ambassadors from abroad, Olympic victors, and others judged worthy of exceptional honour, were entertained at public expense.

30. *Theorus . . . King Sitalces*: Theorus is mentioned several times in Aristophanes' early plays as a political hanger-on of Cleon. Sitalces, the (non-Greek) king of the Odrysians in Thrace, had become an ally of Athens early in the war, but had given them little effective help.

31. *Theognis*: See note 2.

32. *his son . . . an Athenian citizen*: Sitalces' son, Sadocus, had been given Athenian citizenship at the time when the alliance was made.

33. *Festival of the Clans*: The Apaturia, an autumn festival at which (among other things) children and new citizens were admitted, amid much feasting, to the phratries (religious guilds united by a supposed common ancestry). It is not clear whether sausages (*allantes*, strictly

black puddings) are mentioned here because they were specially associated with this festival, or because they were a cheap food for which
only a stupid 'barbarian' would long passionately.

34. *The Odomantian army*: The Odomantians were a Thracian tribe,
living near Mount Pangaeus (west of present-day Kavalla).

35. *Who cut . . . fig-trees?*: The Odomantians are apparently equipped
(against all ethnographic probability) with circumcised phalli ('fig-tree'
was sometimes used to mean 'penis').

36. *two drachmas a day*: An absurdly high rate for a soldier of this
type; twelve years later one drachma was the going rate for Thracian
troops. One drachma was also the regular pay of naval oarsmen,
though the 'top-grade' men (*thranitai*, those who worked the highest
and longest oars) sometimes received a bonus.

37. *garlic . . . fighting mad*: Fighting-cocks were fed with garlic, which
was supposed to make them more pugnacious.

38. *sent a sign . . . drop of rain*: A 'sign from Zeus' such as a rainstorm
or, especially, thunder meant that the Assembly had to be dissolved
immediately. Not for the first time, Dikaiopolis gets his way with
remarkable ease.

39. *Marathon*: The Athenians defeated the Persians at Marathon in
490; so these old men should, strictly speaking, be at least eighty-
five.

40. *peace terms*: Greek *spondai* means both 'libations' (normally of
wine) and 'a treaty'; see Introduction, p. xxxix. The designations
'five-year', 'ten-year', 'thirty-year' can refer both to the duration of a
treaty and to the age of a wine.

41. *pitch and shipbuilding*: Pitch was used both for caulking ships and
for flavouring inferior wines. A five-year 'peace', it is suggested, would
be merely a period of frantic preparation for a new war.

42. *playing for time*: The suggestion here is that the allied states might
evade or delay the payment of tribute if they hoped that before long
Athens would be distracted by a major war and Sparta willing to give
aid to a revolt.

43. *'three days' rations'*: Soldiers were required to bring this with them
when reporting for active service.

44. *chase him . . .* : In this song the Chorus never distinguish clearly
between the person *by whom the treaty was brought* (Amphitheus)
and the person *for whom it was made* (Dikaiopolis). They were chasing
the former; they eventually catch the latter.

45. *Phaÿllus*: A famous runner from south Italy, who commanded a
ship at the battle of Salamis in 480.

46. *Peltingham*: In the Greek 'Ballên', playing on *balein*, 'to throw (a

stone etc.), to pelt (a person)', and *Pallene*, the name of a village east
of Athens.

47. *Speak fair!*: A call to all present to abstain from ill-omened speech
(i.e., in practice, from all unauthorized speech) during the performance
of the ritual which is about to commence.

48. *with a really sour look on your face*: The point is probably that a
virtuous, modest maiden ought not to smile in public.

49. *Phales*: Divine personification of the processional phallus.

50. *home to my village once more*: This is the only indication in the
play that Dikaiopolis is to be imagined as actually having returned to
his home in the countryside. It is given here purely for the purpose of
creating an appropriate atmosphere for the Country Dionysia procession, and in subsequent scenes it is forgotten.

51. *throw her down ... how sweet!*: It will be seen that no stigma
attaches to rape as such if the victim is a slave (provided her owner
does not get to know of this interference with his property). Even when
the woman is of citizen status, it is taken for granted in the New
Comedy of a century later that the rapist can atone completely for his
offence by marrying her.

52. *shoe the Knights*: Alluding to Cleon's association with the tanning
and leather-selling trades. It seems quite illogical for this pro-war
chorus to express hostility to the pro-war politician Cleon; but here
they are speaking not as Acharnians, but as a comic, or an Aristophanic
chorus, and foreshadowing the ferocious attack on Cleon which Aristophanes, it seems, was already planning to make, a year later, in *The
Knights*.

53. *that lot ... worthless*: In all Aristophanes' 'peace' plays – and in
other texts of the period as well, such as Euripides' *Andromache* – the
enemies of peace and of Sparta harp on the theme that a Spartan's
word, no matter how solemn, cannot be trusted. This feeling doubtless
stems from a belief (later shared by Spartans themselves) that Sparta,
by declaring war and invading Attica in 431, had directly violated the
peace treaty of 446/5 (which provided, among other things, that any
differences between the two sides which negotiation could not settle
should be referred to arbitration).

54. *head over a butcher's block*: An idea derived from Euripides'
Telephus (a play of which we will hear much more), where Telephus
told Agamemnon that, having justice on his side, he would not keep
silent even if threatened with decapitation. In Euripides' play this
was probably only a verbal extravagance; Aristophanes turns it into
concrete physical form.

55. *turning*: Literally, 'carding' – which in its ordinary sense is an early stage in the making of woollen clothes, but which also has the figurative sense 'lacerating'.

56. *I'll kill this one*: Telephus again – this time it is a scene in which Telephus wins himself a hearing by seizing and threatening to kill the infant son of Agamemnon. The same scene is also parodied in *The Poet and the Women*.

57. *sword*: Dikaiopolis is not necessarily holding an actual sword (as Telephus no doubt did); a kitchen knife would be funnier (in the corresponding scene of *The Poet and the Women* a sacrificial knife is used).

58. *who's to be stung next*: Literally, 'biting with a vote'.

59. *last year's play*: *The Babylonians*; see Preface.

60. *wretched and downtrodden*: Defendants in court would use their appearance, as well as their speech, to arouse the pity of the jury – though they would not state publicly in advance that they intended to do so!

61. *invisibility hat*: The long hair of Hieronymus (a tragic and dithy-rambic poet) is compared here to the mythical 'cap of Hades' which was said to make the wearer invisible.

62. *all the tricks from Sisyphus's store*: Sisyphus was a mythical king of Corinth renowned as 'the most crafty of men'; when he died, he was even able to trick the underworld gods into restoring him to life.

63. SERVANT: The ancient commentators identify this speaker as Cephisophon, a man mentioned in *The Frogs* as an associate of Euripides (and apparently as having associated rather too closely with Euripides' wife). Cephisophon, however, is never referred to before about 408 BC, and in any case is unlikely to have been a slave (he was probably a young musical composer who collaborated with Euripides in his last years).

64. *Sweet Euripides!*: In the Greek Dikaiopolis uses the diminutive form *Euripidion*.

65. *Cholleidae*: A village whose exact location is uncertain but which was probably not far from Acharnae.

66. *have yourself wheeled out*: The *ekkyklema* brought the interior of a house into the spectators' view, and enabled a character to remain notionally inside the house and yet converse with those outside. Dikai-opolis is suggesting that Euripides might thus be able to talk to him without interrupting his writing.

67. *renounced the use of your legs*: The implication is that the charac-ters a poet creates can be expected to resemble him in personality and habits; this principle is expounded explicitly and in detail by another tragic dramatist, Agathon, in *The Poet and the Women*. That Euripides'

tragedies were full of beggars and cripples was a stock joke, no doubt much exaggerated (his sixteen or seventeen surviving tragedies contain only one such character, whereas Sophocles' seven surviving plays contain two!).

68. *that old play of yours*: Dikaiopolis does not remember the title of the play or the name of the character he is thinking of, and there are so many to choose from!

69. *Oeneus*: A king of Calydon, who was deposed by his nephews and became a penniless exile. Euripides' play *Oeneus* depicted his restoration to the throne by the aid of his grandson Diomedes.

70. *blind Phoenix*: The son of Amyntor, who refused to sleep with his father's concubine Phthia. She accused him to Amyntor of attempted rape; the accusation was believed, and Amyntor banished Phoenix and (in Euripides' *Phoenix*, though not in other accounts) blinded him. He was later taken in by Peleus and made tutor to Achilles.

71. *Philoctetes*: Crippled from a snake-bite in the leg, he was abandoned for ten years on the island of Lemnos by the Greek army sailing to attack Troy, until a prophecy told them that he, or his bow, was essential if the city was to be captured. In Euripides' *Philoctetes* he was dressed in the skins of animals he had shot.

72. *Bellerophon*: In Euripides' *Bellerophon*, he tried to fly to heaven on his winged horse Pegasus, fell to earth and suffered serious leg injuries.

73. *Mysian Telephus*: Telephus, king of Mysia (a region to the south of Troy), was wounded by Achilles when defending his country against Greek invaders who thought they had landed at Troy. In Euripides' *Telephus*, having been told by an oracle that 'your wounder will also be your healer', he travelled, disguised as a Greek beggar, to seek out Achilles at Argos where the Greek chiefs had assembled.

74. *Ino . . . Thyestes*: Ino, wife of the Thessalian king Athamas, had been given up for dead by her husband, who had remarried; when he learned that she was alive, he had her seized and imprisoned. The new queen, Themisto, not knowing who Ino was, sought Ino's aid in killing her stepsons: Ino tricked Themisto into killing her own sons instead. Thyestes, brother of Atreus, appeared in two plays by Euripides; the reference here is probably to one that showed him as an exile, after Atreus had banished him for adultery.

75. *'For I this day . . . appear to be'*: Adapted from Euripides' *Telephus*.

76. *'O be thou blest . . . desire for him'*: Said, in Euripides' play, by someone who was believed to be an enemy of Telephus, but who was in fact Telephus himself.

77. *as once your mother was*: It was widely believed that Euripides' mother had once sold vegetables in the market.

78. *Vexer! You're a fine one to talk!*: Literally, 'By Zeus, you don't yet know what sort of bad things you yourself do'. It is tempting (compare p. 8) to think in terms of what was said twenty years later in *The Frogs* about Euripides' corrupting influence on the family and society, but 'vexer' (Greek *okhlēros*, 'tiresome, irksome') suggests he is being accused of nothing worse than being (sometimes) a bore.

79. *'Yet . . . hate me so'*: Another quotation from *Telephus*.

80. *'O hold it not . . . to speak'*: The whole speech which follows is based on one by the disguised Telephus in Euripides' play, in which, addressing Agamemnon and other leaders of the Greek army, he argued that the Greeks were wrong to go to war against Telephus and the Mysians.

81. *when I'm a comic poet*: Literally, 'when composing (*poiōn*) a comedy', an expression which makes no sense if taken as an utterance of Dikaiopolis: it has to be taken as being spoken in the name of Aristophanes (or possibly of his producer Callistratus, if he was still publicly believed to be the author of the play).

82. *immigrants*: This is the literal meaning of Greek *metoikoi*. Since, however, the descendants of *metoikoi* could neither become nor marry citizens (except by special dispensation of the Assembly), the word had come to mean, in practice, any free, permanent resident of Attica who was not an Athenian citizen (including the descendants both of immigrants and of freed slaves).

83. *Mount Taenarum . . . earthquake*: Alluding to the great Spartan earthquake of 465/4 BC, which was regarded by many as the revenge of Poseidon (god of earthquakes, among other things) for the killing of some Helots (serfs) who had taken sanctuary at the temple of Poseidon on Cape Taenarum (now Cape Matapan).

84. *confiscated and auctioned the same day*: This has usually been taken to refer to prosecutions for evasion of import duties, but it seems to imply that for some time *before* the famous decree of Pericles any goods whatever of Megarian origin found in Attica were liable to automatic confiscation. Dikaiopolis–Aristophanes carefully ascribes the *denunciations* to individuals, 'not the City', but it must of course have been the Assembly that imposed the embargo which made the denunciations possible.

85. *normal Athenian behaviour*: For the idea that the denouncer (*sykophantēs*) was a distinctively Athenian phenomenon, compare lines 902–4.

86. *Aspasia's tarts*: Aspasia of Miletus had lived openly with Pericles

for many years (they could not marry, since she was not an Athenian citizen) and had given him a son, also named Pericles, who was granted legitimacy and citizenship after Pericles' two older sons had died in the plague. Pericles' enemies (and the comic poets, in his time and long after) spoke of Aspasia as a whore, and accused her of running a brothel/harem for Pericles or of setting up assignations for him with married women.

87. *whores*: Literally, 'practitioners of fellatio'.

88. *Pericles the Olympian*: Cratinus and other comic dramatists of Pericles' time frequently spoke of him in language normally used about Zeus.

89. *'No Megarian ... be Megarian-free!'*: Adapted from a drinking song by Timocreon of Rhodes (early fifth century). This decree was much stronger than the one which may be alluded to in lines 515–22: it excluded all citizens of Megara from the Athenian Agora and from all harbours in the Athenian empire – thus making it very difficult for them to buy, as well as to sell, in any territory under Athenian control.

90. *'sailed forth his bark'*: This phrase comes from *Telephus*; in its present context it is meaningless, merely serving to remind us of the Euripidean speech on which this one is modelled.

91. *Seriphians*: Seriphos is a small island in the western Cyclades (south-east of Attica), one of the most insignificant states in the Athenian alliance. The following line is yet another quotation from *Telephus*.

92. *figureheads ... groaning*: Presumably the 'groaning' comes from the boards of raised wooden platforms where dealers stood. The emblems here called 'figureheads' were actually borne on the *stern* of Athenian warships.

93. *garlands ... black eyes*: These last four items no doubt relate to pre-departure parties, and their possible aftermath.

94. *boatswains and warblings*: The crew of each warship included a boatswain (*keleustēs*) who shouted orders to the oarsmen, and a piper (*triēraulēs*) whose playing helped them maintain their rhythm and spirits.

95. *'And ... Telephus would not?'*: This, and the previous quoted line, are straight quotations from Euripides' play: 'Telephus', of course, here means in effect 'the Spartans'.

96. *Lamachus ... tribal champion*: Lamachus was probably a member of the deme Oë, which belonged to the same tribe (Oeneis) as Acharnae did.

97. *my Gorgon from her case*: The Gorgon, the hideous monster whose face turned all who looked on it to stone, was frequently used in archaic and classical Greece as a suitably fearsome emblem for a warrior's shield. 'Case' is an anticlimactic reference to the cloth or leather covering in which a soldier's shield was kept when not in use.

98. *give me a bit of a thrill*: Literally, 'cause my foreskin to retract', i.e. give me an erection (by engaging in anal or intercrural sex, perhaps accompanied by manual stimulation).

99. *in the pay queue*: As the following lines indicate, this refers to service as ambassador rather than as general.

100. *by three cuckoos*: I.e. by a thinly attended Assembly that was not thinking what it was doing.

101. *young fellows like you*: Lamachus must in fact have been well into his forties, but Dikaiopolis is still old enough to be his father.

102. *Chares*: Otherwise unknown; probably the ruler of some tribe on the northern fringes of Greece.

103. *Chaonia*: A people in Epirus (on both sides of the present Greek–Albanian border) with a warlike reputation.

104. *Geres . . . from Diomeia*: None of the Athenians mentioned here – all of whom, evidently, had recently served on embassies – can be confidently identified.

105. *Gelaughatus*: Greek *Katagela*, a name (blended from the Sicilian place-names Gela and Catana) that suggests *katagelōs*, 'derisive laughter'.

106. *Coesyra's boy*: Coesyra was an aristocratic woman, probably from Eretria on the island of Euboea, who early in the fifth century married into the noble Athenian family of the Alcmeonidae; her name became proverbial for haughtiness and ostentatious wealth. The man referred to here is probably her grandson Megacles (the same Megacles whose niece is the wife of Strepsiades in *The Clouds*).

107. *And yet . . . evening*: The implication is that Megacles and Lamachus had saved themselves from financial ruin by getting elected to lucrative ambassadorships.

108. *you all*: Literally, 'the People'.

109. *our producer*: In this speech the words *didaskalos*, 'producer', and *poiētēs*, 'poet', are used interchangeably to denote the same person – who might be either Aristophanes or Callistratus.

110. *'violet-crowned'*: This epithet (Greek *iostephanoi*), together with 'shining' (*liparai*), had been used by Pindar in a famous dithyramb in praise of Athens.

111. *what 'democracy' means in a subject state*: This could refer to the democratic regimes in the subject ('allied') states themselves, or to the way they were ruled by democratic Athens; in either case, as the

following sentence shows, the line taken had been that the inhabitants of these states were hard done by.

112. *Aegina . . . take away this poet*: At the beginning of the war the Athenians had expelled the inhabitants of the nearby island of Aegina (their old enemy, but since the 450s their subject), and had given the land to Athenian settlers. Aristophanes (or Callistratus, as the case may be) must have had some connection of family, property or residence with Aegina, but we have no hard evidence at all as to the nature of that connection.

113. *me*: The chorus-leader shifts from talking *about* the poet/producer in the third person to talking *as* the poet/producer in the first person.

114. *Acharnian Muse . . . ardent fire*: The Muse is thought of as 'fiery' because the Acharnians are charcoal-burners.

115. *'Poseidon . . . slippeth not'*: Alluding to Poseidon's title *Asphaleios*, 'He who keeps men safe'.

116. *So off we go . . . I owe*: It is striking that nowhere in this speech is there anything to suggest that the defendant is not guilty of the offence with which he was charged: sympathy is being stirred for him not because he is innocent, but simply because he is old.

117. *get pursued . . . as the expression goes*: Greek *diōkein* (like French *poursuivre*) meant both 'pursue' and 'prosecute'.

118. *Grabber*: Greek 'Marpsias', probably the nickname (rather than the actual name) of a regular prosecutor (according to the ancient annotator, 'a quarrelsome and noisy orator who talked much nonsense').

119. *Thucydides*: Not the historian, but Thucydides, son of Melesias, long a rival of Pericles, who had been exiled for ten years (by 'ostracism') in 443; the trial referred to here (also mentioned in *The Wasps*), at which he broke down and was unable to make his defence speech, must have taken place after his return.

120. *Son of Cephisodemus*: The son, Euathlus, is mentioned several times again in comedies of the 420s. He is called a Scythian and an archer because one of his ancestors, most probably his paternal grandmother, had come from the northern shores of the Black Sea; nearly a century later, again because of the origin of a grandmother, the great orator Demosthenes was the victim of similar slurs.

121. *from a giant*: The text is corrupt here; a plausible recent suggestion is that the corruption conceals the name of Artachaees, a Persian of gigantic stature and stentorian voice, who had died at Acanthus (on the neck of the Athos peninsula) during the expedition of Xerxes in 480 and had come to be worshipped as a 'hero' there.

122. *wrestled down*: Thucydides' father, Melesias, had been a famous wrestling trainer.

123. *Alcibiades*: He had already been attracting attention in the courts two years earlier, at the age of twenty-two, when a peculiar feature of his vocabulary earned a mention in Aristophanes' *Banqueters*.

124. *young men . . . old*: The proverb was 'drive out like with like'.

125. *Lepri*: Said to have been the site of a tannery; but it may be an invented place-name derived from the verb *lepein*, 'give (someone) a hiding'.

126. *bird of that feather*: Literally, 'pheasant-man', with a pun on *phasianos*, 'pheasant', and *phases*, 'denunciation'.

127. *porkers*: This begins a play, which runs through most of this scene, on the word *choiros*, which meant both 'young pig' and '(especially immature) vulva'.

128. *porkers . . . at Eleusis*: Candidates for initiation at the Eleusinian Mysteries had to sacrifice a sucking-pig as a preliminary rite.

129. *Very agreeable . . . if there's also music*: In the Greek the misunderstanding is based on the similar sound of the words *peinames*, 'we go hungry', and *pinomes*, 'we drink'.

130. *Salt . . . Garlic . . . uproot them*: Salt and garlic were thought of as typical Megarian products. The Athenian occupation of the island of Minoa in 427 will have deprived the Megarians of access to their main salt workings on the facing mainland coast.

131. *Diocles*: A prominent figure, apparently, in the local mythology of Megara (and of Eleusis), who received worship there as a 'hero'.

132. *a beaver*: I owe this rendering of Greek *kusthos*, '(especially mature) vulva', to Ken Kesey's *One Flew Over the Cuckoo's Nest*, in which this term is repeatedly used.

133. *have*: He means 'have inside it'.

134. *can't . . . to Aphrodite*: This prohibition was regular throughout most, though not all, of the Greek world. In the Megarian's lines, the 'sacrifice to Aphrodite' is to be understood metaphorically, and the 'spit' as a thing of flesh and blood.

135. *Eat-olia*: In the Greek he suggests they may have come from Tragasae, whose name can suggest an association with *tragein*, 'to eat (especially sweet things)'.

136. *bunch o' garlic . . . twa pints o' salt*: The Megarian is having to buy, at a high price, the very commodities his country had traditionally exported.

137. *wick*: Most probably meaning a phallus.

138. *Cleonymus*: See note 19.

139. *Hyperbolus*: Though still a young man, he was already becoming prominent in the courts and (as quotations from lost comedies indicate) in politics. After Cleon's death in 422, he became the chief target of political satire in comedy until he was exiled by 'ostracism' c. 416.

140. *Cratinus, whose coiffure looks so unchaste*: The leading comic poet of the generation before Aristophanes, and one of his rivals at this very Lenaea. Adulterers were sometimes informally punished by having their pubic hair plucked out, and possibly also (though direct evidence is lacking) by having their heads shaved; so the meaning may be that Cratinus (who was probably about sixty) was totally bald.

141. *whose life ... smells in the market*: Literally, 'who has in his armpits the evil smell of his Tragasaean father' (punning this time on *tragos*, 'he-goat'), i.e. 'who smells so bad, you'd think his father was a goat'.

142. *Pauson*: A painter, specializing in caricature, who never made much of a living (in *Wealth*, nearly forty years later, his name is still a byword for poverty).

143. *Lysistratus*: Mentioned twice in *The Wasps* as a lover of verbal and practical jokes.

144. *the Chaeris clan*: See note 3.

145. *Iolaus*: Heracles' nephew, and his companion in many of his adventures; like Heracles himself, Iolaus was born at Thebes.

146. *with two wings or four*: I.e. birds or insects (cicadas, locusts); being Boeotian and stupid, he forgets to mention the many quadrupeds he has brought (let alone the eels, a much-prized – and in wartime a much-missed – delicacy).

147. *'O ... daughters'*: Adapted from Aeschylus' play *The Award of the Arms*, where it was addressed to Thetis, as 'eldest born of *Nereus*' fifty daughters'.

148. *gastronomes*: The Greek text names one of them, Morychus, who also figures as a lover of luxury in *The Wasps* and *Peace*.

149. *for nor alive ... my beet-wrapped love*: Parodied from Admetus' words to his dying wife in Euripides' *Alcestis*.

150. *We've got those*: He is, once again, too stupid to be aware that what he could buy at Athens was of far better quality (at least in the opinion of Athenians!).

151. *the Two Gods*: Amphion and Zethus, who built the walls of Thebes.

152. *unmanned boat ... ablaze in no time*: Attempts were certainly being made at this time to develop devices and techniques for using fire as a weapon in war; this particular device (a boat filled with combustible material, launched downwind at a hostile fleet) was familiar by

413, for when the Syracusans tried to use it against Athenian ships the Athenians had defensive measures ready and no damage was done.

153. *Festival of Pitchers*: The second day of the Dionysiac festival of the Anthesteria (held midway between the Lenaea and the City Dionysia).

154. *mighty crests that cast a fearful shade*: A quotation from Aeschylus' *Seven against Thebes*, where it describes the warrior Tydeus. Tydeus, significantly, was also the name of Lamachus' son.

155. *Let him shake . . . at the salt-fish vendors!*: In effect, 'Let him see if he can frighten cheap fishmongers in the Agora; he can't frighten *me*!'

156. *Eros . . . picture*: Alluding to a famous painting of Eros by Zeuxis, in the temple of Aphrodite in Athens.

157. *Vines . . . their oil*: It is clear that in this passage agricultural activities are being used (as often happens) as a metaphor for sexual activities – which in turn, it might be said, are a metaphor for the reunion between the Athenian people and the peace from which/whom they have been separated so long. Some of the details of the metaphor are less clear, and have been compressed in this rendering.

158. *pitchers*: The capacity of these vessels was one *chous* (more than three litres, or nearly six pints).

159. *Ctesiphon*: Not otherwise known, but evidently a fat man and probably (reputed to be) a heavy drinker.

160. *Phyle*: A village high on Mount Parnes, near the Boeotian border.

161. *Dercetes*: We happen to know from two inscriptions that there really was at this time a member of the deme Phyle who bore this name. Whether there was something about this person that made him a suitable target for comic satire, or whether Aristophanes, having happened to encounter the name (which means 'one who can see'), merely exploited it because of its topsy-turvy appropriateness to a man seeking eye treatment, we cannot tell.

162. *Pittalus and Co.*: Pittalus was the best-known medical practitioner in Athens; the expression used here (literally 'the ones of Pittalus') indicates that he ran a team practice, probably with his sons and/or pupils as assistants.

163. *BRIDEGROOM'S SLAVE . . . BRIDESWOMAN*: It has usually been supposed that the male visitor in this scene was the equivalent of a 'best man'; but although such a figure did exist at Athenian weddings, the bridegroom would not have sent him on a routine errand. The woman who accompanies him is the *nympheutria*, a mature woman chosen by the parents of the bride to be her companion on the wedding-day and to escort her to the bridal chamber.

164. *flask*: It is certainly not without significance that the type of flask referred to (an *alabastos*) was of a distinctly phallic shape.

165. *Pitcher and Pot Feasts*: The Pot Feast (*Chytroi*) was the day following the Pitcher Feast, and a day on which, to judge by a casual remark in *The Frogs*, a large percentage of the Athenian population could be expected to be suffering from hangovers.

166. *four-plumed monster*: In the Greek text Lamachus is apparently (though the text is uncertain) addressed as 'Geryon', the monster with three bodies who was slain by Heracles.

167. *'Harmodius' beloved'*: Among the most popular of Athenian drinking songs was one in honour of Harmodius and Aristogeiton, who had assassinated Hipparchus, brother of the tyrant Hippias, in 514 BC. Its lyrics varied, but one common version began 'Harmodius, beloved' (*philtath' Harmodie*); here this is distorted into 'Harmodius' beloved' (*philtath' Harmodiou*) – with, of course, a sly implication that this national hero had had something of an eye for the ladies. (And indeed a story attached to the Harmodius–Aristogeiton legend – though not attested till later – tells of Leaena, the mistress of one or other of the assassins, who died under torture without revealing anything about the conspiracy.)

168. *pork fat*: Only the main filling is mentioned; like the stuffed vine-leaf of today, the fig-leaf would contain several other fillings too.

169. *Orestes*: 'Orestes' (meaning 'madman', for the Orestes of myth had gone mad after killing his mother Clytaemestra) was the nickname of a man who had the reputation of a nocturnal mugger and clothes-stealer (*lōpodytēs*) – meaning probably that he had once committed such a crime in his youth and had subsequently never been allowed to forget it. We do not know the man's real name, only that of his father (Timocrates).

170. *[Enter DIKAIOPOLIS ... with a DANCING-GIRL on each arm.]*: The girls would probably be nude (played, that is to say, by male performers costumed as nude females). Dikaiopolis has exchanged his previous stage phallus for an erect one.

171. *Lammie*: In the Greek, Lamachus' name is extended by two suffixes, *-hipp-*, 'horse' (a common element in personal names), and the diminutive ending *-ion* (see note 64). As the first suffix is grandiose and the second intimate, the overall effect is grotesque.

172. *Paean*: A title of Apollo, especially in his role as healer.

173. *judges ... King*: The 'King' or Basileus (see Introduction, p. xxv) presided over the Anthesteria *and* the Lenaea; and the reference to 'judges' is likewise ambiguous between the judges of the drinking contest which Dikaiopolis has won, and those of the dramatic contest which Aristophanes hopes to win.

174. *A . . . hostile spear has pierced my bones*: It was made clear previously that Lamachus' injuries were the work of no human hand; are we meant to infer that he is now delirious?

175. *Hail to the champion!*: The opening words of an Olympic victory-hymn in honour of Heracles, attributed to Archilochus (seventh century BC).

THE CLOUDS

1. *One can't even discipline one's own slaves*: For fear they may run away and be given asylum by the enemy.

2. *his long hair*: An upper-class affectation.

3. *the date gets past the twentieth . . . another step up*: Interest on debts was calculated by the month, each new tranche being added to the debt on the last day of the month.

4. *twelve hundred drachmas*: Other evidence suggests that this was a fairly typical price for a horse. An Athenian in regular work might well take three or four years to earn this amount.

5. *koppa-bred horse . . . copped it right then and there*: The horse was one branded with the obsolete letter *koppa*, to denote the breed to which it belonged; Strepsiades' comment is, literally, that he wishes that before buying it he had had an eye knocked out (*exekopēn*).

6. *the niece of Megacles . . . a Coesyra of a woman*: Megacles, son of Megacles, was the head of the senior branch of the extremely blue-blooded family of the Alcmeonidae. Coesyra, his long-dead grand-mother, had been in her day a byword for wealth and arrogance.

7. *'Missus . . . my resources!'*: The Greek has a complex pun on the verb *spathān*, which means (i) to pack threads closely when weaving, (ii) to be extravagant, and (iii) to exhaust someone's sexual energies.

8. *Xanthippus, Chaerippus, Callippides*: These names mean 'Bay-horse', 'Enjoyhorse' and 'Fitz-Fairhorse' respectively. Xanthippus had been the name of Pericles' father, who had married a daughter of the Coesyra mentioned above. Pheidonides, the name preferred by the boy's father, means 'Fitz-Thrifty'.

9. *Pheidippides*: This was a genuine Greek name (similar, though not identical, names are attested at Athens), but the way it is led up to here makes it seem self-contradictory: thrift and horses do not go together.

10. *galloping consumption*: Greek *hipperos*, an invented word that sounds like a disease (compare *ikteros*, 'jaundice') caused by horses (*hippoi*).

11. *put your right hand in mine*: A strong pledge of fidelity, almost as binding as an oath.

12. *intellectual souls*: Possibly alluding to Socrates' frequent, and eccentric, use of the word *psyche*, 'soul, life, ghost', in the sense of 'mind, personality'.

13. *the sky is like a baking-pot ... charcoal inside it*: One way of making bread was to bake it under a dome-shaped cover (*pnigeus*). The interior would first be pre-heated by burning charcoal under it; the coal would then be heaped round the outside of the cover, and the dough put under the cover to bake. This suggests that the thinker(s) here referred to had a decidedly naïve model of the universe consisting of a flat earth and a hemispherical sky.

14. *Leogoras' pheasants*: Leogoras (father of the orator Andocides) was a rich man and a big spender, and pheasants were rare and expensive birds.

15. *an obol*: One sixth of a drachma.

16. *nor any of your damn thoroughbreds*: Literally, 'nor your yoke-horse [one of the inner pair of a team of four] nor your *san*-bred [a horse branded with another obsolete letter, compare note 5 above]'.

17. *Cicynna*: The location of this village is not certain, but it was probably to the south-east of Athens. It appears from lines 138 and 1322 that Strepsiades is to be imagined as actually living there, even though on stage the two houses adjoin each other and it never takes more than a moment or two to go from one to the other.

18. *kicking of the door*: It is not clear whether Strepsiades actually did kick the door (perhaps after his calls were not answered) or whether the Student is exaggerating.

19. *treat this as a holy secret*: The language is that of mystery-cults, whose sacred words and/or actions could not be divulged to those who had not been initiated.

20. *Chaerephon of Sphettus*: It is odd that he should thus be formally identified by name and deme, when he has already been mentioned in the conversation. Possibly his name has supplanted another similar name in the text (e.g. that of his brother Chaerecrates).

21. *this gecko ... from the ceiling*: Before this moment the audience will have thought that 'gazing upwards' meant 'gazing at the sky'; but Socrates, typically, prefers to do his research indoors. The gecko was walking upside-down on the ceiling, as small lizards often do.

22. *sprinkled a little ash ... nicked somebody's cloak ... wrestling*: Again we are taken by surprise – it looks as though the students are

going to have nothing for dinner except some mathematical 'food for thought' (the ash is for drawing diagrams in), but Socrates has a more practical (if criminal) device to supply them with a meal (the cloak will, of course, be sold).

23. *old Thales*: Thales of Miletus (early sixth century) was a famous sage, about whose wisdom and ingenuity many stories clustered. For Aristotle (and for many subsequent historians of Greek thought) he was the earliest figure who deserved to be called a philosopher.

24. *Spartan prisoners from Pylos*: The Spartans captured on the island of Sphacteria in 425 (see p. 9) were in effect held hostage at Athens to prevent any future Spartan invasion of Athenian territory.

25. *measuring out land*: The literal meaning of the word 'geometry' itself.

26. *overseas settlement*: The reference is to 'cleruchies', territories outside Athens which the Athenian state had appropriated (usually by force) and divided into lots which were given to selected Athenian citizens.

27. *It's there*: This may be interpreted (and played) either as implying that the Student knows what part of Attica this village is in, or that he does not.

28. *stretched it flat . . . the rest of us*: Referring to the suppression of a revolt in Euboea in 446.

29. *attacking the mystery . . . attack the Mysteries*: In the Greek Strepsiades misunderstands Socrates' word *periphronō*, 'I contemplate (the sun – which was, of course, a god)', as if it bore its other meaning 'I despise, hold in contempt'.

30. *The same thing . . . cress*: Cress seeds soak up moisture greedily.

31. *sacrifice . . . Athamas*: Alluding to a tragedy by Sophocles in which Athamas was on the point of being sacrificed to Zeus (he was standing at the altar, wearing the garland appropriate to a sacrificial victim), apparently as punishment for having supposedly caused the death of his son Phrixus, but was rescued by Heracles who brought news that Phrixus was still alive (having been safely conveyed to Colchis by the ram with the golden fleece). It is doubtless relevant that Phrixus' mother was named Nephele ('Cloud').

32. *[Turning . . . points of the compass]*: Of the places mentioned where the Clouds might be at this moment, the Ocean was thought of as being in the far west (beyond the Straits of Gibraltar; Ocean's 'bower' was the Garden of the Hesperides); Egypt was in the south, Mount Mimas (near Erythrae, on the coast of Asia Minor) in the east, and Lake Maeotis (the Sea of Azov) in the north.

33. *To the sky*: Literally, 'to the peaks of the high tree-crowned hills'.

34. *to make a great big noise down below*: I.e. to shit myself in terror (the Greek word means, literally, 'fart off', but is often used in circumstances where the context strongly suggests that something more than wind is being emitted).

35. *Where the initiated . . . contest sing*: It is very remarkable that the Clouds here praise the Athenians for their pious worship of the traditional gods (with particular reference to the Eleusinian Mysteries), when Socrates claims that *they* ought to be worshipped to the *exclusion* of the traditional gods (and has just performed an 'initiation ceremony' on Strepsiades as if for a special, private mystery-cult). This is the first of many indications that will gradually make it evident to the audience (though not to the characters, until it is too late) that the Clouds are not what Socrates takes them for. Their song is appropriately climaxed by mention of the festival (the City Dionysia) in which (outside the fictive framework) they are actually competing as a chorus.

36. *They're not . . . female heroes, are they?*: Strepsiades is still afraid; 'hero(in)es' – the spirits of great (wo)men of the past – were believed sometimes to walk the earth, and if one encountered one of them, especially at night, it was thought that one risked being struck with paralysis (see *The Birds*, lines 1490–93).

37. *[At this point . . . cloudlike.]*: This reconstruction of the movements of the Chorus was proposed, in a slightly different form, by Peter von Möllendorff in E. Pöhlmann et al., *Studien zur Bühnendichtung und zum Theaterbau der Antike* (Frankfurt, 1995), pp. 147–51.

38. *Mount Parnes*: Forming the northern frontier of Attica; in the Theatre of Dionysus the auditorium is to the north of the performing area.

39. *high-powered prophets*: Literally, 'prophets from Thurii', with particular reference to the distinguished Athenian seer Lampon, who twenty years earlier had been the official founder of the colony of Thurii in southern Italy and who was still prominent in public life.

40. *they get feasted*: By their *choregoi*, after a successful performance. For the *choregoi* the dithyrambic competitions, with their choruses of fifty members, were often more expensive and more prestigious than those in tragedy or comedy; but tragic and comic dramatists alike must have felt with good reason that dithyrambic *poets* (whose compositions were far shorter, whose music and choreography were far simpler, and who needed no theatrical skills) had a very easy time of it compared with themselves!

41. *son of Xenophantus*: This is apparently the poet Hieronymus (see

The Acharnians, note 61). 'Savage' (*agrios*) and 'centaur' were both expressions for men who pursued boys more persistently and more indiscriminately than was thought acceptable.

42. *Simon*: Probably, like Cleonymus and Theorus (mentioned with him in lines 399–400), a political associate of Cleon.

43. *Cleonymus . . . Cleisthenes*: See *The Acharnians*, notes 19 and 25.

44. *Prodicus*: A scientist, philosopher and writer from the island of Ceos, who had acquired a considerable reputation even outside intellectual circles.

45. *You swagger . . . with disdain*: In Plato's *Symposium* (221b) Alcibiades is made to quote this line as a correct portrayal of Socrates' bearing, with particular reference to the retreat from Delium in 424 (see p. 66).

46. *Panathenaea*: The great summer festival of Athena.

47. *'thunderous fart'*: In the Greek, Strepsiades' comment refers to the similarity between the words *pordē*, 'fart', and *brontē*, 'thunder'.

48. *headland of Sunium*: At the south-eastern tip of Attica; it had temples of Poseidon and Athena.

49. *Diasia*: A major festival of Zeus, held a few weeks before the City Dionysia.

50. *I assume . . . speak to him*: This last question and response stand eleven lines later in the manuscripts (after 'get to work on me'); I have adopted a proposal by F. V. Fritzsche to transpose them to this earlier position, which gives a smoother and more logical sequence.

51. *you'll gain a reputation . . . every nation*: This alluring vision of Strepsiades' future glory seems to be modelled on the renown of Antiphon, the first Athenian to be regarded as an expert consultant on legal problems and the first to write speeches for clients to deliver in court.

52. *Do Greeks come this stupid?*: Literally, 'this man is stupid and barbarian', i.e. so stupid that one would have thought he was not a Greek.

53. *no outer garments . . . stealing it*: A man who suspected another of stealing from him had the right to search the suspect's house, but he was required to remove his outer garment before entering.

54. *honey-cake . . . into that cave*: Alluding to the cave-sanctuary of the hero Trophonius in Boeotia, where those consulting the oracle took with them a honey-cake to placate the resident snakes.

55. *[addressing the audience]*: This speech, which discusses the failure of the original production and criticizes other plays produced subsequently, is a new composition for the revised play (see pp. 69–70).

56. *Model Son and Pansy Boy*: Referring to his first play, *The Ban-*

queters, which featured a father and two sons, one traditionally educated (and manly), one sophistically educated (and effeminate).

57. *like an unwed mother . . . she brought it home to you*: The Banqueters was produced for Aristophanes by (probably) Callistratus. It
would normally have been taken as insulting to speak of Callistratus
as a woman ('she'), but Aristophanes has here defused the insult by
speaking of *himself* as a woman too!

58. *like Electra . . . cut from her brother's hair*: In Aeschylus' *Libation
Bearers*, Electra, going to the tomb of her father Agamemnon to make
offerings, finds a lock of hair there, resembling her own, which she
guesses correctly to be that of her brother Orestes. The play was
famous, but it was forty years old (though it had probably been restaged
more than once during that period), and Aristophanes expects his
audience's recall of it to be rather vague – for Electra was certainly not
looking for her brother's lock.

59. *what a modest girl she is*: Most of the claims made about this play
in the next few lines will be proved totally false before it ends.

60. *She doesn't play the fool . . . red-tipped leather tool*: If this is true,
it is probably only true because no one in the play had, or had any
reason to have, a phallus that was 'red-tipped', i.e. circumcised.

61. *making fun of men who are bald*: Hardly surprising, since Aristophanes was bald himself!

62. *cordax*: A ribald comic dance.

63. *a repeat*: Of course, the production for which these words were
written, had it ever been staged, *would* have been virtually a repeat –
though it would have been avowedly so, with no attempt at 'pretending
[it was] new'.

64. *Hyperbolus*: A politician of similar style to Cleon and appealing
to a similar constituency, who became the leading butt of comedy after
Cleon's death in 422. He was exiled by 'ostracism' in 417 or 416, and
assassinated by anti-democratic conspirators at Samos in 411.

65. *in Maricas*: At the City Dionysia of 421.

66. *Phrynichus . . . drunk old woman*: Probably the Phrynichus meant
here is the contemporary comic dramatist, rather than his namesake,
the tragic dramatist of the early fifth century; the play of his allegedly
plagiarized by Eupolis was apparently a parodistic version of the story
of Perseus and Andromeda with a 'drunk old woman' substituted for
Andromeda.

67. *eels*: In *The Knights* (lines 864–7) Aristophanes had compared
Cleon to a man fishing for eels, who could only catch them by stirring
up the mud ('and similarly *you* gain by setting the City astir').

68. *Zeus, thou almighty Ruler . . .*: Here again (compare note 35

above) the Clouds appear as pious worshippers of the traditional gods, though their hymn does include one non-traditional deity in the shape of their own father Ether; and here again (lines 605–6) they end with mention of Dionysus.

69. *stops the expedition*: The rain or thunder would be taken as an adverse omen (compare note 38 to *The Acharnians*).

70. *Paphlagonian tanner*: Cleon, who had been portrayed in *The Knights* as a slave from Paphlagonia (in northern Asia Minor), was soon afterwards (in February or March 424) elected, for the first time, as one of the ten generals. For his association with tanning, see *The Acharnians*, note 52.

71. *the moon forsook her path*: There had been a total eclipse of the moon on 9 October 425.

72. *sun . . . quench his flame*: There was an annular eclipse of the sun on 21 March 424, probably a few weeks after the election.

73. *Cynthus' rocky summit*: Mount Cynthus is the highest point of Apollo's sacred island of Delos.

74. *blest Maid*: Artemis.

75. *our Protectress*: The Chorus are here momentarily speaking not in the role of Cloud-goddesses but in that of Athenians performing at an Athenian festival.

76. *calendar all topsy-turvy*: The calendars of Athens and other Greek states were theoretically lunar, but the actual dates were often out of step with the phases of the moon. In what follows it is assumed that the gods' calendar follows the moon strictly.

77. *instead of feasting . . . sue*: The lawcourts did not sit on festival days.

78. *Memnon, Sarpedon – keeping solemn fast*: Memnon and Sarpedon, sons of Eos (Dawn) and Zeus respectively, were killed fighting as allies of Troy in the Trojan War. For fasting as a mark of mourning, compare Achilles' refusal to eat on the day after the death of Patroclus (*Iliad* 19.209–15, 305–8).

79. *chief envoy to Thermopylae*: Greek *hieromnemon*, the leader of the Athenian delegation to the twice-yearly councils of the Amphicytonic League at Thermopylae and Delphi.

80. *took his wreath away*: 'Perhaps by blowing it off at an embarrassing moment' (Dover).

81. *Measures?*: Socrates means verse measures (metres), but Strepsiades misunderstands him.

82. *the three-measure or the four-measure*: Socrates is referring to two metres much used both in tragedy and in comedy, the iambic trimeter and the trochaic tetrameter. Strepsiades can still think only of measures of capacity.

83. *four measures in a gallon*: One *hemiekteon* (about 0.95 UK gallon or 1.15 US gallons) was equal to four *choinikes*.

84. *armamental . . . digital*: I have latinized the names of these types of rhythm, which metricians usually refer to by the Greek terms 'enoplian' (though no one quite knows what that means!) and 'dactylic'.

85. *sticking out his middle finger*: An obscene and contemptuous gesture.

86. *And feminine? . . . fowl*: This question and response are not in the manuscripts but seem to me necessary to the sense of the passage; when, as would be the case here, two successive lines of the text end in the same word, it is a very easy slip for a copyist to omit the second of the two. That a line or two had been lost at this point was suspected by Richard Bentley nearly three centuries ago; the tentative restoration here translated was proposed in my 1982 edition of the play.

87. *'Fowless' . . . 'fowler'*: Socrates recommends that *alektruon*, the regular word for a domestic fowl of either sex, should be replaced by *alektor* (an existing but rather poetic word) for the male and *alektruaina* (a new coinage) for the female.

88. *You call it a trough . . . feminine object*: Socrates' point, which cannot really be expressed in a language without grammatical gender, is that the word for 'kneading-trough', *kardopos*, is of feminine gender and yet has an ending (*-os*) that is typical of masculine nouns; he wants the word changed to *kardopē*.

89. *In the same way as Cleonymus is*: For Cleonymus has shown himself to be unmanly by displaying cowardice in battle (see lines 353–4).

90. *in a round mortar*: The point of this gibe appears to be that at one time (before he gained notoriety and profit through politics) Cleonymus was so poor and wretched that he could not get himself either proper food or proper sex.

91. *Philoxenus . . . Melesias . . . Amynias*: Philoxenus is elsewhere (e.g. *The Wasps*, line 84) spoken of as a person of dubious masculinity, and doubtless the other two names are chosen for the same reason. The third name, Amynias, has the comically useful property that most of its Greek inflectional forms could equally well be those of a hypothetical woman's name Amynia (represented in this translation by 'Minnie').

92. *These buggers*: Literally, 'Corinthians' (in 423 an enemy state), with a pun on *koreis*, 'bugs'.

93. *glass*: At this time, in Greece, glass was so rare as to be almost as precious as gold (compare *The Acharnians*, line 74), and it is not surprising that Strepsiades has forgotten what it is called.

94. *stinking rich women*: The Greek text calls them 'daughters of Coesyra' (compare note 6 above).

95. *Socrates of Melos*: Socrates had no connection with the island of Melos; but to call him a Melian, in such a context, associates him with Diagoras of Melos, a notorious atheist who mocked all religious observances and especially the Eleusinian Mysteries, and who was eventually prosecuted for impiety, condemned to death in his absence, and a price put on his head.

96. *sons of the soil*: Greek *gēgeneis*, 'children of earth', which means (i) stupid clods but also (ii) the Titans and/or the Giants who once warred against the Olympian gods.

97. *as Pericles once said*: When the Spartans invaded Attica in 446/5, Pericles was said to have given the Spartan king Pleistoanax a bribe of 60,000 drachmas to withdraw and to have entered the amount in his accounts as spent 'for essential purposes'.

98. *tied up . . . a good lashing*: Like a delinquent slave.

99. *I won't be there*: This is a transparent, and decidedly artificial, device to get Socrates off stage during the debate between Right and Wrong; it is necessitated by the competition rule limiting the number of speaking actors to four (see Introduction, pp. xxix–xxx) – and by Aristophanes' wish to have Strepsiades hear the debate, so that he is fully aware of the kind of instruction his son will receive if allowed to attend the school.

100. *claim at all*: Had the revised play been produced, there would have been a choral song at this point, before the entry of Right and Wrong.

101. *Zeus . . . father in chains*: The chaining of Cronus, ex-king of the gods, by his son Zeus, was the classic instance used by philosophers and others seeking to prove the 'immorality' of traditional myth.

102. *drop out of school*: That is, to abandon *traditional* education (which, by the mid-teens, would be mainly in music, dancing and athletics).

103. *Mysian Telephus*: See *The Acharnians*, note 73.

104. *Pandeletus*: According to the ancient commentators, an informer who was also active in politics; we can safely assume that to say that Wrong's ideas came from Pandeletus was equivalent to saying that they were unjust or immoral – particularly since Pandeletus' name could be understood as meaning 'he who entraps everyone'.

105. *happy to let him start*: Wrong knows – and Right apparently does

not – how great an advantage it is to have the last word, especially in an Aristophanic *agon*!

106. *our friends*: Designedly ambiguous and misleading, many (among them probably Strepsiades) will take them to be referring to Socrates and his associates – but the phrase could just as well denote the gods, whose agents they actually are.

107. *Phrynis*: A celebrated lyre-player, who won the song contest at the Great Panathenaea in (probably) 446.

108. *cicada brooches*: In the early fifth century it had been fashionable to wear hair-brooches in the shape of cicadas.

109. *oxslaughter trials*: The summer festival of the Dipolieia had as its best-known feature a bizarre rite called the *bouphonia* ('oxslaughter') in which, after an ox had been sacrificially slain, the knife that had killed him was put on trial, condemned, and thrown in the sea; subsequently the ox was stuffed, stood on its feet and yoked to a plough as if alive.

110. *Cedeides*: A contemporary lyric poet, evidently regarded as very old-fashioned.

111. *dancing at the Panathenaea*: The dance was a martial one, and the dancers were naked but carried a hoplite shield. It is not clear whether the lowering of the shield is to be understood as due to bashfulness, physical weakness, or both.

112. *do anything ... defile the face of Modesty*: This expression (even more convoluted and obscure in the Greek) is probably to be understood as referring to sexual transgressions which Right finds too disgusting to mention.

113. *chucks an apple ... as a come-and-get-me*: This method of issuing a coded sexual invitation survives in Greece to the present day, but the apple is virtually always thrown by the man (as in the myth of Melanion and Atalanta), not by the woman.

114. *antediluvian*: The Greek has 'call him Iapetus' (a god of the generation before Zeus).

115. *a boring little baby*: Literally, 'one who feeds like a baby on blite [an insipid vegetable]'.

116. *Academe's Park*: This precinct of the god or hero Academus, north of the city walls, had been laid out as a public park in the 460s with shaded walks and running-tracks. Ironically, it later became the site of Plato's philosophical school and so gave to the world the words 'academy' and 'academic'.

117. *e-lection*: The Greek text at this point, having set up an expectation that Right will say 'a big prick' (which, it should be explained, was regarded as something ugly and semi-bestial), makes him say

instead 'a long decree' (implying that Wrong's devotees often become politicians proposing motions in the Assembly). I have replaced this by a play on 'election' and 'erection'.

118. *Heracles having a cold bath*: Warm springs were called 'Heraclean baths'.

119. *Homer ... 'marketeers'*: A multiply flawed argument: *agora*, which in Aristophanes' time meant 'market-place', meant for Homer '(place of) assembly', and its derivative *agorētēs*, which Homer does apply to Nestor and some other wise elders (though certainly not to 'all' of them), meant correspondingly 'public speaker'. In the Greek of Aristophanes' time *agorētēs* was obsolete, but there was a similar-sounding word, *agorastēs*, which meant 'person who does shopping in the market'.

120. *Peleus ... given a knife*: Peleus, when a guest of Acastus, resisted the amorous advances of his host's wife, and she then accused him to her husband of attempting to rape her. The enraged Acastus abandoned Peleus unarmed on a mountain to be devoured by wild beasts, but the gods, impressed by his chastity, gave him a knife to defend himself.

121. *Thetis as his wife*: The sea-goddess Thetis was courted by Zeus and Poseidon, but their pursuit of her ended abruptly when they learned of an oracle that said she was destined to bear a son mightier than his father. She was therefore married off at once to a mortal, Peleus being chosen as the most virtuous mortal alive.

122. *she deserted him as well*: The usual story was that Thetis left her husband when he angrily abused her on finding her holding the infant Achilles over a fire, not realizing that she was trying to make him immortal; i.e. Peleus lost his wife not (as Wrong claims) because he had too many inhibitions, but because he had too few.

123. *indicates ... 'no'*: See *The Acharnians*, note 24.

124. *radish-buggered ... ash-plucked*: A husband who caught an adulterer with his wife had a rich repertoire of methods of punishment available to him, up to and including summary killing. Two of these, which might (as here) be used together, were a symbolic anal rape performed with a radish root, and the pulling out of the man's pubic hair with the aid of hot ash.

125. *advocates ... actors ... politicians ... faggots*: Regarding *advocates*, compare *The Acharnians*, lines 715–16; regarding *actors*, compare the modern stereotype of the male ballet dancer. That most politicians were former male prostitutes was a standard comic assumption, which is even put in Aristophanes' mouth by Plato in the *Symposium*: in actual fact anyone who had been a male prostitute was forbidden by law to address the Assembly, but this law was only rarely enforced.

126. *[He throws ... at the rear.]*: This stage-direction is again based on a suggestion by Peter von Möllendorff (see note 37 above).

127. *You'll come to regret it!*: This is the decisive moment of the play; it is nearly three quarters over, but only now has Strepsiades finally committed himself to having his son undergo a full course of sophistic education. And only now, with the die cast, do the Clouds begin to predict his subsequent fate – though only when he is either not present or paying no attention. Had the revised play been produced, more lyrics and another speech would probably have been added here to make a full 'second *parabasis*' (see p. 71, note 15).

128. *in Egypt*: To a Greek, Egypt was a remote country, inhabited mainly by liars and cheats, and with a particularly alien civilization; but at least it didn't rain there!

129. *Old and New Day*: The last day of the month was probably so called because it belonged to the *old* month and yet (since the calendar day ended at sunset) the *new* moon might already be visible before the end of the day (provided, of course, that the calendar was actually in step with the moon – see note 76 above).

130. *court deposits*: In most types of lawsuit the complainant/prosecutor had to lodge a deposit (called *prytaneia*) with the magistrate in charge of the relevant court; he lost the deposit if he withdrew the case, but if he won he could demand reimbursement from the defendant.

131. *accept this*: We cannot tell what the present was – except that the Greek word for it was of the masculine gender; but it was doubtless of small value, perhaps nothing more than a cake or the like.

132. *Solon ... a good democrat*: Solon (early sixth century) had been the creator of the Athenian law-code, and in the fifth and fourth centuries the whole corpus of Athenian law, though it included many later additions, was commonly referred to as 'the laws of Solon'. And if Athens was a democracy, and its laws were the laws of Solon, it seemed to follow that Solon must have been a democrat – and so, as we know from surviving oratory, most classical Athenians believed, in the teeth of the evidence of Solon's own poetry.

133. *Old Day ... New Moon*: I.e. not (as was actually the practice) on the last day of a month, but on the first day of the next month. Evidently, when lawsuits are brought against Strepsiades, Pheidippides will argue that they should all be dismissed because the complainants' deposits had been accepted on the wrong day.

134. *put Athens to shame*: On the comic assumption that at Athens litigation was virtually the duty of every citizen.

135. *in a place of my choosing*: An oath could be given added solemnity by being taken in a sacred place, where a god was close at hand to hear it.

136. *Zeus, Hermes and Poseidon*: Chosen, no doubt, as being, respectively, the supreme god, the god of commerce, and the god of horses.

137. *Carcinus' gods*: Carcinus was a tragic dramatist (he and his sons have walk-on, or rather dance-off, parts at the end of *The Wasps*). Presumably some play of his had included a scene in which a god uttered laments.

138. *O cruel divinity . . . destroyed me utterly*: Quoted or adapted from the tragedy *Tlepolemos* – not by Carcinus but by his son Xenocles.

139. *fell off the proverbial donkey*: 'To have fallen *off a donkey*' (Greek *ap' onou*) was an expression often used punningly to mean 'to be *out of one's mind*' (Greek *apo nou*).

140. *criminal outrage*: The Greek word is *hybris*, which means (any action displaying) wanton and contemptuous disregard for the rights or dignity of another; it was a serious crime which, if the prosecutor so demanded and the jury agreed with him, could be punished by death.

141. *this sophist*: Strepsiades is meant, the Chorus ironically accepting him at his own recent valuation.

142. *loathsome young hooligan*: Literally, 'foul father-beating burglar'.

143. *'The Shearing of Mr Ram'*: This song (whose opening survives) by the lyric poet Simonides was a victory-ode for a wrestler who had defeated Crius ('Ram') of Aegina at the Nemean Games, perhaps around 510.

144. *myrtle branch*: It was customary to hold a branch of bay or myrtle when singing at a symposium, if one was not accompanying oneself on an instrument. Strepsiades is no longer demanding that his son should sing, but he does ask for the myrtle branch as a token concession to tradition.

145. *Euripides . . . full sister*: The brother and sister will have been Macareus and Canace, the children of the title character in Euripides' *Aeolus*. The point of specifying that she was his *full* sister is that a half-brother and half-sister could lawfully marry at Athens, provided that they were born of different mothers.

146. *'The son gets thumped . . . the father shouldn't?'*: An adaptation of a famous line from Euripides' *Alcestis* (line 691) – which was later to be quoted verbatim (at Euripides) in *The Poet and the Women* (line 194). In Euripides' play, Admetus, who had been saved from death by the willingness of his wife Alcestis to die in his stead, found life

insupportable without her and bitterly reproached his father Pheres
for not having volunteered to sacrifice *his* life; Pheres retorted, 'You
want to live; do you think your father doesn't?'

147. *over your dead face!*: At this point the transmitted text has
Strepsiades saying, apparently to a group of older men in the audience:
'To me, you men of my age, his point of view seems to be fair, and I
think we should make reasonable concessions to it. It's proper that we
should suffer if we do wrong.' Not only is this very clumsy in itself,
but it is also surprising that such a surrender by Strepsiades does not
end the debate (as the surrender by Right in lines 1101–4 ends his
debate with Wrong). I suspect that these lines are a remnant of an
alternative, rejected draft for the transition to the revised ending of the
play.

148. *off the Acropolis*: Literally, 'into the Barathron', a rocky gully
(actually outside the city, close to the Peiraeus road), into which
condemned criminals (or their corpses – the evidence is ambiguous)
were sometimes thrown.

149. *you turned*: Greek *strepsās*, playing on Strepsiades' name.

150. *Chaerephon*: Chaerephon's prominence is surprising; perhaps
this too is a relic of changes of plan in the process of revision, if at one
time Aristophanes had envisaged giving Chaerephon a major role in
the revised play.

151. *this image here*: We are apparently to understand that seeing this
cup (*dīnos*) standing outside the Thinkery, as (for instance) an image
of Hermes stands outside Strepsiades' own house, encouraged Strepsiades to understand Socrates' reference to 'a celestial vortex' (also *dīnos*)
as if he were giving the name of a new supreme god.

152. *[He goes inside.]*: It has been suggested that Pheidippides may
make his exit here into the school, rather than into his father's house.
If so, the lines assigned to 'Student' in the finale should perhaps be
transferred to him – and in that case Strepsiades, having earlier threatened to disown his son if he does *not* study with Socrates, finishes by
stoning him because he *has* studied with Socrates.

153. *prosecution against them*: Most likely he is to be understood as
envisaging a prosecution for 'impiety' – the very charge that was
actually brought against Socrates in 399.

154. *save them this time!*: From this point on, both the staging, and
the assignment of lines among the various inmates of the school, are
very uncertain; what I have offered is not necessarily the only possible
reconstruction that makes sense of the transmitted words. In particular,
there is no direct evidence whatever for the idea that Chaerephon, in
jumping for his life, knocks Socrates over – but if he is going to jump,

such a collision will be useful both for its comic effect and because it will break his fall!

155. *let's light things up*: It appears that backstage fires were sometimes created simply by setting light to a suitably placed heap of combustible material; this had been done in a play called *The Sack of Troy* by Iophon (son of Sophocles), and in Aristophanes' first play, *The Banqueters*, someone had referred to this and spoken of 'Hecuba wailing and the heap of straw burning'. It is to be hoped that some precautions were taken to ensure the safety of the performers on such occasions.

156. *'I am walking . . . mystery of the sun'*: Strepsiades quotes Socrates' own words (line 225) back to him.

157. *back side*: Greek *hedrā*, which, like English 'seat', could mean (among other things) both 'place of abode' (of, for instance, the moon as a celestial object) and 'buttocks' (of, for instance, the moon as an anthropomorphic goddess).

LYSISTRATA

1. *tambourines*: Strictly speaking, these were associated only with Bacchus (Dionysus) of the three divinities mentioned; but on standard comic assumptions, also reflected in this play, women were likely in any case to turn *any* festivity into a Bacchic one.

2. *Big and meaty*: Or 'long and thick'; Lysistrata, somewhat artificially, is not allowed to understand the *double entendre* until her next response but one.

3. *country*: Literally, 'city', as if Greece were one state – which it never had been, and would not be until the Byzantine age. This is not the last time that Lysistrata will speak and act as a citizen of the Greek world rather than just of Athens: contrast Calonice's cheerful welcome for the prospective destruction of enemy peoples.

4. *eels*: Compare *The Acharnians*, lines 880–96.

5. *giant slippers*: Greek *peribārides*, slippers that looked as broad and flat as a Nile barge (*bāris*).

6. *the Holy Twain*: Demeter and her daughter Persephone or Kore, the goddesses worshipped in the women-only festival of the Thesmophoria.

7. *they are Athenian . . . relied on to be late*: Alluding probably to a series of occasions during the preceding twelve months when Athenian naval forces had appeared before cities in the eastern Aegean (Miletus, Cnidus, Rhodes) too late to prevent their revolting from the Athenian alliance.

8. *Paralia . . . Salaminians*: There is again a nautical allusion, this time to the two extra-fast galleys *Paralos* and *Salaminia*; but the reference to the latter provides a feed for a joke by Calonice on the sexual tastes and/or stamina of the males of the island of Salamis.

9. *Acharnians*: It is striking that now (in contrast with fourteen years earlier) it is assumed that the Acharnians, or rather their wives, are eager for peace – or at least that it does not sound absurd to suggest that they are.

10. *Well . . . to get here*: The text is uncertain here, and its interpretation obscure. Theogenes was a shipowner and minor politician, and Calonice may be making a (weak) joke about his trade; 'putting on all sail', if correctly read, must be metaphorical, since one could not travel by boat from Acharnae (or even Peiraeus, if, as seems likely, that is where Theogenes actually lived) to central Athens.

11. *Stinking Trefoils*: The village of Anagyrus abounded in this malodorous shrub (*Anagyris foetida*), and was named after it (no doubt to the occasional embarrassment of its inhabitants). 'To bump a stinking trefoil' (like the English phrase 'to open a can of worms') meant 'to disturb something that would have been better left alone'.

12. *I'm thinking . . . by the Twa Gods*: In Greek, *oiō* and *nai tō siō* (the two gods are Castor and Pollux); these are both, for Athenian hearers, stereotypical markers of Spartan speech.

13. *CALONICE*: It is particularly difficult in this scene to distinguish one speaker from another, especially as between Calonice and Myrrhine. Calonice, however, appears to be the older and coarser of the two, and following a recent suggestion by Giuseppe Mastromarco (*Eikasmos* 6 [1995], pp. 71–89), I have given her mainly those lines which are distinctly bawdy or boozy.

14. *as if . . . sacrifice me*: The comparison is with sacrificial victims (in other words, animals to be killed for meat) being examined to see how much flesh and fat they had on them.

15. *not one of you has a husband at home*: This statement, immediately confirmed by the other women, creates a glaring inconsistency (for if the husbands are all away from home, there is no one for a sexual boycott to target); but Aristophanes is evidently confident that the inconsistency will not be noticed, and is prepared to accept it so as to add extra strength to Lysistrata's argument at this point.

16. *our general*: The Greek text names the general as Eucrates; the implication of Calonice's remark is that he is a greater threat to Athens' interests than the enemy are (an attitude towards generals that was already becoming common when an expedition was not as successful, or not successful as quickly, as the public had expected).

17. *Pylos*: On the western coast of the Peloponnese; captured by Demosthenes in 425, it was still in Athenian hands (it was retaken by the Spartans in 410/09).

18. *drink up*: Greek *ekpiein* means literally 'drink up' and figuratively 'spend entirely'; it is designedly uncertain in which of these senses Calonice is using the word.

19. *cut . . . like a flatfish*: Flatfish (flounder, sole, turbot, etc.) can be thought of as looking like ordinary fish cut in half vertically and laid flat; Aristophanes is made to use the same comparison during his speech in Plato's *Symposium*.

20. *Mount Taÿgetum*: This range rises almost sheer from the plain of Sparta to a height of nearly 8000 feet.

21. *shag . . . that's the way we live*: Literally, 'we are nothing but Poseidon and a tub', with reference to the story of Tyro, who was seduced by Poseidon, gave birth to twins and exposed them in a tub or trough on a river-bank (they were, of course, rescued, as exposed babies always are in myth, and grew up to be the heroes Neleus and Pelias).

22. *real woman*: Lysistrata's notion of what it means to be a 'real woman' is clearly very different from the standard male stereotype.

23. *Menelaus . . . glimpse of . . . apples*: After the capture of Troy, when he had intended to kill her for her infidelity.

24. *Pherecrates*: A contemporary comic poet, somewhat older than Aristophanes.

25. *fall back on a dead dog*: Literally, 'skin a skinned dog', meaning a leather dildo (made of dog's skin).

26. *if they beat us, what then?*: Note how it is taken for granted that a husband who is refused sex by his wife can be expected to attempt to beat her into submission. Lysistrata's reply reveals a great deal about contemporary (male) assumptions regarding rape (not all of which, unfortunately, have yet vanished from the world).

27. *feet*: Probably meaning oars, which are elsewhere occasionally called the feet of ships.

28. *the limbs of the sacrificial victim*: An oath of special solemnity, as this one would be, was often taken over the severed limbs of a sacrificial animal. In this case no sacrifice has yet been made, and we might expect someone to say 'What victim?'; but in fact the dialogue takes a different course and the illogicality is forgotten.

29. *Aeschylus talks about somewhere*: The reference is probably to *Seven against Thebes*, lines 42–8, where the Seven swear over a shield filled with *bull*'s blood that they will sack Thebes or perish in the attempt.

30. *white stallion*: Horse sacrifices were very rare in Greece; Myrrhine is probably thinking of the oath administered in this fashion to the suitors of Helen by her (foster-)father Tyndareos – another inappropriate precedent, since this oath was one of the main causes of the Trojan War.

31. *sacrificial victim*: Literally, 'boar'.

32. *how well it flows*: It was a good omen if the blood from a sacrificial victim flowed freely.

33. *adopt the lioness-on-a-cheesegrater position*: That is, stand bending forward with hands resting on the bed (in a posture reminiscent of a lion crouched to spring), ready for penetration from behind. According to an ancient commentator, cheese-grater handles were often made in the form of crouching animals.

34. *wholly consumed*: In sacral language, the Greek verb used here, *kathagizein*, means 'cause to be consumed *by fire*'; that is not what Lysistrata has in mind!

35. *The Citadel of Athena . . . in the women's hands*: By these words the audience is notified that the *skene* henceforth represents the entrance to the Acropolis, as it will do for the rest of the play.

36. *our own Acropolis*: Implicitly excluding women from the Athenian civic community – but forgetting that the civic community was also a religious community, that the Acropolis was sacred to Athena, and that her cult there was largely performed by women.

37. *image of the Maid*: The ancient olive-wood image of Athena Polias.

38. *Lycon's wicked wife*: A notorious adulteress; since they see the seizure of the Acropolis as due to a criminal conspiracy, the men assume that the most criminal woman in Athens must have been responsible for it.

39. *great Cleomenes*: Cleomenes I, king of Sparta, intervened militarily at Athens in 508 BC to support the oligarchic regime of Isagoras against the nascent democracy led by Cleisthenes. Popular opposition forced him to retire into the Acropolis, where he was besieged for two days (not 'six whole years'!) and then surrendered on condition that he and his men were allowed to leave unharmed.

40. *enemies . . . of Euripides*: Euripides had the reputation of a hater and slanderer of women – an idea which forms the basis of Aristophanes' comedy *The Poet and the Women*, produced two months after *Lysistrata*.

41. *trophy . . . at Marathon*: This trophy, commemorating the Athenian victory over the Persians in 490, is frequently mentioned with pride by Aristophanic characters. It has not occurred to the old men that in attacking the Acropolis – and with fire – they are re-enacting

what the Persian king himself did when he captured and sacked Athens in 480.

42. *'The pig ... the styes'*: In the Greek the flame is called 'Lemnian' (which could mean either 'volcanic' or 'vicious'), with a pun on *lēmai*, 'styes in the eye'.

43. *slaves with bold tattoos*: They would have been tattooed for misconduct, or after running away and being recaptured.

44. *Child of the Lake*: Greek *Tritogeneia*, an epithet of Athena used appropriately to remind her that she was born near water – Lake Tritonis in North Africa.

45. *Bupalus*: A sixth-century sculptor from Chios, made famous by his enemy, the iambic poet Hipponax; the allusion here is to the latter's line, 'Take my cloak, I'm going to give Bupalus a sock in the eye' (Hipponax, fragment 120).

46. *no other bitch ... grab your bollocks again*: Implying that *she* will be the 'bitch' (shameless woman) who grabs them – and tears them right off!

47. *'There is no beast ... as a woman!'*: Many Euripidean characters (some of them female) express detestation of the whole female sex in extravagant terms, but it is not clear whether this particular sentence is quoted, paraphrased or pastiched.

48. *wedding bath*: Athenian brides and bridegrooms, before their marriage, were ritually bathed in water from the Enneakrounos fountain-house, not far from the Acropolis – the very place from which the women have drawn the water they now have with them.

49. *you're not sitting on a jury now*: Old men sitting on juries have the power of life and death; old men *not* sitting on juries have no power at all.

50. *Sabazius ... Adonis ... roofs of houses*: Sabazius was a Phrygian god (sometimes wholly or partly identified with Dionysus), whose worship had become popular at Athens in the late fifth century, especially among women and slaves. The cult of Adonis (the mortal youth who was loved by Aphrodite and killed by a boar), though as yet it had no official status at Athens, was very widespread, particularly among women, who sang laments over effigies of Adonis and sowed seeds of quickly growing, quickly withering plants in trays called 'Adonis gardens' which they carried up to the house roof.

51. *Demostratus ... let the Sicilian expedition sail ... 'O woe for Adonis!'*: The expedition sailed in the high summer of 415, shortly after the Adonis festival; Demostratus is mentioned by Plutarch as one of the politicians who most strongly supported it. The Assembly meeting referred to cannot be identified with certainty, and may indeed

be a conflation of two meetings held at different times. The woman's laments for the youthful Adonis, at a time when a decision was about to be taken that would send thousands of young men on a hazardous expedition, would be seen as an obvious portent of disaster – all the more so once disaster had indeed struck.

52. *Ragers clan*: Demostratus was a member of the aristocratic *genos* (clan) of the Buzygae ('Ox-yokers'); here, in the Greek, the clan's name is perverted into Cholozygae ('Rage-yokers').

53. *pin*: Greek *balanos* (literally, 'acorn') had among its other senses (i) 'pin, bolt' and (ii) 'glans penis'.

54. *little pinkie*: Greek *daktulidion*, depending on the length of the vowel in the third syllable, could mean either 'little toe' (which is what the speaker does mean) or 'little ring' (which in turn can mean 'anus').

55. *member of the Advisory Board*: Greek *proboulos* (see p. 134).

56. *timber to make oars*: After the Sicilian disaster Athens suffered from a chronic shortage of timber suitable for this purpose, almost all of which had to be imported.

57. *Pandrosus*: A daughter of the mythical Athenian king Cecrops; there was a precinct on the Acropolis dedicated to her.

58. *What language!*: Hard-core obscene words such as *khezein*, 'shit', and *bīnein*, 'fuck', are normally avoided, even in comedy, by women when addressing men (whereas men have no compunction about using them in the presence of women).

59. *Bringer of Light*: An epithet of the goddess Hecate, who was also worshipped on the Acropolis.

60. *I'm going to put a stop to these sallies*: And the audience think he will succeed (even though he has no more policemen to spare), because there are now four speaking actors on stage, and there cannot be a fifth; but they have forgotten about the Chorus!

61. *Bull Goddess*: Greek *Tauropolos*, a title under which Artemis was worshipped at Halae in eastern Attica; her cult-image was said to have been brought back by Iphigeneia and Orestes from the land of the Tauri (the Crimea), whose inhabitants were Scythians (the story is told in Euripides' *Iphigeneia in Tauris*), and this makes it appropriate to use her name in threatening a Scythian.

62. *Stop . . . no stripping the corpses!*: Parodying the orders a military commander might give after a successful skirmish, even though on this occasion there are no corpses to strip.

63. *Why did Peisander . . . keep stirring up trouble?*: In view of the past tense, this probably refers not to Peisander's current anti-democratic intrigues (which in any case were probably as yet unknown to the public – see p. 134) but to his previous record as a typical 'demagogue';

as early as 426 Aristophanes had depicted him as one who favoured war from corrupt motives.

64. *what did you decide to inscribe on . . . the Peace Treaty?*: In the winter of 419/8, on the urging of their Argive allies (to whose enemies the Spartans were giving active aid), the Athenian Assembly decided that to the stone bearing the text of the peace treaty of 421 should be added the words 'The Spartans have not kept their oaths', and also that Pylos should again be made a base for guerrilla operations against Spartan territory. These actions could easily have resulted in a renewal of full-scale war, and did lead within a few months to the campaign which ended at the battle of Mantinea, in which the Athenians and their allies were defeated and Athens lost nearly 200 dead.

65. *'Let war be the care of the menfolk!'*: Hector says these words to his wife Andromache in the *Iliad* (6.492) – and proceeds so to misman-age the war that he is killed, and Troy's cause thereby rendered hope-less, a few days later.

66. *chew beans*: A common practice among Athenian peasants (and their wives, no doubt) when engaged on monotonous tasks.

67. *Aphrodite of Cyprus*: Cyprus was the first land on which Aphrodite stepped after being born from the sea-foam, and Paphos remained a major centre of her cult.

68. *Liquidators of War*: In the Greek she uses the plural form of Lysimache, the name of the incumbent priestess of Athena Polias; see p. 136.

69. *Corybantes*: Minor divinities usually associated with Cybele ('the Great Mother'), with Phrygia in north-western Asia Minor, and with ecstatic dancing, but not with anything martial; here they seem to be identified, or confused, with the Curetes, who belong to Crete and who danced in armour around the infant Zeus.

70. *that's what a brave man should do*: I.e. he should be prepared to fight at a moment's notice (in case, say, of a surprise attack on the city walls by the Spartans based at Decelea).

71. *King Tereus*: A central figure in a famous tragedy by Sophocles, in which he had doubtless appeared in the armour supposed to be typical of a Thracian warrior. He married the Athenian princess Procne; their son Itys was later killed by his mother in revenge for Tereus' rape of her sister Philomela. Tereus was finally transformed into a hoopoe, Procne into a nightingale and Philomela into a swallow. Both he and Procne appear, after their transformations, in Aristophanes' *Birds*.

72. *colonies of Athens*: The reference seems to be to the Ionic-speaking states of Asia Minor and the Aegean, which were believed to have been founded from Athens. Most of these had long been tribute-paying

'allies' of Athens, and quite a number were currently in rebellion. The proposal appears to be that their peoples should be given Athenian citizenship; it is doubtful how much this would have appealed either to the intended beneficiaries (many of whom must have thought Athens was doomed) or to Athenians (who would be swamped by the numbers of new citizens).

73. *to stand erect* –: We cannot tell whether Aristophanes had considered, or expected his audience to be able to infer, how this sentence would have continued if not interrupted; one possibility might be, '. . . would be only too willing to take one of those women as a *concubine*'.

74. *honey-cake*: This is the only surviving reference in Greek literature to the practice of burying the dead with a (honey-)cake in their hand. It was evidently meant to be used for propitiating underworld powers that might otherwise be malevolent.

75. *Charon*: The ferryman who rows or punts the dead across the infernal lake.

76. *post-funeral offerings*: Literally, 'third-day offerings'; they were brought to the tomb on the third day (reckoned inclusively, i.e. the next day but one) after death.

77. *Hippias' tyranny*: Hippias, son of Peisistratus, had been autocrat of Athens from 527 to 510; his expulsion had been quickly followed by the establishment of democracy. Had the Persians' invasion of 490 not been defeated at Marathon, they would have restored him to power. Even in 411, when his family had long since vanished from the scene, 'tyranny', and in particular the tyranny of Hippias, remained the opposite against which Athenian democracy defined itself and the great bogy in Athenian democratic thinking.

78. *Cleisthenes*: See *The Acharnians*, note 25; he makes a good intermediary in a conspiracy involving men and women, because he has many of the characteristics of both!

79. *steal our jury fees*: If democracy is abolished, jury pay will disappear (as indeed it did when the Four Hundred took power a few months later).

80. *he who trusts a Spartan, trusts a snake*: Literally, 'with Spartans . . . who can no more be trusted than can a ravening wolf'.

81. *'I'll bear my . . . bough', And stand beside them, thus*: Quoting the first line of a famous symposiac song about Harmodius and Aristogeiton, who had assassinated Hippias' brother Hipparchus in 514 and whom Athenians, somewhat unhistorically, regarded as the heroic overthrowers of tyranny and founders of their free constitutional state (in fact, as Lysistrata will say later, there was at least as strong a case

for giving credit for this to the Spartans). The attitude he apparently proceeds to strike will be that of the Harmodius figure in the statue of the two liberators by Critius and Nesiotes, which stood in the Agora. This is particularly incongruous because Harmodius had been, and was portrayed in the statue as, a very young and very handsome man.

82. *an Acropolis child priestess*: That is, one of the *arrhephoroi* (aged from seven to eleven – so the singers received this honour at the earliest possible age), who lived for a year on the Acropolis under the supervision of the priestess of Athena Polias, and performed important ritual duties at the Panathenaea and several other festivals. This, and some at least of the other ritual functions mentioned below, were reserved for girls from the old Athenian nobility.

83. *served as a Grinder*: Grinding flour for sacrificial cakes offered to (probably) Demeter.

84. *Brauron ... saffron-dyed gown*: The quadrennial festival of the Brauronia, held in honour of Artemis (here called *Archegetis*, 'the Foundress') at Brauron in eastern Attica, was notable particularly for the ritual of the *Arkteia* ('being a bear') performed by girls who, to judge by vase-paintings, were usually about ten years old. The paintings suggest that the girls at first wore a saffron robe, then shed it and performed part of the ritual in a state of nudity, and finally put on the long, white garments appropriate to their future role in the community as adult women.

85. *the ritual basket to bear*: In a procession at the Panathenaea or another major festival. The basket contained the sacrificial knife and other ritual requisites; those chosen for the honour of bearing it were virgins approaching marriageable age.

86. *dried figs for a necklace*: For the original audience this detail probably identified the festival concerned.

87. *the gold ... live instead on tax*: The cash reserve accumulated (largely from the tribute of the allied states) during the half-century between the Persian and Peloponnesian wars had now run very low, and much revenue was now raised internally through property taxes (*eisphorai*).

88. *wrapped in fig-leaves*: Stuffed fig-leaves (*thria*) were as popular a dish as stuffed vine-leaves are today.

89. *[The MEN remove their tunics.]*: They are now 'stage-naked', i.e. wearing only close-fitting bodysuits and, of course, phalli.

90. *who ... against the tyrants went to war*: Literally, 'who went to take Leipsydrium'. In or about 513 BC Leipsydrium, in the hills of northern Attica, was occupied and fortified by aristocratic opponents

of the tyrant Hippias; Hippias' forces besieged them and drove them out of the country. The men of the Chorus, who elsewhere always cast themselves as foes of tyranny, presumably here intend to identify themselves with the rebels. The sobriquet 'Whitefeet' is not found elsewhere, but presumably was attached to the rebels at the time; its meaning is obscure.

91. *just like Artemisia did*: Artemisia, queen of Halicarnassus, took personal command of the squadron her city sent to fight in Xerxes' fleet when he invaded Greece in 480 BC, and distinguished herself at the battle of Salamis.

92. *don't slip off easily*: Everything said in this speech up to this point carries a sexual innuendo.

93. *Micon's painting*: Either in the Painted Portico (Stoa Poikile) or in the temple of Theseus, both of which had murals showing the battle between the Athenians under Theseus and the Amazons.

94. *Tear out your hair*: Literally, 'shear you' (the old men's hair being as white as sheep's wool).

95. *[The WOMEN remove their remaining garments.]*: While (simulated) female nudity is not uncommon in Aristophanes (see note 170 to *The Acharnians*), all the other instances involve *young* females, normally either divine or quasi-divine beings (like Reconciliation later in this play) or professional sex-workers. The action of this semi-chorus in stripping completely is probably to be understood as an assertion of confidence and power.

96. *celery*: The Greek actually says 'garlic'. The women mean, of course, that anyone who attacks them will have his teeth knocked out.

97. *the beetle in the fable*: Alluding to a famous fable ascribed to Aesop. The beetle (said the fable) had a grudge against the eagle and pursued it wherever it nested, rolling its eggs out and breaking them, until the eagle sought sanctuary (unavailingly) in the bosom of Zeus. The men's 'eggs' are no doubt their testicles.

98. *a fine Boeotian eel ... asked round*: The neighbour/eel, of course, would have *been* the meal; but, as in *The Acharnians*, Boeotian eels are 'enemy goods', whose importation is forbidden and which are liable to confiscation if discovered.

99. *pulley-cable*: Evidently building work was in progress on the Acropolis, possibly on the temple now called the Erechtheum.

100. *yesterday*: This indicates clearly, for the first time, that we are to imagine that a considerable time has passed (five or six days, as we later learn) since the strike and occupation began.

101. *Orsilochus ... sparrow-back*: The sparrow was the sacred bird

of Aphrodite, and had strong erotic and phallic associations. Ancient commentators make various and inconsistent statements about Orsilochus, the most plausible of which is that he was a man with a reputation as a seducer of married women.

102. *Eileithyia*: Goddess of childbirth.

103. *rather hard . . . must be a boy*: Greek *sklēros*, 'hard', could also mean 'tough, virile'.

104. *Athena's sacred helmet*: Probably that on Pheidias' great free-standing bronze statue of Athena (called by modern writers the Athena Promachos), which stood in the open air on the Acropolis.

105. *stay here . . . round the hearth*: Alluding to the ceremony (probably, but not certainly, performed on the fifth day of life) when a baby was ritually introduced to the household and the hearth-goddess Hestia. Evidently the mother was not permitted to leave the house until after this ceremony.

106. *Guardian Serpent*: Said to dwell in the temple of Athena Polias; a honey-cake was offered to it every month. Herodotus (*History* 8.41) makes it clear that he did not believe the serpent actually existed, and strongly implies that no one had ever claimed to have seen it; it is thus likely that the Third Woman's latest excuse would seem a very tall tale indeed.

107. *owls . . . honking*: The call of the Little Owl (Athena's sacred bird, which frequented and frequents the rocky citadel of many a Greek town) is here phoneticized in the Greek text as *kikkabau* (in modern Greek it is *koukouvaou*).

108. *swallows . . . hoopoes*: In the myth of Tereus (see note 71 above), Tereus after his transformation into a hoopoe is destined eternally to pursue (but not to capture) the nightingale (Procne); here, however, the nightingale is replaced by the swallow (Philomela), doubtless because *chelidōn*, 'swallow → swallowtail → fork', was a slang term for the female genitals.

109. *cock-birds*: Greek *phalētes*, 'phalli', possibly with a pun on *phalēris*, 'coot'.

110. *I heard in boyhood many a tale . . . Detest the creatures too!*: The men are shamelessly selective in their citation of myth. Melanion was certainly a famous hunter in the wilds of Arcadia – and may for all we know, in some versions of his story, have gone there to avoid an unwelcome marriage; but he subsequently accepted the challenge set by the huntress maiden Atalanta to her would-be suitors (to run a race against her, on pain of death if defeated) and won the race, and Atalanta, by a ruse.

111. *Myronides . . . Phormio*: Respectively, a successful general of the

450s and a successful admiral of the 420s. The expression 'shaggy-arsed' (Greek *melampugos*) was in common use meaning 'macho'.

112. *Timon*: The archetypal (but probably legendary) misanthrope. The women, like the men, edit the story to suit themselves; in no other account is Timon described as hating only *male* humanity, and at least once he *is* described as rejecting marriage.

113. *prickly brier and thorn*: I.e. thick matted hair.

114. *a Fury*: The Furies (Erinyes) were hideous goddesses of vengeance, often portrayed with snakes entwined in their hair.

115. *use the lamp . . . closely singed*: Women whose business it was to make themselves attractive to men (whether as wives or as sex-workers) were expected to remove their pubic hair, or at least keep it short, by plucking or singeing or both.

116. *shrine of Chloe*: Close under the Acropolis, a little to the south of the great west entrance (the Propylaea), and thus to the left of an observer looking down from above it.

117. *Cinesias from Paeonidae*: Cinesias was a moderately common Athenian name, and Paeonidae was a real Attic deme; but they can be linked with two verbs (*kinein* and *paiein*) which are frequently used in comedy to mean 'copulate'.

118. *Myrrie baby*: When expressions of this type are used in the translation, the Greek text has a diminutive form of Myrrhine's name (*Myrrhinidion* or the shorter *Myrrhion*).

119. *Absence . . . grow fonder!*: This sentence is not in the Greek text as transmitted; but the next sentence is shown by its wording not to be the beginning of Cinesias' speech, so a line or two must have been lost here in the 1400 years between Aristophanes and our earliest manuscript.

120. *the goods we own together*: This is a rhetorical rather than a legal statement; the contents of the matrimonial home were legally the property of the husband, except for the wife's dowry and any items (e.g. clothing, jewellery, slaves) which she had brought with her at the time of the marriage.

121. *What . . . in front of the baby?*: It will be observed that Myrrhine takes no notice of the presence of the Chorus – which suggests that they have moved to a relatively inconspicuous location well away from the *skene*.

122. *there's nowhere we can do it here*: Because they are in the open with no buildings near (except on the Acropolis, where, as in most sanctuaries, sex was forbidden). Of course, the place they eventually choose is one that is in full view of some 14,000 theatre spectators!

123. *Pan's Grotto . . . Clepsydra Spring*: The cave would be not only

convenient but mythically appropriate, since it was here (as told in Euripides' *Ion*) that Creusa was raped by Apollo and conceived Ion, the ancestor of the Ionian and Athenian peoples. That it was a sanctuary apparently does not matter (note that Myrrhine, for once, raises no objection on this point); probably Pan, as a very highly sexualized god himself, was assumed not to mind what mortals got up to on his property. The spring lay conveniently between Pan's Grotto and the Propylaea.

124. *cheap little fart though you are*: Literally, 'though you are of such a kind', a rather obscure phrase. Giuseppe Mastromarco (in A. López Eire, ed., *Sociedad, politica y literatura* [Salamanca, 1997], p. 115) has observed that not only is 'by Apollo' normally a *man*'s oath, but that the whole sentence (with a minor adjustment of grammatical gender) would come more appropriately from a man. (In the translation, the effect of this may be tested by changing 'fart' to 'tart'.) He sees the sentence as one of numerous indications, in this passage and elsewhere, that the usual power relations between men and women have been reversed.

125. *Heracles' supper*: Heracles was traditionally a voracious eater, and when he appeared in comedy he was often kept waiting for his dinner. This is mentioned in *The Wasps* and *Peace* as a comic cliché which Aristophanes loftily shuns.

126. *Philostratus*: A pimp of considerable experience in the business (he had been casually mentioned in *The Knights* thirteen years earlier). The Greek text uses not his name but his nickname 'Fox-dog' (i.e. 'cunning and shameless').

127. *heart . . . soul . . . bollocks*: The Greek text also mentions various other body parts (kidneys, loins, crotch).

128. *Senate*: Greek *gerōkhia*, the name of the council of elders which advised the Spartan kings; there was no such body at Athens.

129. *CINESIAS*: The identity of the Herald's interlocutor has long been disputed. In my original Penguin translation I identified him with 'the Athenian magistrate we met before', but the state of his phallus makes it likely that he is someone much younger. Most recent scholars have taken the view that this character is none other than Cinesias, largely because nothing in Cinesias' last lines before the Herald's entry indicates that he is about to leave the scene. Cinesias, to be sure, does not make a very dignified representative of the Athenian state, but then by now *every* male Athenian is either undignified or decrepit.

130. *walking-stick*: Spartans (and those upper-class Athenians who aped Spartan ways) used a distinctive type of walking-stick with a knobbly head.

131. *Laconia*: The region (the SE quarter of the Peloponnese) of which Sparta was capital; also called Lacedaemon.

132. *we've got no Pellene*: This joke has never been convincingly explained. Pellene was a state allied to Sparta in the northern Peloponnese, but the name must evidently, in one way or another, here carry a secondary, sexual connotation. The least unlikely explanations – though neither has any positive evidence in its favour – are (i) that Pellene was the name of a courtesan well known at Athens or (ii) that there is a pun on an (otherwise unknown) word meaning 'vagina' or (in view of Spartans' supposed sexual preferences – see note 155 below) 'anus'.

133. *Pan was responsible*: Being often represented himself with an erect phallus, he might logically be supposed responsible for causing erections in others.

134. *stooped . . . carrying lamps*: A man carrying a lit oil lamp would bend his body over it to protect it from the wind.

135. *wee berries*: I.e. clitorises.

136. *you look more like a man now*: It is paradoxical, especially in a culture in which male nudity was so important, that a man should be said to look *more* like a man when clothed; but the point is, of course, that there was nothing very virile about these old men's bodies.

137. *take this ring of mine . . . scoop it out*: The lower eyelid will be pulled downwards and the ring used to wipe the insect out of the eye.

138. *Two hundred drachmas*: Enough to maintain a family for six months.

139. *What's more . . . money that we lend!*: Having given the impression that they were offering gifts of money, they turn out to be merely offering loans – and interest-bearing loans at that (as the vocabulary choices in the Greek text make clear). This is the first of four songs (lines 1043–71 and 1188–1215) in which the Chorus make magnificent free offers which they then cancel in the 'small print' in a manner that would make any present-day advertising executive proud. It will be noted that here (reflecting the hard reality outside the comic fiction) they assume that the war can be expected to continue indefinitely.

140. *Carystus . . . nice*: Several words in this part of the song ('Carystus' – compare line 1181 – 'soup', 'porker', 'tender [flesh]') have strong potential for a sexual connotation, hinting (as I have put it elsewhere) 'that the flesh of the human female will be as important a part of the evening's entertainment as the flesh of the pig'. Carystus was a town on the island of Euboea; its men seem to have had something of a

reputation for sexual prowess, perhaps because the town's name was suggestive of *karya*, 'nuts', whence 'testicles'.

141. *pig-cage*: Many Athenians kept pigs in the courtyards of their houses, usually in portable wicker cages.

142. *leaning forward like wrestlers*: Referring to the Greek wrestler's usual preliminary stance, leaning slightly forward and thrusting out his hands in front of him.

143. *excess abdominal fluid*: Referring, ostensibly, to dropsy; the Greek has a pun on the adjectives *askitikos*, 'dropsical', and *askētikos*, 'connected with athletics'.

144. *sacred emblems mutilated*: Referring to the mutilation of many images of Hermes in Athens in 415 BC shortly before the Sicilian expedition sailed. The images consisted essentially of a square pillar with a carved head and an erect phallus; this passage shows that the mutilation included (and perhaps consisted chiefly of) knocking the latter off (Thucydides speaks euphemistically of *ta prosōpa*, usually rendered 'the faces', but probably in fact meaning 'the front parts').

145. *those men*: I.e. the mutilators of the Hermae.

146. *Lysistratus*: The name was common, and apparently more than one bearer of it was mentioned in late fifth-century comedy; the reference here is probably not to the Lysistratus mentioned in *The Acharnians* (see note 143 to that play) but to one Lysistratus, son of Macareus, who had a reputation as a passive homosexual (and might thus have a special appeal to Spartans – see note 155 below).

147. *the brutal way our menfolk used to do*: Probably alluding to Athenian lack of diplomatic finesse in past negotiations with Sparta.

148. *I am a woman . . . older men*: This opening is based on, and part of it is quoted from, a speech by the title character in Euripides' play *Melanippe the Wise*.

149. *lustral water*: Sprinkled on altars to purify them, as a preliminary to a sacrifice.

150. *threatened by barbarian foes*: The Persians were trying to take advantage of Athens' weakness by reclaiming sovereignty over the Greek communities of Asia Minor; their logical next step might be another attack on Greece itself (not that there is any evidence that any Persian king after Xerxes ever contemplated this). Lysistrata diplomatically makes no mention of recent Spartan negotiations with Persia.

151. *Cimon . . . saved all Lacedaemon*: In 464 BC Sparta was almost destroyed by a catastrophic earthquake, and the helots (serfs), especially those of the subject territory of Messenia to the west of Laconia, rose in revolt. This developed into a prolonged guerrilla campaign based on the stronghold of Mount Ithome, and in spring 462 Sparta sought aid from her allies, including Athens; Pericleidas was the leader of the Spartan delegation, and a close friend of the then leading Athenian politician, Cimon, who persuaded the Assembly to send a force to Sparta's aid. Lysistrata omits to mention that the Spartans sent the Athenian force home on discovering that many of them sympathized with the rebels, that shortly afterwards Cimon was 'ostracized', and that within two or three years Athens and Sparta were at war.

152. *Hippias*: See notes 77 and 90 above. Hippias was expelled, at the second attempt, by a Spartan force under King Cleomenes, which invaded Attica at the request of exiled Athenian aristocrats opposed to Hippias. Hippias was supported by some Thessalian cavalry, forty or fifty of whom were killed in the fighting. Lysistrata omits to mention that two or three years later Cleomenes intervened at Athens again in an unsuccessful attempt to strangle Athens' newborn democracy (see note 39 above).

153. *Pylos . . . to revolt*: Pylos had been an important base for Messenian guerrilla operations against Spartan territory.

154. *Prickly Bushes . . . everything*: In the Greek the first place demanded is Echinus in southern Thessaly; *echinos* means 'hedgehog' or 'sea-urchin' – but also 'pubic hair'. It will be evident from this what the Malian 'Gulf' represents, why it is said to be 'behind' Echinus when in geographical fact Echinus was behind (beyond) the gulf, and why the Spartan is exaggerating only mildly when he complains that, with these two areas and the 'Long Legs' as well, the Athenians are demanding 'everything'.

155. *some husbandry . . . muck*: The agricultural language used by both delegates has, as often in Greek, a sexual connotation – and the Spartan's sexuality is anal; for the Spartans were believed to have a liking for anal copulation with women as well as boys. This also explains why, given first pick in the share-out of Reconciliation's body, they choose her bottom.

156. *a basket to bear*: See note 85 above.

157. *Open the door here! . . . [The SLAVES are driven away.]*: It is very difficult to be sure what is going on in this scene, or even what characters are involved in it. My identifications and stage directions are based on the assumption that the Athenians, being drunk, drive the Spartans' slaves away (as they will later do a second time) in the mistaken belief that they are doing their new-found friends a good turn.

158. *we go to Sparta sober*: This must allude to some embassy before (we cannot tell how long before) the Spartan declaration of war in the

winter of 414/3, whose members evidently made contradictory reports on their return.

159. *'Telamon' . . . 'Cleitagora'*: Two popular symposiac songs. We need not necessarily assume that to sing one instead of the other was a grave impropriety; part of the point may well be that trivial issues like this are the only things that can now divide Athenians from Spartans – and another part of the point is that even issues like this are *not* in fact allowed to become divisive.

160. *bagpipes*: In the Greek the instrument is called *physallides* or *physatēria*, which means, literally, 'things that can be expanded by puffing'; it is not certainly identifiable, but is more likely to have been some kind of bagpipe than anything else (though the earliest definite evidence for the existence of bagpipes in the Greek world comes a century or two later).

161. *Send me thy child . . .* : The song recalls the simultaneous battles of Artemisium and Thermopylae in 480 BC. The Spartan is rather generous in crediting the Athenians with a victory in the sea-battle, which was indecisive and did not halt the Persian advance; of Thermopylae he mentions only the courage of King Leonidas and the Spartans, and the enormous numerical superiority of the enemy – he does not need to mention that the Spartans who fought there were killed to the last man.

162. *cunning foxes*: I.e. self-seeking politicians.

163. *aegis of Athena*: The priestess of Athena Polias – a figure with whom Lysistrata has strong associations (see pp. 136–7) – wore the *aegis* of the goddess on certain occasions, and in particular when she visited brides shortly after their marriage; and the present scene is, in effect, a mass renewal of marriage. The *aegis* is represented in art as a garment, often with a scaly surface, fringed with tassels (sometimes with snakes), either worn over the shoulders or hung over the left arm.

164. *maenad crew*: Maenads were ecstatic female devotees of Dionysus/Bacchus.

165. *pray for victory*: In the dramatic competition.

166. *Evoi . . . evai!*: An exclamation of joy associated with Bacchic worship.

167. *Eurotas*: The river that flows by Sparta.

168. *Apollo's noble seat*: At Amyclae, near Sparta.

169. *holy rods*: The maenads carry the *thyrsos*, a fennel rod tipped with ivy leaves.

170. *Helen, the pure*: Helen is normally thought of as anything but 'pure'; but at Sparta she was worshipped as a goddess, and thought of as the ideal type of the Spartan maiden and wife. Ten months before

the production of *Lysistrata*, Athenian theatregoers too had been presented with a chaste Helen in Euripides' *Helen* (which Aristophanes was about to parody extensively in *The Poet and the Women*).

171. *hymn*: The final hymn is not included in the surviving script, possibly because it was traditional and not composed by the poet.

PENGUIN ⓟ CLASSICS

The Classics Publisher

'Penguin Classics, one of the world's greatest series.' JOHN
KEEGAN

'I have never been disappointed with the Penguin Classics. All
I have read is a model of academic seriousness and provides
the essential information to fully enjoy the master works that
appear in its catalogue.' MARIO VARGAS LLOSA

'Penguin and Classics are words that go together like horse and
carriage or Mercedes and Benz. When I was a university teacher
I always prescribed Penguin editions of classic novels for my
courses: they have the best introductions, the most reliable
notes, and the most carefully edited texts.' DAVID LODGE

'Growing up in Bombay, expensive hardback books were
beyond my means, but I could indulge my passion for reading
at the roadside bookstalls that were well stocked with all the
Penguin paperbacks ... Sometimes I would choose a book just
because I was attracted by the cover, but so reliable was the
Penguin imprimatur that I was never once disappointed by the
contents.

Such access certainly broadened the scope of my reading,
and perhaps it's no coincidence that so many Merchant Ivory
films have been adapted from great novels, or that those novels
are published by Penguin.' ISMAIL MERCHANT

'You can't write, read, or live fully in the present without knowing the literature of the past. Penguin Classics opens the door
to a treasure house of pure pleasure, books that have never
been bettered, which are read again and again with increased
delight.' JOHN MORTIMER

CLICK ON A CLASSIC

www.penguinclassics.com

The world's greatest literature at your fingertips

Constantly updated information on over 1600 titles, from
Icelandic sagas to ancient Indian epics, Russian drama to
Italian romance, American greats to African masterpieces

•

The latest news on recent additions to the list, updated
editions and specially commissioned translations

•

Original scholarly essays by leading writers: Elaine Showalter
on Zola, Laurie R King on Arthur Conan Doyle, Frank
Kermode on Shakespeare, Lisa Appignanesi on Tolstoy

•

A wealth of background material, including biographies
of every classic author from Aristotle to Zamyatin, plot
synopses, readers' and teachers' guides, useful web links

•

Online desk and examination copy assistance for academics

•

Trivia quizzes, competitions, giveaways, news on
forthcoming screen adaptations

•

eBooks available to download

READ MORE IN PENGUIN

In every corner of the world, on every subject under the sun, Penguin represents quality and variety – the very best in publishing today.

For complete information about books availabale from Penguin – including Puffins, Penguin Classics and Arkana – and how to order them, write to us at the appropriate address below. Please note that for copyright reasons the selection of books varies from country to country.

In the United Kingdom: *Please write to* Dept EP, Penguin Books Ltd, Bath Road, Harmondsworth, West Drayton, Middlesex UB7 0DA

In the United States: *Please write to* Consumer Services, Penguin Putnam Inc., 405 Murray Hill Parkway, East Rutherford, New Jersey 07073-2136. *VISA and MasterCard holders call 1-800-631-8571 to order Penguin titles*

In Canada: *Please write to* Penguin Books Canada Ltd, 10 Alcorn Avenue, Suite 300, Toronto, Ontario M4V 3B2

In Australia: *Please write to* Penguin Books Australia Ltd, 487 Maroondah Highway, Ringwood, Victoria 3134

In New Zealand: *Please write to* Penguin Books (NZ) Ltd, Private Bag 102902, North Shore Mail Centre, Auckland 10

In India: *Please write to* Penguin Books India Pvt Ltd, 11 Community Centre, Panchsheel Park, New Delhi 110017

In the Netherlands: *Please write to* Penguin Books Netherlands bv, Postbus 3507, NL-1001 AH Amsterdam

In Germany: *Please write to* Penguin Books Deutschland GmbH, Metzlerstrasse 26, 60594 Frankfurt am Main

In Spain: *Please write to* Penguin Books S. A., Bravo Murillo 19, 1°B, 28015 Madrid

In Italy: *Please write to* Penguin Italia s.r.l., Via Vittoria Emanuele 451a, 20094 Corsico, Milano

In France: *Please write to* Penguin France, 12, Rue Prosper Ferradou, 31700 Blagnac

In Japan: *Please write to* Penguin Books Japan Ltd, Iidabashi KM-Bldg, 2-23-9 Koraku, Bunkyo-Ku, Tokyo 112-0004

In South Africa: *Please write to* Penguin Books South Africa (Pty) Ltd, P.O. Box 751093, Gardenview, 2047 Johannesburg

HOMER
The Iliad

*'Look at me. I am the son of a great man. A
goddess was my mother. Yet death and inexorable
destiny are waiting for me'*

One of the foremost achievements in Western literature,
Homer's *Iliad* tells the story of the darkest episode in the Trojan
War. At its centre is Achilles, the greatest warrior-champion of
the Greeks, and his refusal to fight after being humiliated by his
leader Agamemnon. But when the Trojan Hector kills Achilles'
close friend Patroclus, he storms back into battle to take revenge
– although knowing this will ensure his own early death.
Interwoven with this tragic sequence of events are powerfully
moving descriptions of the ebb and flow of battle, of the domestic world inside Troy's besieged city of Ilium and of the conflicts
between the gods on Olympus as they argue over the fate of
mortals.

E. V. Rieu's acclaimed translation of Homer's *The Iliad* was one
of the first titles published in Penguin Classics, and now has
classic status itself. For this edition, Rieu's text has been revised,
and a new introduction and notes by Peter Jones complement
the original introduction.

Translated by E. V. RIEU
Revised and updated by PETER JONES *with* D. C. H. RIEU
Edited with an introduction and notes by PETER JONES

EURIPIDES
Medea and Other Plays

*'That proud, impassioned soul, so ungovernable
now that she has felt the sting of injustice'*

Medea, in which a spurned woman takes revenge upon her
lover by killing her children, is one of the most shocking of all
the Greek tragedies. Dominating the play is Medea herself, a
towering figure who demonstrates Euripides' unusual willingness to give voice to a woman's case. *Alcestis*, a tragicomedy, is
based on a magical myth in which Death is overcome, and *The
Children of Heracles* examines conflict between might and right,
while *Hippolytus* deals with self-destructive integrity and moral
dilemmas. These plays show Euripides transforming awesome
figures of Greek myths into recognizable, fallible human beings.

John Davie's accessible prose translation is accompanied by a
general introduction and individual prefaces to each play.

'One of the best prose translations of Euripides I have seen'
ROBERT FAGLES

'John Davie's translations are outstanding . . . the tone throughout is refreshingly modern yet dignified' WILLIAM ALLAN,
Classical Review

Translated by JOHN DAVIE
With introductions and notes by RICHARD RUTHERFORD